ABRAM'S EYES

The Native American Legacy of Nantucket Island

ABRAM'S EYES

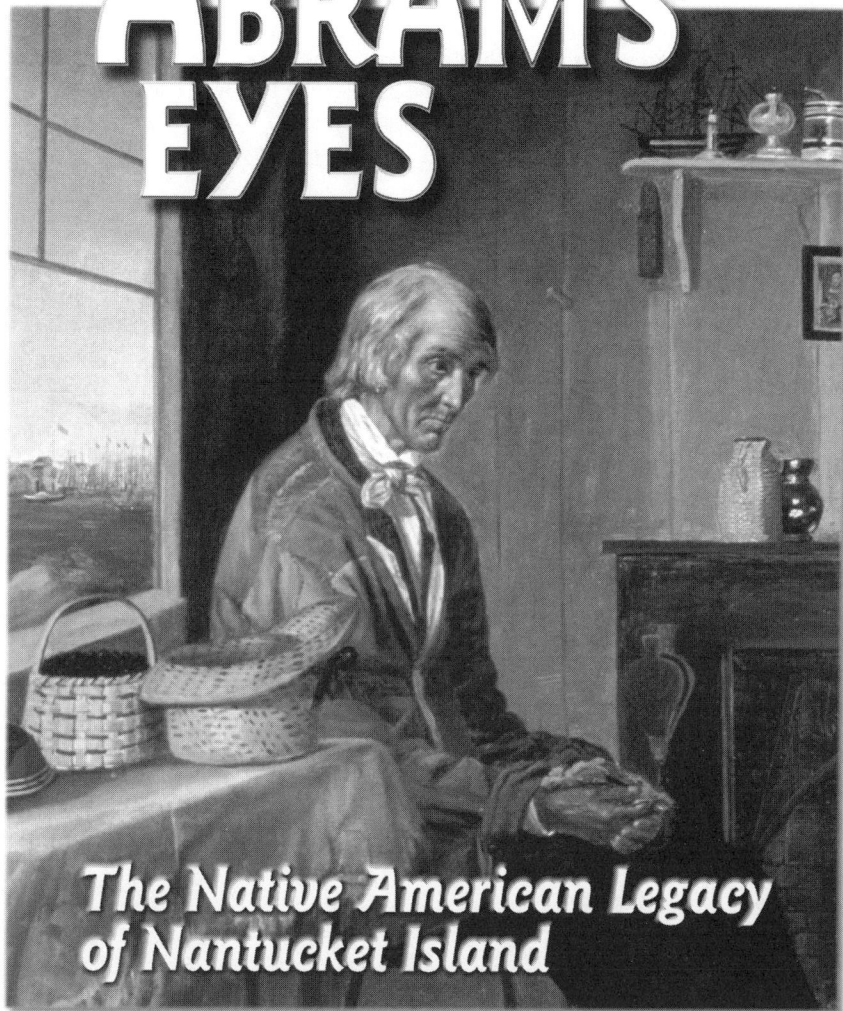

The Native American Legacy of Nantucket Island

NATHANIEL PHILBRICK

MILL HILL PRESS, NANTUCKET ISLAND

Mill Hill Press was established to preserve and record the history of Nantucket Island and the people who live by the sea—for therein lies, in great part, the story of America.

Hope you enjoy this offering from Mill Hill.

Albert F. Egan

Albert F. Egan, Jr., Publisher
Mill Hill Press

Mill Hill Press

124 Orange Street

Nantucket, Massachusetts

First Edition

Copyright ©1998 by Nathaniel Philbrick

Library of Congress Catalog Card No. 97-076393

ISBN 0-9638910-8-1

Manufactured in the United States of America

Once again, for Melissa

CONTENTS

ILLUSTRATIONS

FIGURES

MAPS

ACKNOWLEDGMENTS

My sincere thanks to Albert F. Egan, Jr., and Dorothy H. Egan, whose support through the Egan Foundation and the Egan Institute of Maritime Studies has made this book possible. No one knows more about Nantucket Native Americans than Elizabeth Little; her generosity and insight have helped to make this a better book. The efforts of Wampanoag Tribal Historian Russell Gardner, or Great Moose, on my behalf are greatly appreciated. Special thanks to Helen Vanderhoop Manning and June Manning, who made my stay on Martha's Vineyard as enjoyable as it was productive.

Thanks also to the staffs of the Nantucket Historical Association (especially Jean Weber, Michael Jehle, Betsy Lowenstein, and Peter McGlashan) and the Nantucket Atheneum (Charlotte Maison, Barbara Andrews, Betsy Tyler, and Sharon Carlee). The Nantucket Town Building contains a wealth of documents relating to Native Americans; my thanks to the staffs of the Registry of Deeds, Probate Court, Superior Court, and Town Clerk's Office.

Research off-island was greatly facilitated by the staffs of the Mashpee Indian Museum, Mashpee Archives (especially Rosemary Burns), Martha's Vineyard Historical Society (Jill Bouck and Peter Vascella), Research Library at the Wampanoag Tribal Office at Gay Head Aquinnah, American Antiquarian Society, Massachusetts Historical Society, New Bedford Whaling Museum (Mary Jean Blasdale), Massachusetts Archives, Massachusetts Historical Commission, Supreme Judicial Court Archives (Elizabeth Bouvier), Kendall Whaling Museum (Stuart Frank), and Rhode Island Historical Society (Linda Eppich).

For reading and commenting on all or a portion of the manuscript, I am indebted to Elizabeth Little, Kathleen Bragdon, Michael Gibbons, Russell Gardner, Wes Tiffney, Susan Beegel, Timothy Lepore, Mary Lynne Rainey, Thomas and Marianne Philbrick, Andrew Spielman, Phil and Ursula Austin, Dwight Beman, and Helen Winslow Chase–although all errors are mine and mine alone. More than anyone else, Peter Gow, managing editor at Mill Hill Press, has helped give this manuscript its final shape. Thanks also to Libby Oldham for her careful copyediting and to Fred and Diane Swartz for designing and producing the book. Special thanks to Margaret Moore, Curator at the Egan Institute of Maritime Studies, for help in assembling the images contained in this book, along with countless other tasks associated with the writing and editing of the manuscript.

Others who helped in a variety of ways are Daniel Vickers, Paul Morris, Adelaide Cromwell, Rebecca Roth, Robert diCurcio, Klaus Barthelmess, C. S. Lovelace, Jean MacAusland, Elizabeth Mansfield, Jeffrey Brain, Maggie Philbrick, Augie Ramos, John Peters, Paul Manning, Robert Leach, Paul LaPaglia, M. J. Dickson, and Alicja Mann. Final thanks to my wife, Melissa D. Philbrick, and to our children, Jennie and Ethan, for their patience and understanding.

AUTHOR'S NOTE

Although the text contains no footnotes, an extensive section of endnotes includes not only sources but additional information, anecdotes, legends, and a bibliography. In an effort to make the writings of Native Americans and other historical sources more accessible, the spelling and punctuation of quotations have been modernized. Since, sadly, the pilfering of native artifacts remains a concern on Nantucket, I have been purposefully vague in describing the sites where there is evidence of Indian occupation. Little enough is left of the island's Native American legacy to put what remains at risk.

–Nathaniel Philbrick
November 1997

Whoever attempts to write Native American history must admit in advance to fallibility.... It depends on the imperfect evidence of archaeology; the barely disguised, self-focused testimony of traders, missionaries, and soldiers, all of whom had their own axes to grind and viewed native peoples through a narrow scope; and last and most suspect of all, common sense. The making of cross-cultural, cross-temporal assumptions is enough to send every well-trained Western academic into catatonia, but there is no avoiding it. If we stipulate only a few givens–that Indian societies were composed of people of the normal range of intelligence; that human beings *qua* human beings, where and whenever they may live, share some traits; that Indians were and are human beings–then we have at least a start. We can dare, having amassed and digested all the hard data we can lay our hands on, to leap into the void and attempt to see the world through the eyes of our historical subjects.

–Michael Dorris

Every living thing on an island has been a traveler. Every species of tree, plant, and animal on an island has crossed the beach. In crossing the beach every voyager has brought something old and made something new. The old is written in the forms and habits and needs each newcomer brings. The new is the changed world, the adjusted balance every coming makes. On islands each new intruder finds a freedom it never had in its old environment. On arrival it develops, fills unfilled niches, plays a thousand variations on the themes of its own form.

–Greg Dening

Historical sense and poetic sense should not, in the end, be contradictory, for if poetry is the little myth we make, history is the big myth we live, and in our living constantly remake.

–Robert Penn Warren

PROLOGUE

ABRAM'S EYES

On a sunny morning in July of 1852, Abram Quary emerged from his cottage. Almost eighty years old and with a decided stoop, he shuffled through the beach grass, the sea breeze blowing back his long, graying hair.

He wore an overcoat covered with patches. His dark pants hung loosely and needed mending at the knees. His feet were bare and pointed inward, giving his otherwise arthritic shamble the rolling, pigeon-toed gait of the whaleman he had once been. In his left hand was a white flag.

He lived on a point of land that pierced the narrow confines of the harbor at its western third. On either side of the point were tidal streams and pools, stained the color of tea by the mucky peat, where he fished for eels and crabs. Across the harbor, several miles to the west, was the town: a crowded knoll of houses, church steeples, windmills, and wharves. He attached the flag to a halyard and raised it up a pole.

They would be coming soon, perhaps as many as a dozen of them on a "squantum," the local word for picnic. An hour or so after seeing his signal, they would arrive with their baskets and blankets and Abram would provide them with his roasted "pooquaws," or quahogs. But they didn't come just to taste his shellfish. As he doubtless knew all too well, most made the three-mile trek to his house in Shimmo not to eat, but to see him: Abram Quary, Nantucket Island's last Indian.

Just about every New England town had a "last Indian"—an old man or woman whom white residents regarded as the finish of their town's

Native American legacy. But Abram Quary was not a typical last Indian, just as Nantucket was not a typical New England town.

For almost a hundred years this tiny island twenty-four miles off the south coast of Cape Cod had been the whaling capital of the world–a fishery that had been native long before it ever was American. Without the island's Indians, English Nantucketers would never have had the manpower required to establish a major whaling port. By 1852, however, the Indians had gone the way of the region's whales. Besides Abram, the only other Nantucket Indian was an old woman named Dorcas Honorable.

But it was Abram upon whom white Nantucketers lavished their attention. Out there at the end of a lonely point, he both lived and looked the part of the quintessential last Indian. He wore his hair long, in the traditional Indian manner; he had the requisite high cheekbones and coppery skin; he still spoke Massachusett, the almost extinct language of the Wampanoag. He cooked his pooquaws the way native Nantucketers had been doing for centuries–roasting them in a hole lined with heated stones and covered with seaweed. And best of all, as far as Christian Nantucketers were concerned, it was said that he still sought solace for the loss of his wife and child (both of whom died tragically) through his faith in the Almighty.

Only the year before, thirty-four "Friends of Art" had raised the money necessary to purchase a portrait of Abram for the Nantucket Atheneum Library. The painting had been an immediate sensation. It showed the Indian in his cottage, a pot simmering on the fire. Through an open window behind him the town was visible beneath a thin blue sky. But it was Abram's eyes that almost everyone commented on. Dark brown and clear, they stared at the floor with a soul-wrenching sorrow, a wistfulness that made more than a few visitors to the Atheneum shake their heads and sigh.

Truth be told, the real Abram was something more than a sad, contemplative figurehead for a vanishing people. For one thing, he was by no means alone. Besides Dorcas Honorable, there were many others on Nantucket, particularly in the town's African-American community, who were keenly aware of their Native American ancestry. Abram also had contact with Indians from beyond his island. Some years after the loss of his wife, he began seeing an Indian woman in Sandwich whose descendants would proudly display a lithograph of his portrait well into the twentieth century. As late as the 1920s, a Mrs. Sturgis from the Mashpee Indian community remembered accompanying her father, Ezra Attaquin, on a trip out to see Abram. Then a little girl, she was impressed by his long hair and that he still "spoke Indian."

Part of a regionwide Native American network, Abram was far more connected to the world beyond his island than many white Nantucketers. He was also not about to sit idly by as people trivialized or even desecrated the memory of his Nantucket ancestors. At one point he was hauled into court for threatening to shoot some trinket gatherers who were digging in a nearby Indian burial ground. When the judge (who ultimately dismissed the case) asked if he really would have shot the people if they had continued to dig, he replied without hesitation, "Yes, I would."

According to Benjamin Franklin Folger, one of the few white people who knew him well, Abram Quary was "always distant and reserved with strangers, but friendly with his acquaintances." Still, there were limits. If you made the mistake of asking him a personal question, his "decided taciturnity" would, according to Folger, "run into obstinacy" and he would refuse to speak.

Instead of talking about himself, Abram seems to have preferred to tell stories about his people. Indeed, it is no accident that Folger, who lived in a Quary-like shack of his own at the east end of the island, in Siasconset, was recognized as the leading source of Indian legends on the island.

Although Folger contributed to a handful of articles for the local paper, he was well aware that the written word did not do justice to the stories that Abram and other Nantucket Indians had told him. According to Eliza Mitchell, who remembered visiting Folger when she was twelve years old, "He never seemed willing to give me an opportunity to write any [of his stories] down. But simply said, 'Your memory is good enough, and you'll remember, because you cannot forget.' And so he would, when all was just right, tell me stories of the past."

The white Nantucketers' unwillingness to forget Indian oral traditions meant that even as the island's native population dwindled, the stories they told lived on. As late as 1877, Arthur Gardner recorded "an old Indian tradition…as remembered by many of our older inhabitants." According to Gardner, the Indians had told of how a French ship full of gold had been driven ashore on the eastern end of the island "some time previous to the settlement of the island by the whites." After burying their treasure in an area known as the "Gulch" (not far, as it so happens, from where Folger lived in 'Sconset), the Frenchmen "were compelled to cut their way through the forest" in search of the nearest Indian settlement.

White Nantucketers apparently regarded the story as something more than a legend. Gardner reported that "the beach in that vicinity has been thoroughly dug over within a hundred years, in the vain hope of unearthing the ship's treasure." If this tale is any indication, Nantucket's native traditions remained a vital and respected part of the island's cultural life long after the death of the island's last Indian.

White Nantucketers lent less credence, however, to another group of traditions: tales that told about a giant named Maushop (pronounced "MOSH up") who created Nantucket. Some claimed that Maushop slept on the south shore of Cape Cod. Irritated by the sand that kept accumulating in his moccasins, he eventually threw them into the ocean and formed Martha's Vineyard and Nantucket.

Another legend told of how the giant pursued an eagle with a child

Fig. 1
Purchased by the "Friends of Art" for the Nantucket Atheneum in 1851, this painting by
Herminia Dassel shows Abram Quary in his cottage at Abram's Point in the Shimmo section of the island. With his back to Nantucket's bustling waterfront, Abram is portrayed
as a kind of cultural dead end: a barefooted "last Indian" meditating on his people's sad
and inevitable demise. For white Nantucketers nostalgic for a past that never was, this
painting was both moving and comforting even as it played to their own mounting anx-
ieties concerning their island's future in the wake of the Great Fire of 1846, the disastrous
decline in whaling, and the discovery of gold in California. *Photo by Jack Weinhold. Courtesy of the Nantucket Atheneum Library.*

Fig. 2
By focusing on his eyes, Herminia Dassel's second study of Abram Quary emphasizes the
"sad and mournful countenance" that was so often attributed to the island's last Indian
by white Nantucketers. Of interest is the degree to which Dassel has sanitized Quary of
his pronounced Native American features, clearly visible in Figures 3 and 4. *Photo by Terry
Pommett. Courtesy of the Nantucket Historical Association.*

ABRAHAM QUARY.

The last Indian of the Nantucket tribe.

Presented to the Author by Col. J. C. Hart of New York

Fig. 3

Instead of the retiring and contemplative "last Indian" of the Dassel portraits, this lithograph by an unknown artist portrays a much younger Abram Quary possessed of considerable dignity and resolve, proudly wearing an undetermined medal. The image first appeared in 1836 in the booklet *Abraham Quary: A Sketch* by J. O. Lewis. The note beneath the portrait reads, "Presented to the Author by Col. J. C. Hart of New York." Hart was the author of *Miriam Coffin, or The Whale-Fishermen*, the 1834 historical novel set on Nantucket, which contained a detailed description of Abram Quary. Quary gave a woman friend on Cape Cod a copy of this portrait that was subsequently displayed by her descendants in Sandwich as late as the 1950s. *Courtesy of the Nantucket Historical Association.*

Fig. 4
The eyes that stare out at us from this remarkable daguerreotype of Abram Quary, circa 1848, are very different from those portrayed by Herminia Dassel, providing clear evidence of the degree to which popular portrayals of Quary, both visual and literary, represented him as a symbol instead of a man. *Courtesy of the Nantucket Historical Association.*

Fig. 5

A split-ash, handwoven basket, circa 1850, attributed to Abram Quary. Other evidence of Quary's handiwork can be seen in the Dassel painting in Figure 1, which includes a large basket full of huckleberries. According to Benjamin Franklin Folger, Quary's mother, Sarah Apie, was known for her skill as a basketweaver. Folger also recalled the time when Quary visited him at his house in Siasconset (see Figure 8) and "amused himself by making for a present a basket of beach grass." *Photo by Terry Pommett. Courtesy of the Nantucket Historical Association.*

Fig. 6

If Abram Quary was considered Nantucket's last Indian male, Dorcas Honorable, shown here in the middle of the nineteenth century, was the island's last Indian woman, dying a few months after Quary in the town's poorhouse in 1855. According to Eliza Mitchell, Honorable was the granddaughter of the Indian minister Benjamin Tashama and was an imposing presence: "six feet tall, a noble woman of her tribe, always kept aloof from bad company, lived to be over eighty." Proving that neither Dorcas Honorable nor Abram Quary qualified as the end of the Native American line on Nantucket is the fact that Dorcas is known to have had a granddaughter named Isabel Castro who by 1895 had married a man named Hiram Reed. *Courtesy of the Nantucket Historical Association.*

Fig. 7
Mrs. R.H. Sturgis, shown here in the 1920s, was one of ten children of Ezra and Sara Jones Attaquin of Mashpee. Mrs. Sturgis lived to be ninety-seven years old and remembered the time when as a child she accompanied her father on a trip out to Nantucket Island to visit with Abram Quary. She recalled being impressed by his long hair and that he still "spoke Indian." *From the photo collection of Earl Mills, Sr., courtesy of Word Studio.*

Fig. 8
This photograph of the Upper Broadway whale cottages in Siasconset was taken in the 1860s, only a few years after the death of Benjamin Franklin Folger, a hermit and preserver of the island's oral traditions. Folger lived in the fourth cottage from the left, known as Nonantum, which was said to mean welcome in the Massachusett language. It was here that Folger frequently entertained Abram Quary and learned the legends and stories he would pass on to future generations of Nantucketers. Rather like the Native Americans themselves, Folger, according to Eliza Barney, "eschewed the use of the pen himself," leaving it to others to record the information he had learned. Although several articles appeared in the *Nantucket Inquirer* under his byline, they appear to have been ghostwritten by others. *Courtesy of the Nantucket Historical Association.*

in its talons to the previously undiscovered island of Nantucket. After finding the child's bones beneath a tree, Maushop sat down for a long, contemplative smoke and created Nantucket's notorious fog.

Others claimed that Maushop lived on Martha's Vineyard, where he feasted on whales and smoked his pipe in a crater beside the cliffs of Gay Head. Initially the giant welcomed the Indians who began to gather around him, sharing his whales with them and creating Nantucket as a gift with the ashes from his pipe. Then Maushop turned sullen and unpredictable, ultimately transforming his five children into killer whales and throwing his wife onto the rocky shores of Rhode Island before disappearing altogether.

As far as white Nantucketers were concerned, the Maushop legends were the Indian equivalent of fairy tales. According to Eva Folger, who recorded the legend of Maushop's moccasins in 1911, "While these make pleasing additions to folklore, yet their true bearing on history is of very little value."

It is only recently that we have begun to appreciate the importance of Maushop. In 1976, Meredith Marshall Brenizer published *The Nantucket Indians: Legends and Accounts Before 1659*, in which the various stories about the giant and Nantucket were collected for the first time. Meanwhile, the archaeologist and historian Elizabeth Little began to explore the treasure trove of documents (many of them authored by Nantucket Indians) in town and state archives, providing a previously unavailable historical context for the legends collected by Brenizer. In 1982 the anthropologist William Simmons brought Maushop to the attention of academic folklorists, claiming that the tales of Maushop may be "the oldest continuously recorded body of living Indian legends known anywhere in North America."

Eventually Simmons published *Spirit of the New England Tribes*, including a definitive collection of Maushop legends extending from the seventeenth century to 1983. In Simmons's view, Maushop is one of the few remaining connections to a culture that would otherwise be lost: "Whereas language, kinship organization, and subsistence patterns have all disappeared, these legends have been an important part of Indian identity in this region throughout the historic period." But how far back do they go?

Nantucket became an island between 5,000 and 7,000 years ago, when rising sea levels associated with melting of the glaciers flooded the low-lying area we now call Nantucket Sound. Since there is archaeological evidence that the region had been inhabited for thousands of years prior to this event, the possibility exists that the Maushop legends have truly ancient origins.

But as anthropologists studying the still-evolving traditions of native peoples in South America have found, Indian legends do not exist in "a timeless, unchanging state." Historic events are continually working their way into the mythic time frame described by a preexisting oral tradition, thus blurring the boundaries between mythic and historical times.

One of the most catastrophic historic events an indigenous culture can experience is European contact. According to George Hamell, the oral traditions of Indians throughout North America began to change "within the span of a single generation [to] explain the present reality of that community's...contact experience." This suggests that even if the Maushop legends (the first was recorded in 1702) existed prior to the arrival of the English, they rapidly evolved to reflect the devastating experiences of Indians after contact.

Certainly the story of Maushop bears an unmistakable similarity to what happened to his people during the seventeenth century. In the beginning the giant is a free man—luxuriating on the expansive beaches of Cape Cod or feasting on the whales that once frequented the waters off Gay Head. Then things begin to change: The sand in his moccasins irritates him to the point that he flings his shoes into the sea; a predatory bird appears in the skies above the Cape; Indians from the mainland begin to move out to his island home beside the cliffs. It is during this period of disturbing flux that Nantucket comes into the picture. Whether it is a hurled moccasin or the ashy contents of Maushop's pipe, the island's origin/discovery is attributed to events first set into motion either on Cape Cod to the northeast or Martha's Vineyard to the west.

Although they may be partially based on myths that date back thousands of years, Maushop's actions relative to Nantucket display a desperation and immediacy in keeping with the disastrous and late-breaking changes associated with European contact—an event that, according to Simmons, clearly had a "formative effect" on the legends. The question then becomes, if these traditions are not describing the literal creation of Nantucket, what are they *really* talking about?

From the perspective of Native American culture, Nantucket is an extinct volcano: a place that once burned with a tumultuous, even explosive heat, but which has now grown cold. Almost every place-name on Nantucket (which means "faraway land") is Massachusett in origin, but no Indians of Nantucket descent still call the island home. Arrowhead collectors and archaeologists may have their stones and bones, but for those looking to imbue the artifacts with a flicker of life, very little remains—with the exception of the portrait in the Nantucket Atheneum with its brown, pensive eyes.

Abram's eyes are at once a mirror and a mask, inviting us into the world of the Nantucket Indian yet ultimately denying access—leaving us, in the end, with our own vulnerable and yearning selves. Indian legends might be considered the literary equivalent of those eyes: once-living stories that have been preserved and, of course, distorted by white people as written texts. Yet the distortions are also part of the story, telling us as much about the turbulent times through which the legends have traveled as they do about the events that inspired them.

Fully recognizing the impossibility of identifying an authentically

Indian point of view, this book looks to Maushop as a way to recover an understanding of how native Nantucketers experienced their world. As Simmons has said, "Despite…the deadening effect that the arrival of Europeans had on the mythical age, the legends still convey a self-contained magical world where the ancestors, landscape, weather, sounds, and sea creatures are alive in distinctly Indian ways."

However, as several Native American scholars have pointed out, what is "magical" to a Westerner is literally true to an Indian. If we are to appreciate legendary giants such as Maushop for who they really are, we must enter a universe where myth is more than mere fiction; it is a higher reality. According to Robin Ridington, "Unless we can find some way to understand the reality of mythic thinking we remain prisoners of our own language, our own thoughtworld. In our world one story is real, the other, fantasy. In the Indian way of thinking both stories are true because they describe personal experience."

With Maushop serving as a kind of Native American Virgil to our Dante, this book attempts to retrieve a sense of the island's mythic past in the context of the documented record we call history. And if, like Virgil, Maushop must leave us part way through our journey (with the arrival of the English), he is never completely gone. As Ridington says, "Historical events happened once and are gone forever. Mythic events return like the swans of spring…. They are essential truths, not contingent ones."

To this day, Abram Quary's cultural, if not literal, descendants in Mashpee and Gay Head still speak of Maushop–a giant who transformed himself, according to one account, into a white whale known as Moby Dick. Using the Wampanoag's own lead, this book looks to Melville's novel as a way to trace the mythic continuities between the worlds of the Nantucket Indian and the Nantucket whaleman. By accepting the Indians' legends as flexible and renewable truths (instead of "flawed history"), perhaps we can begin to see the Native American legacy of Nantucket Island through Abram's eyes.

1

AN ISLAND IN TIME

On the west end of Martha's Vineyard are high cliffs of variegated colored earths, known by the name of Gay Head. On the top of the hill is a large cavity, which has the appearance of the crater of an extinguished volcano, and there are evident marks of former subterranean fires. The Indians who live about this spot have a tradition that a certain deity resided there before the Europeans came into America, that his name was Maushop; that he used to step out on a ledge of rocks which ran into the sea, and take up a whale, which he broiled for his own eating on the coals of the aforesaid volcano, and often invited the Indians to dine with him, or gave them the relics of his meal. That once to show their gratitude to Maushop for his very great kindness to them, they made an offering to him of all the tobacco which grew upon the island in one season. This was scarcely sufficient to fill his great pipe, but he received the present very graciously, smoked his pipe, and turned out the ashes of it into the sea, which formed the island of Nantucket. Upon the coming of the Europeans into America, Maushop retired in disgust, and has never since been seen.

—Anonymous, 1787

Today we think of Nantucket as a whaling port turned summer resort, a place of historically correct houses and wide, picture-perfect beaches. But Nantucket's present-day reputation does not justly reflect its past. Instead of the birthplace of the Quaker whaleman (who flourished for a mere century or so), Nantucket should be remembered as, in the words of Massachusetts Governor John Winthrop, "an island full of Indians." For the vast majority of its history, Nantucket had been home to a people who viewed it not as a sandy launching pad to wealth or relaxation, but as an island of remarkable variety and abundance.

It began with a glacier, a giant sheet of ice that pushed its way south from the Arctic Circle and ended where Nantucket is today. When the southern edge of the glacier started to melt between 14,000 and 16,000 years ago, the ocean was as much as 400 feet below its current level, and Nantucket emerged as a ragged pile of glacial deposits more than fifty miles inland.

As the glacier melted, rivers of water ran to the south, carving out channels that would become the basis of valleys and ponds while buried chunks of ice created the round kettleholes that dot the island today. When people first began to venture in Nantucket's direction approximately 10,000 years ago, it was a low ridge of windswept hills overlooking a terrain that had evolved from open tundra and grasslands into groves of pine, spruce, and hemlock. A large glacial lake dominated what is now Nantucket Sound. Perhaps using the Nantucket hills as a break against the ice-cooled northerly winds, those early hunters (called the Paleo people by anthropologists) pursued mastodon, caribou, and moose.

Between 8,000 and 10,000 years ago (known as the Early Archaic era), the climate became significantly warmer. The caribou and other large game animals moved north. Oaks replaced the spruce and pine as the most common tree. The area's human inhabitants were forced to adjust, relying on new forms of plants (nuts, berries, and roots) as well as fish (Atlantic salmon, alewives, and shad) that migrated up rivers and streams. Instead of caribou, the Early Archaic people hunted deer. To assist in killing this smaller, swifter prey, hunters developed a spear-throwing device known as an *atl-atl*: a weighted, hooked stick that afforded the thrower added leverage to hurl a spear farther and with greater accuracy.

As the temperatures rose, so did the sea level. Some time during the Archaic period, more than 5,000 years ago, this ridge of hills became the island of Nantucket. Ocean currents quickly transformed the island into a rough approximation of what it is today. As the south shore became a relatively featureless stretch of sand, tidal rips teased the extreme northeast tip of the island into the narrow curl of sand known as Great Point. Meanwhile, Nantucket's north shore benefited from the formation of a barrier beach now called Coatue, creating a lagoon-like breeding ground for fish and shellfish.

The Late Archaic Indians fished with hooks and spears equipped with slender stone points manufactured from materials found, for the most part, along the harbor's pebbly south shore. Fish weirs, made of sticks interwoven among stakes arranged to create a fence-like maze, were used to capture the fish feeding in estuaries.

Trade seems to have flourished at this time, providing the islanders with materials that were otherwise unavailable. Chert for spear points and soapstone bowls from quarries on the mainland made their way to the island.

By three thousand years ago, when what is called the Woodland period began, new technologies from the west were being introduced that would revolutionize the Indians' way of life. Vessels made of ceramic pottery were much lighter than those made of soapstone. By the Late Woodland period, between 400 and 1,000 years ago, the Native Americans had become committed agriculturists, growing squash, gourds, beans, and, finally, maize, specifically a strain known as flint corn distinguished by eight- to nine-inch cobs of multicolored kernels. The Indians also had a new and much more effective weapon: the bow and arrow, allowing them to hunt with an efficiency that would ultimately reduce the island's deer population to dangerously low levels.

Instead of hunter-gatherers who roamed over a large territory, these people were tied to a specific portion of the island, shifting their village sites within a limited range according to the season. By relocating their wigwams (dome-shaped houses made of bent saplings covered with grass mats) to the shore during the summer, the Indians kept fish and shellfish close at hand while sea breezes dispersed insects.

Two or more families typically shared a wigwam (which they

called a "wetu"), reclining on low sleeping platforms around a central fire. In this companionable, often smoky space, the Indians cooked, ate, told stories, picked the fleas that infested the wigwams' dirt floors, and often, at night, chanted among themselves. Daily life was crowded with activity—the women tending the crops, caring for the children, gathering shellfish, and ceaselessly grinding corn while the men hunted and fished. According to Roger Williams, "They are full of business, and impatient of hindrances (in their kind) as any merchant in Europe."

Since some of Nantucket's most fertile land lies along the harbor, the northeastern portion of the island was ideally suited to their fishing and farming lifestyle. The Indians' habit of burning the land prior to spring planting permanently changed the entire ecology of the island, eventually limiting woodlands to where ponds and swamps protected the trees from the flames. In the swamps to the southwest of Siasconset grew large numbers of groundnuts—fleshy, potato-like tubers that were an important food source for the Indians. In winter it was to such low, protected areas, where the natural contours of the land maximized southerly exposure to the sun while deflecting northerly winds, that the Indians moved their wigwams.

Necessity and culture gave the Indians an intimate, visceral, and decidedly spiritual connection with their island. It was part of their very beings. According to Roger Williams, an Indian could "picture the face of the country on his mind." Onto the Indian's consciousness was printed the image of many landscapes: the grassy sweep of Nantucket's western half; the sheltering undulance of the main harbor's southern edge; the swampy warmth of the eastern interior, where the Indians lived on islands of higher ground; and the wave-battered, whalebone-whitened southern beaches.

These landscapes were also part of the Indians' collective memory. In the vicinity of Plymouth, the Native Americans were in the habit of digging round, foot-deep holes in the ground where "any remarkable act" had occurred. According to the Pilgrim Edward Winslow, the holes ensured that "many things of antiquity are held fresh in memory." Thus an Indian walking Nantucket's many narrow, hard-packed trails was also traversing a mythic land where trees and ponds, rocks and dunes connected him with the past.

The Indians' internal landscapes also included the waters surrounding the island. In the Pacific Northwest, native fishermen and whalers relied on songs that preserved "everything we ever knew about the movement of the sea" to guide them on their voyages. Native Nantucketers who voyaged to and from the island in dugout canoes undoubtedly possessed their own traditional knowledge of the currents, rips, and shoals that make these waters some of the most dangerous in the world.

While the Indians regularly negotiated the virtual maze of shoals and islands stretching to the west toward Martha's Vineyard and to the northeast toward Cape Cod, it would be another story altogether for European explorers and fishermen. For the vast majority of these navigators, who also had to contend with the network of sand, rock, and gravel (known as the Nantucket Shoals) that extends out for almost fifty miles to the south of the island, Nantucket remained well hidden. This meant that as Europeans infiltrated nearby Cape Cod and Martha's Vineyard in the early seventeenth century, Nantucket became something more than an island in the ocean; it became, from a Native American perspective, an island in time.

For more than five thousand years, the ever-rising waters have been nibbling at Nantucket's edges. In as little as another six hundred years, the flood that first created the island will have completely washed Nantucket away. All Nantucketers—past, present, and future—are awaiting a burial at sea.

In the meantime, significant archaeological evidence of the island's first inhabitants remains. Nantucket is so littered with arrowheads ("projectile points" to the archaeologist) that if you know where to look and the conditions are right (the day after a hard rain is perfect), you are almost guaranteed of finding, if not a point or a scraper or some other tool, at least the flakes left by an ancient stoneworker.

More than fifty shell middens (the equivalent of garbage dumps) have been identified on the island, containing not only shells but also the remains of fish, birds, seals, foxes, whales, turtles, deer, and other animals. Pieces of clay pottery, bone fishhooks, stone sinkers, weapons, and other implements have also been found on the island, as have human remains. In at least two instances, the skeleton of a small, fox-like native dog has been discovered curled up at its master's feet.

In the summer of 1995, as part of a federally mandated repatriation project, the skeletal remains of more than thirty Indians in the holdings of the Nantucket Historical Association were analyzed prior to their return to the earth. The preliminary results of the survey (conducted by the anthropologist Michael Gibbons) are at once surprising and predictable, particularly if we bear in mind the legends of the giant Maushop.

The evidence suggests that the average Nantucketer from between 500 and 1,000 years ago was significantly taller and healthier than the average Indian from the mainland, with one notable exception: bad teeth. It is an interesting detail in light of one legendary claim that Maushop, the creator of Nantucket, had only two teeth "green as the ooze raked up by the winds from the bottom of the sea."

Gibbons estimates that the average Nantucket male was five feet nine inches tall, while a female stood five feet three and a half inches, making both of them more than an inch and a half taller than their mainland counterparts. They also lived longer by an average of three and a half to four years. These findings are indirectly corroborated by

Fig. 9
A soapstone vessel found on the farm of George West in Chilmark on Martha's Vineyard in 1903. A bowl of this type was uncovered on Nantucket in the 1950s during the grading of a driveway at the Nantucket High School. Unfortunately, it was inadvertently crushed by a bulldozer. *Photo by Jill Bouck. Courtesy of the Martha's Vineyard Historical Society.*

Fig. 10
From Nantucket, possibly a grooved sinker for a fishing line or net. *Photo by Terry Pommett. Courtesy of the Nantucket Historical Association.*

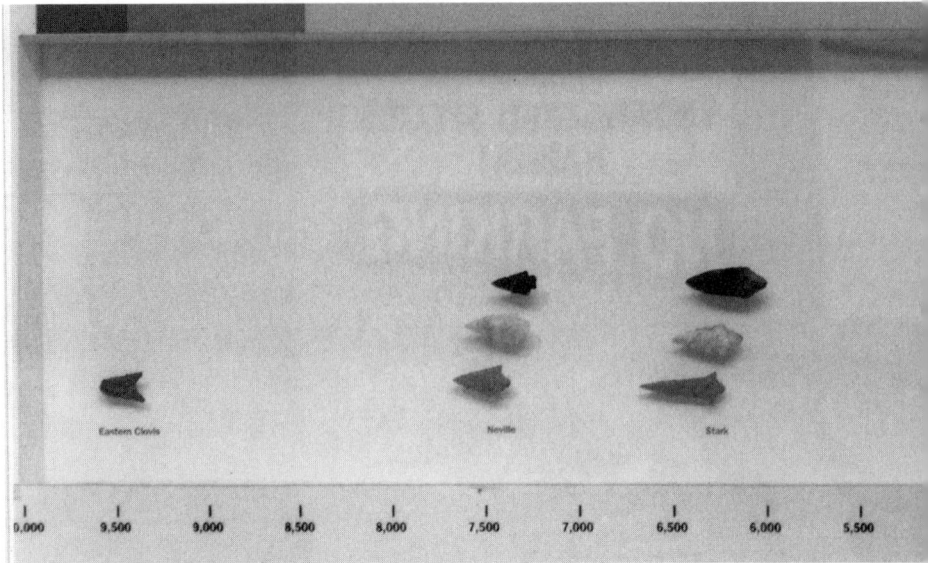

Fig. 11
A display of projectile points found on Nantucket Island that demonstrates how the shape of the points changed over time. *Photo by Terry Pommett. Courtesy of the Nantucket Historical Association.*

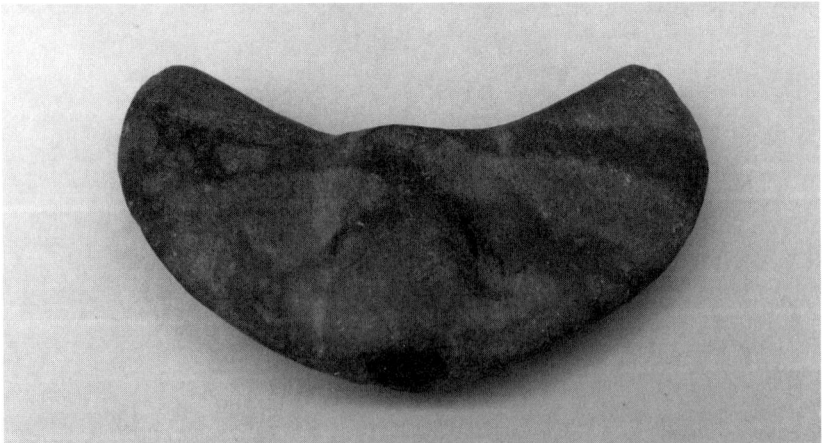

Fig. 12
A beautifully crafted, whale-tail-shaped *atl-atl* weight found in 1980 in Tisbury, near Lagoon Pond on Martha's Vineyard. *Photo by Jill Bouck. Courtesy of the Martha's Vineyard Historical Society.*

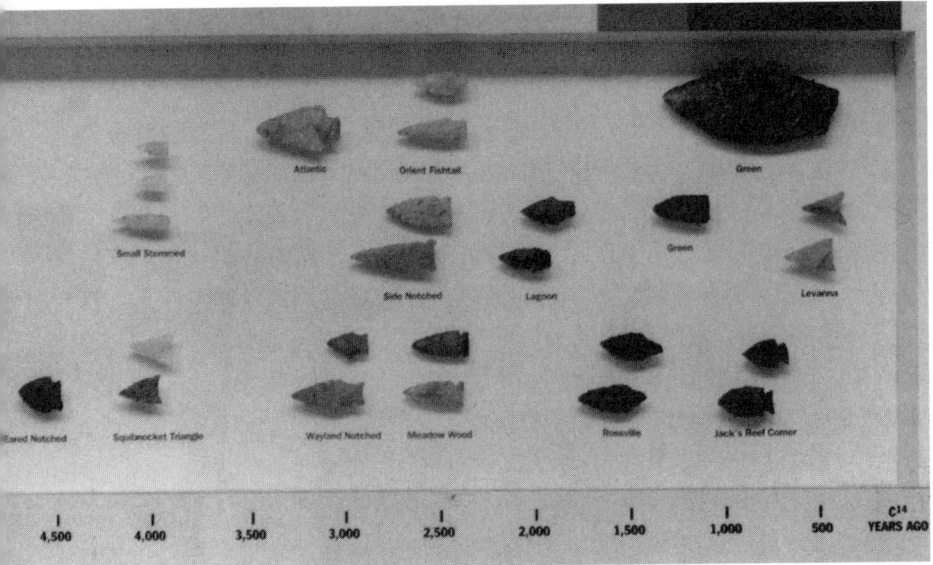

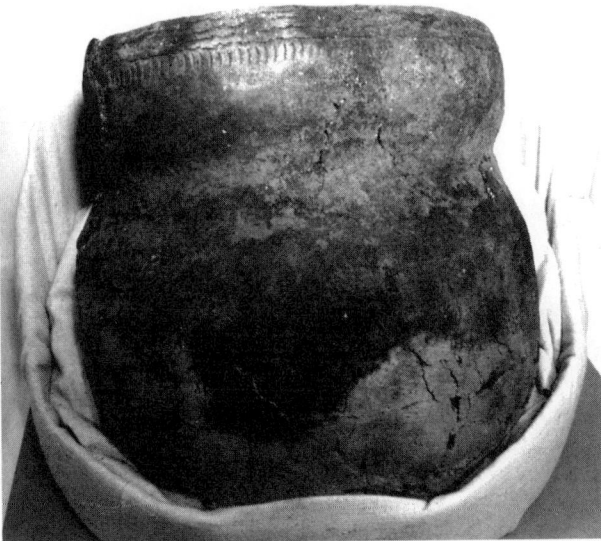

Fig. 13
A ceramic vessel, approximately 700 years old, from Chilmark, Martha's Vineyard. Although numerous potsherds have been found on Nantucket, this remarkable find, discovered by Richard Burt in 1952, bears witness to the functional beauty of Native American pottery. *Photo by Jill Bouck. Courtesy of Martha's Vineyard Historical Society.*

Figs. 14 and 15
An ax head (top) and gouge from Nantucket that may have been used to cut wigwam frames and dugout canoes. *Photos by Terry Pommett. Courtesy of the Nantucket Historical Association.*

Fig. 16
A mortar and pestle, circa 1750, made by Indians in Nantucket's Miacomet village. *Photo by Terry Pommett. Courtesy of the Nantucket Historical Association.*

Fig. 17

Whalebone tools from Nantucket. The two smaller tools, which may be spades, were found in Madaket; the larger, shovel-like tool is from Quidnet, on the opposite end of the island. *Photo by Nathaniel Philbrick. Collection of Paul Morris.*

Fig. 18
Hide-working tools from Nantucket collected by Nelson O. Dunham and Alfred F. Shurrocks. The stone scraper was used to clean the hide, and the bone awl and needles were used to make holes in the hide for sewing. *Photo by Terry Pommett. Courtesy of the Nantucket Historical Association.*

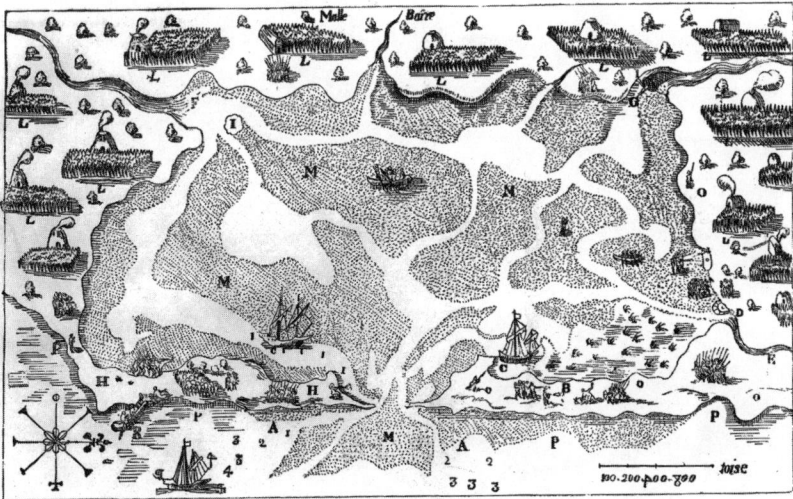

Fig. 19
This 1613 chart representing what the French explorer Samuel Champlain encountered in the Nauset area of Cape Cod illustrates what the settlement pattern around Nantucket Harbor may have been like prior to the arrival of English settlers. Note the many shoreside wigwams, each surrounded by its own plot of farmland. *By permission of the Houghton Library, Harvard University.*

Fig. 20

Although portraying Native American activity in the Virginia area, scenes such as this undoubtedly occurred on Nantucket, where Indians also fished from dugout canoes and used weirs similar to the one shown in the upper left. By Theodor de Bry. *Photo courtesy of Edward E. Ayer Collection, The Newberry Library, Chicago.*

the observations of English explorers at the beginning of the seventeenth century. Indians along the southern edge of Cape Cod were, according to the English (who averaged a measly five feet seven inches), "of stature much higher than we," while Indians just a few miles to the north on Cape Cod Bay were "only somewhat taller than our ordinary people." Moving up the coast to Maine, the English found the Indians to be "not tall...in stature like us."

If these observations are to be trusted, height variations in keeping with Gibbons's findings were clearly discernible along the New England coast and may have contributed to the association of a mythical giant with Cape Cod and the islands to the south. But why were these Indians so tall? To account for the height variations, we must look to the Indians' environment.

Nantucket, Martha's Vineyard, and the south shore of Cape Cod have much in common. But Nantucket is something more than a fifty-square-mile piece of the Cape. It is an island with an almost thirty-mile buffer between itself and the mainland.

As observers from Sir Thomas Moore to Charles Darwin have noted, islands are ecological and cultural laboratories where trends that might be only dimly perceived on the mainland are brought into bold relief. Islands tend toward extremes. The highs are higher, the lows are lower. To live on an island is to be in a permanent state of schizophrenia—booming and busting with an abandon that resonates across the waters. As David Quammen has said, "Islands are distinct from mainlands in that they represent simplified, exaggerated versions of exactly those evolutionary processes that occur on mainlands."

Whereas deer were relatively plentiful throughout the Cape and Martha's Vineyard, on Nantucket their numbers would begin to decrease. At some point during the seventeenth century (if not before), overhunting killed them all off. The scarcity of deer on Nantucket would have forced the Indians to rely on what they could either grow or catch in the sea, requiring them to eat what may have been a healthier, height-enhancing diet.

More than compensating for the lack of game animals were the astonishing quantities of fish, especially shellfish, supported within what is one of the most estuary-riddled terrains on the planet. Indeed, it would be difficult to design an environment better suited for breeding shellfish than Nantucket. The intricate convolutions of Nantucket Harbor, along with the many ponds and inlets scattered throughout the western and eastern extremes of the island support-ed (and continue to support) extraordinary levels of quahogs, scal-lops, clams, oysters, and mussels. Crabs were so plentiful on Nantucket that one legend claimed that Maushop had personally delivered them to the island.

Nantucket's remote, offshore location also worked to its advan-tage. Huge schools of bluefish, sea bass, cod, and sturgeon (some as long as eighteen feet) frequented island waters on a seasonal basis. Right whales migrating down the coast every fall were virtually fun-neled in Nantucket's direction by the arm of Cape Cod; as a result, the many shoals surrounding the island produced more than their share of stranded whales throughout the fall, winter, and early spring. Birds migrating up and down the eastern seaboard regularly stopped at Nantucket.

Being so far out to sea placed the island within the warming influ-ence of the Gulf Stream, providing for the longest frost-free growing season in the region. And while corn is a wonderful and nutritious food, it has a tendency to stick to the teeth and cause cavities–hence the native Nantucketers' dental problems, a deficiency that the grit associated with shellfish only exacerbated.

Living on an island that was like the rest of the Cape and islands, but only more so, Nantucketers seem to have established their own identity. The pots Nantucketers fashioned from the blue and yellow clay found along the island's northern shore may have been cruder, thicker, and perhaps bigger than pots found elsewhere in the region, according to a comparative analysis performed by Barbara Luedtke. While blue and white shell beads known as wampum became the accepted form of currency throughout New England in the sixteenth and seventeenth centuries, Nantucketers, in typical island fashion, chose to go their own way, using instead strings of sun-dried clams "in their mutual exchanges," even though, according to one account, "they had all the materials [for wampum] on the shore."

Nantucketers may have also developed their own approaches to clothing and cooking–approaches that were, in Quammen's words, "simplified, exaggerated versions" of what already made the Indians from this part of the New England coast unique. Whereas European explorers reported that Indians on the Cape had "but few skins," Nantucketers appear to have had even fewer, dressing themselves, according to one account, in "coarse mats, made of grass." Another tradition insisted that Nantucket Indians were "acquainted with roast-ing, but not with boiling." This may be a garbled reference to the rou-tine use of an underground oven of heated stones for cooking–a method well adapted to Nantucket's sandy, easily worked soils and the wide range of foods available on the island. This type of roast-ing/steaming is also relatively fuel-efficient compared to boiling, par-ticularly advantageous on an island where supplies of firewood were never great. One Maushop legend even claimed that before knocking out the ash from his pipe to create the island, the giant first dug a hole in the ocean floor and filled it with heated stones. On an island of relatively tall people who cooked just about everything–from fish to clams to corn–in a shoreside "subterranean oven," perhaps it was inevitable that Nantucket's creation be associated with a giant and a hole full of heated stones.

The portraits we have of Maushop in his early days–of a good-natured, even shy, giant who freely shared his bounty with all those who made their way out to his island–may reflect the congenial, simple, and unaffected way of life that typified Nantucket's Indians in the beginning of the seventeenth century. But if Nantucketers were the affable, green-toothed Maushops of southern New England, then why didn't the island's first English settlers (who began to appear in 1659) make any mention of the Indians being especially large or, for that matter, cavity prone?

To begin to appreciate how life was forever changed on Nantucket almost half a century before the arrival of the first white settlers, we must now approach the moment when this island of myths finally entered the methodical succession of days called history.

2

AN EAGLE IN THE YEAR OF *The Tempest*

In former times, a great many moons ago, a bird, extraordinary for its size, used often to visit the south shore of Cape Cod, and carry from thence to the southward, a vast number of small children. Maushop, who was an Indian giant, as fame reports, resided in these parts. Enraged at the havoc among the children, he, on a certain time, waded into the sea in pursuit of the bird, till he had crossed the sound and reached Nantucket. Before Maushop forded the sound, the island was unknown to the aborigines of America.

Tradition says, that Maushop found the bones of the children in a heap under a large tree. He then wishing to smoke a pipe, ransacked the island for tobacco; but, finding none, filled his pipe with poke, a weed which the Indians sometimes used as its substitute. Ever since the above memorable event, fogs have been frequent at Nantucket and on the Cape. In allusion to this tradition, when the aborigines observed a fog rising, they would say, "There comes old Maushop's smoke."

> *—as told to the Reverend Timothy Alden by a*
> *"good old Quaker lady" from Yarmouth, 1798*

Throughout the first decade of the seventeenth century, Nantucket remained virtually invisible to the Europeans. Cloaked by shoals and frequent fog, yet intimately connected to the Native American world around it, Nantucket's inhabitants could, for a time at least, observe the European invasion from a position of relative safety.

It began peacefully enough–at least according to what records have survived–with the arrival of Giovanni da Verrazano on the New England coast in 1524. Although the Italian explorer made his way into Nantucket Sound (where the shoals so frightened and annoyed him that he named the body of water for a hated tax collector), he does not appear to have even seen Nantucket. He did, however, leave a detailed account of the Indians he met forty-five miles to the west in today's Newport Harbor:

> Among them were two kings more beautiful in form and stature than can possibly be described; one was about forty years old, the other about twenty-four, and they were dressed in the following manner: The oldest had a deer's skin around his body, artificially wrought in damask figures, his head was without covering, his hair was tied back in various knots; around his neck he wore a large chain ornamented with many stones of different colors. The young man was similar in his general appearance. This is the finest looking tribe, the handsomest in their costumes, that we have found in our voyage.

In 1602, the English explorer Bartholomew Gosnold was equally impressed with the Indians he saw in the vicinity of Nantucket. After rounding a large, hook-shaped peninsula that he named for the cod caught by his men, he and his crew found themselves in the same dangerous waters that had so perplexed Verrazano almost eighty years before. Eventually the English made it across Nantucket Sound to an island Gosnold called Martha's Vineyard. From there they ventured to Cuttyhunk Island at the end of the Elizabeth group, with an additional exploratory trip to the north shore of Buzzards Bay.

For these seamen what is now the southeast coast of Massachusetts was a paradise made real: "Coming ashore, we stood a while like men ravished at the beauty and delicacy of this sweet soil." Instead of an impenetrable wilderness, they found the New World equivalent of an English park: wide, crystal-clear lakes, endless meadows of green grass, and a most civilized, sun-dappled forest with plenty of open space between the trees. What they were seeing was the result of centuries of Native American land management, but for

Gosnold and his men it seemed as if some supernatural force had been at work, boosting Nature "above her power, artificial."

With plans to establish a settlement, Gosnold's men began building a fort on Cuttyhunk. A few days later, a delegation of fifty Indians in nine canoes arrived from the mainland for the purposes of trade. It was obvious to Gosnold and his men that one of the Indians was looked to with great respect. Some have speculated that this may have been the father of Massasoit, the Wampanoag sachem who would greet the Pilgrims eighteen years later; he may have also been a descendant of the "two kings" Verrazano met in Newport, not far from Massasoit's ancestral seat at Mount Hope, near present-day Bristol, Rhode Island.

After the Indian leader accepted the English gift of a pair of knives and a straw hat (placing it experimentally on his head), he and his people "all sat down in manner like greyhounds upon their heels" and began to trade. With the exception of mustard ("whereat they made a sour face"), the Native Americans seemed to enjoy all the strange foods the English had to offer. For their part, the white men took an immediate fancy to the Indians' tobacco, a dried green powder that when smoked in carefully crafted clay pipes proved addictively pleasant.

Although the Englishmen were at a loss to fathom the natives' language, the Indians proved to have an unnerving ability to mimic the white men's speech. At one point a sailor sat smoking beside an Indian and said, "How now, sir, are you so saucy with my tobacco?" Suddenly, the Indian repeated the phrase word-for-word, "as if he had been a long scholar in the language."

But Gosnold's idyllic introduction to the area and its people turned as sour as his mustard. While foraging for food, two of his men were attacked by four Indians who may have been recent arrivals on the island. Although the English escaped with their lives (in large part because one of the men had the presence of mind to cut the strings of the natives' bows with his knife), Gosnold decided to abandon his initial plan of establishing a year-round trading post. With supplies of food already running dangerously low, the English headed back across the Atlantic with a profitable load of sassafras (used both as an aphrodisiac and to treat syphilis).

Although local historians have been eager to claim Gosnold as the first European to discover Nantucket, there is no proof that he came within sight of the island. Nantucket may have also escaped the roving eyes of the explorer George Waymouth in 1605 whose description of a white sandy cliff was, according to the findings of David and Alison Quinn, the Lower Cape Cod Highlands instead of (as is often claimed) Nantucket's Sankaty Head. There is no evidence that Samuel de Champlain, who voyaged to the south shore of Cape Cod in 1604 and 1606, ever saw Nantucket. Significantly, a 1610 map of the region, known as the Velasco map and thought to have been based on information provided by Gosnold and perhaps others, includes a surprisingly accurate rendering of Cape Cod, Martha's Vineyard, and the Elizabeth Islands but shows no Nantucket.

As the number of European visitors to the region increased throughout the first decade of the seventeenth century so did, inevitably, the outbreaks of violence. A year after Gosnold's voyage, an Englishman named Martin Pring built a palisaded trading camp on the north shore of Cape Cod. Just as had occurred on Cuttyhunk, mounting tensions with the Indians forced Pring and his men to abandon their fort, but not before unleashing their dogs (a pair of giant mastiffs) and firing on the Indians. In 1605, Waymouth and his men kidnapped five Abenaki Indians in Maine. By the time Champlain ventured to Cape Cod, the Indians were prepared for the worst, with several deadly skirmishes breaking out between the natives and the French.

Although they had so far escaped detection by the Europeans, Nantucket's Indians would inevitably have heard stories about those early contact experiences. Their imaginations fired by tales of mysterious ships bringing with them trade goods and violence, native Nantucketers may have begun to look out from the shores of their island home with increasing concern and expectation. And in the early summer of 1611, someone saw a sail.

In the very year that William Shakespeare produced *The Tempest*, about an enchanted island in the throes of European contact, the Earl of Southampton, one of the playwright's patrons, financed an exploratory voyage to "an isle supposed about Cape Cod." Led by Captain Edward Harlow, the expedition first made landfall at Monhegan (an island off the coast of present-day Maine already well known to Europeans), then headed west and south along the New England coast toward Cape Cod. Whether or not the English had heard about this previously uncharted island from the region's Native Americans, Harlow, like so many explorers before him, found nothing but treacherous shoals to the south of the Cape's elbow. Perhaps in hopes of finding an Indian who could help guide him to this fabled island, Harlow decided to postpone his search and head for Cape Cod.

Anchorages were not easy to find along the Cape's south shore, but eventually Harlow found a spot (possibly Stage Harbor in Chatham, where Champlain had been several years earlier) where he could drop anchor. Harlow's interest in the local Indians went beyond finding a guide. In addition to trading with the natives, he planned to cover the cost of his voyage by bringing some of them back to England. Except for perhaps a bear-baiting, nothing drew a paying crowd in London like an Indian from America. (In *The Tempest* Trinculo claims that while the English "will not give a doit [a Dutch coin worth less than a cent] to relieve a lame beggar, they will lay out ten to see a dead Indian.")

It wasn't long before Harlow had enticed three Indians—named

Pechmo, Monopet, and Pekenimme–on board his vessel. When the natives realized what Harlow intended for them, they attempted to escape. Monopet and Pekenimme were quickly subdued, but Pechmo managed to jump over the side and swim to shore.

That evening, Pechmo and a group of other Indians returned to the ship and stole the small boat tied at the stern. They then towed it to shore and buried the cockleshell halfway in the sand. When the English attempted to retrieve the boat, the Indians launched an attack from behind the nearby dunes, forcing Harlow and company to abandon the boat. Whether or not news of the abductions preceded them, the English were attacked once again at their next stop on the Cape, and three of Harlow's men were severely wounded by arrows.

Even if he hadn't taken the two Indian prisoners, Harlow's trading tactics alone were likely to stir up trouble. Three years later he would leave a detailed list of instructions for a subsequent explorer that described the Cape Cod Indians as "very false and malicious." After noting that "they are plentiful in corn and tobacco but have not many skins," he gave this advice: "if you cannot otherwise deal with them, first making trial of all fair courses, then do your best to seize their corn and provision for that will enforce them to commerce...especially when they see they cannot offend you but that you are still offensive unto them."

By his second stop on Cape Cod, this strategy had already resulted in the injury of three of his crew members. It was then, perhaps in hopes of finding shelter from a storm of his own devising, that Harlow headed offshore once again. And this time he found an island.

Given the many shoals surrounding Nantucket, the only direction from which a keel-equipped vessel could safely approach the island was the north, which was just where Harlow's westward cruise along

Cape Cod's south shore would have placed him. Forced to the south by the "false and malicious" Indians on the Cape, and with, perhaps, guidance from his two native captives, Harlow boldly sailed where no other European seems to have ever sailed before: to an island at the farthest reach of Nantucket Sound.

There is no way of knowing with absolute certainty which island Harlow sailed to. For, in truth, he was navigating a sea of islands, many of them (such as Isle of Nauset, Webb's Island, and Ram Island) long since washed into shoals by the inexorably rising sea. All we know is that the English sailed to an island that is referred to as "Nohono," in a brief account of Harlow's voyage by Captain John Smith, and "Natcea," in the 1614 list of instructions attributed to Harlow himself. According to at least one expert, Nohono/Natcea is, in fact, Nantucket, meaning that, even though it has been almost completely overlooked by historians, Harlow's voyage was the first documented European visit to Nantucket.

In the prevailing southwesterly breeze, Harlow and his men would have approached the island on a reach. First, they might have seen the curling tail of Great Point stretched out to eastward. Fearful of shoals, they would have hardened up and sailed toward the low green hills to the west, not far from where a large water tower presently stands.

The English would have been regularly checking the depth of the water, hurling out a sounding lead and calling back to Captain Harlow the latest report. A half mile from the beach, they would have crossed a long shoal running parallel to the shore, known today as the Nantucket Bar. But with the assistance of a favorable tide, they should have made it across without a problem. Where they went from there will never be known, but what follows is a possible scenario.

If the wind was out of the southwest, they would have had little choice but to head east and run along the island's north shore. Up ahead they would have seen a break in the shoreline, tempting them to round the peninsula we now call Brant Point. To the east was the tip of the sand spit that forms the northern edge of Nantucket Harbor. Although it is today tufted with pitch pines and scrub oak, Coatue (which means, according to one account, "at the pine woods") then included salt-stunted groves of pine, cedar, and red oak.

Once through the gap between Brant Point and Coatue, the English entered an immense, well-protected harbor. Harlow had come upon the western rim of what he would soon discover was the island's transportation system. Extending across the entire eastern half of the island, the harbor of Nantucket functioned much like a wide, tidal river; and in what must have seemed like no time at all, dugout canoes from up and down harbor were bearing down on the English ship.

We know none of the details of what may have been the native Nantucketers' first encounter with the English. However, accounts of not only Gosnold's voyage but those of Martin Pring in 1603 and, two years later, George Waymouth, provide possible hints as to what transpired on Nantucket in 1611.

It probably began cautiously, the English urging the Indians to approach in their canoes, the Nantucketers watching the strangely animated and bearded men with a suspicion that finally gave way to curiosity as they focused on the trade goods–knives, bracelets, beads, etc.–that the English held in their gesturing hands. At least one Indian eventually clambered up the cliff-like side of the ship to get a better look. This, the English soon learned, was Sakaweston.

Whether or not they were impressed by the physical size and bearing of this island Indian, the English decided to add him to their collection. As a skuffle broke out on deck, Sakaweston's com-patriots "assaulted the ship," according to John Smith, "till the

MAP OF MASSACHUSETTS COASTLINE

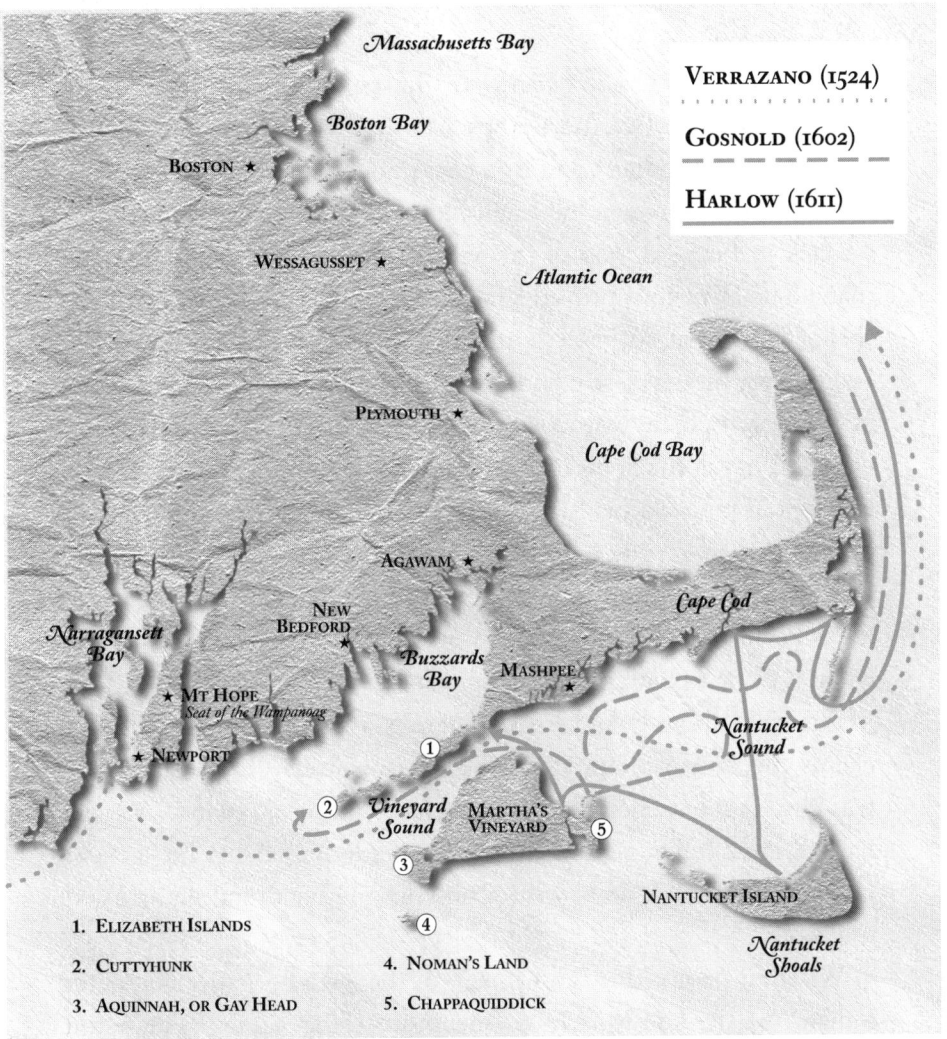

The probable routes of three explorers, only one of whom seems to have made it to Nantucket Island. Working his way up the New England coast in 1524, Giovanni da Verrazano passed through Nantucket Sound and named the shoal-infested waters for a hated tax collector. In 1602 Gosnold approached the region from the north and, after negotiating his way through the shoals, made it to Martha's Vineyard and Cuttyhunk Island. Finally, in 1611, Edward Harlow's search for "an isle supposed about Cape Cod" led him to an island that appears to have been Nantucket. *Map by Frederick Swartz.*

English guns made them retire." And so, in a cloud of gunpowder and arrows and with Sakaweston in their possession, the English set out to sea once again.

But Harlow was not finished in the region. Before returning to England, he made two more stops: Martha's Vineyard, where he captured two more Indians, and Agawam (modern Wareham), where, for once, relations between the English and Indians remained peaceful.

Back in England, one of the Vineyard captives, an extremely tall man named Epenow, proved a financial windfall. According to Smith, "being a man of so great a stature, he was shown up and down London for money as a wonder." A Maushop-like giant in the streets of London, Epenow was also a quick learner, and he soon acquired enough English to tell his captors just what they wanted to hear: there was a gold mine on his island and only he knew its location. (It was in anticipation of this return voyage, led by Nicholas Hobson, that Harlow wrote out his instructions in 1614.) Ultimately Epenow would do as Pechmo had done and leap over the side of the English vessel when it came to within swimming distance of Martha's Vineyard.

But what about Sakaweston? There is a Nantucket tradition that claims the Indian pictured on the Massachusetts Bay seal of 1629 was based on a sachem from the eastern end of the island. Was this Sakaweston? Judging from the rather crude engraving, he seems a tall, fairly muscular man, with a bow in one hand and an arrow in the other.

Whether or not this is an image of the island's first documented Indian, we do know at least one more thing about Sakaweston. According to Captain Smith, "after he had lived many years in England he went a soldier to the wars of Bohemia." Thus Nantucket's "first Indian" disappears into the anonymity of the Thirty Years War, a struggle that might be taken as a harbinger of things to come on Sakaweston's native island.

If in 1611 Harlow had been the first European navigator to penetrate the maze of shoals that surrounds Nantucket, he would have left a profound impression on the island's people–particularly given his unrestrained use of firearms, not to mention the capture of Sakaweston. The seventeenth-century equivalent of an alien abduction, it was just the kind of event to find its way into the island's oral traditions.

Since European ships were unlike anything they had ever seen before, Indians at the time of contact inevitably sought to describe them in familiar terms. Some traditions referred to these high-sided, white-sailed vessels as floating islands–the masts being trees, the sails clouds, and the guns lightning and thunder. Other legends–not only from New England but throughout America–referred to the ships as large predatory birds, particularly if their crews took native hostages. For example, a legend from Dighton, Massachusetts, tells how "a number of white men arrived in the [Taunton] river, in a bird," then relates how the "white men took Indians into the bird, as hostages."

But the legend of the giant eagle that carried children to Nantucket is about much more than an abduction. Central to the story is Maushop's determined pursuit of the bird, even after losing sight of it, and his discovery of an island. A legend recorded on Nantucket in 1807 claimed that instead of Maushop it was the parents of the child who pursued the bird: "an eagle…seized and carried off in his talons a papoose, the parents followed him in their canoe till they came to Nantucket, where they found the bones of their child dropped by the eagle."

By making it a family tale of trauma and loss, this version of the legend may refer to how in 1611 the compatriots of the abducted Indians–specifically Pechmo and company–took it upon themselves to pursue the English ship across the sound to Nantucket. Since Harlow's visit to the island seems to have lasted only a brief time, he would have more than likely been long gone by the time the Cape Codders arrived, which is just how the legend has depicted it.

But what about the bones?

On the most obvious level they evoke a foreboding sense of loss. But to appreciate how this image of death reaches across time, we must also look to Maushop's fog-engendering smoke of pokeweed.

Pokeweed was used on a ceremonial basis by the Indians, particularly on Nantucket where real tobacco, according to several sources, seems to have been relatively scarce. When harvested in the spring before it matures into a toxic plant commonly known as pokeberry, pokeweed is a leafy green that can be smoked. It has been speculated that pokeweed had hallucinogenic properties and was used by the Indians to induce the dream-like visions that a powwow, or shaman, used to predict the future. As it turns out, Indians frequently associated those pipe-induced visions with the flight of birds, and it is, of course, a child-carrying eagle that leads Maushop to Nantucket.

Although we never find out what, if anything, Maushop sees while smoking pokeweed, the giant is said to have dreamed, in another instance, about "strange people, white people" coming to his island and bringing with them nothing but strife. Whether or not he saw a similar vision while puffing his pipe on Nantucket, Maushop's pursuit of an eagle and his use of pokeweed (as opposed to tobacco) underscore the oracular quality of the legend.

Part shamanistic spell, part vision quest (a rite of passage common to Native Americans across the country), and part heroic journey, the tradition of Maushop and the giant eagle created a visionary link between the appearance of the Europeans and the tide of death to come. With each retelling of how Maushop pursued the eagle and then sat down to smoke beside a pile of bones, native Nantucketers were able to explain the unexplainable: how an island almost thirty miles out to sea had been enveloped in a disturbing cloud of conflict and change.

3

ESCAPE FROM GOLGOTHA

Once upon a time there lived on the Atlantic coast a giant who used Cape Cod for a bed. One night, being restless, he tossed from side to side till his moccasins were filled with sand. This so enraged him that on rising in the morning he flung the offending moccasins from his feet, one alighting to form Martha's Vineyard, while the other became the since famous island of Nantucket.

—Eva Folger, The Glacier's Gift, *1911*

There are two, seemingly contradictory traditions concerning the native Nantucketers' relationship to the world around them. One source claimed that the island's Indians had more and bigger canoes than others in the region and were even considered New England's "chief naval power." But in 1781 a visiting Quaker minister heard just the opposite, recording in his diary that "there is no account of [the Indians] using boats" on Nantucket prior to the arrival of the English.

Instead of contradicting each other, these differing claims may speak to the presence of two peoples on the island: one group that paddled out to the island each summer to fish, another that lived on Nantucket all year round, depending on the fish and shellfish that could be easily taken from ponds, creeks, and harbors and, according to the Quaker's account, the "plenty of winter wildfowl and deer" on the island.

Whether or not it dated back to an ancient division between those who regarded the island as a summer-time fishing station and those who lived on it year-round, there is archaeological as well as traditional evidence that two different cultures developed on Nantucket:

47

one centered amid the swamps and hills on the eastern end of the island, the other in the pond-pocked narrows to the west. Bernard Stockley, an amateur archaeologist working in the 1960s, claimed that the points and ceramic pipe pieces found in a particularly rich dig in the Ram Pasture area of the island (to the west) had more in common with natives living to the south of the Hudson River than they did with what had been found in shell middens at the eastern end of the island in Squam.

A native legend recorded in 1827 by the editor of the Nantucket *Inquirer*, Samuel Jenks, describes two very different groups of Nantucket Indians. The Indians to the west, whom Jenks called the "Taumkhods," were the island's shellfish eaters, subsisting on "oysters, crabs, clams, clappers [scallops], lobsters, pooquaws, periwinkles, [and] mussels." The "Khauds" to the east, on the other hand, relied chiefly on birds and fish (cod frequented the eastern shore well into the twentieth century), using bark from the several forests in their part of the island to manufacture fish lines and nets.

Although archaeological evidence may suggest that Nantucket had been an island divided for quite some time, the overwhelming changes associated with European contact would have inevitably introduced a new dynamic to the island, a dynamic that may have modified or even erased former cultural patterns. As the anthropologist Frank Speck pointed out, Nantucket was not the only island in southern New England where territorial rivalries existed in the first half of the seventeenth century. The even smaller Block Island off the Rhode Island coast was also an island divided as the Pequot and Narragansett struggled for control. Speck's conversations with Wampanoags on both Martha's Vineyard and Cape Cod in the 1920s led him to theorize that Nantucket's east-west division was the result of a two-pronged invasion involving Indians from the mainland to the northeast and from the Vineyard to the west. To identify why Nantucket became a battleground, we must return to the historical record.

Three years after Harlow's appearance in 1611, John Smith led an expedition to the region. Besides mapping the coast (and naming the area New England), Smith sought to improve relations with the Indians for the purposes of trade and eventual settlement. But all his efforts went for naught when one of his men, Thomas Hunt, ignored Smith's orders and abducted a total of twenty-four natives (including an Indian named Squanto) from Plymouth and Cape Cod and took them to Spain, where he attempted to sell them as slaves. (Almost a decade later, an old Indian woman from Nauset would tell some of the Pilgrims about how she had lost her sons in the raid—an event that underscored the relevance of the giant eagle.)

A year or so later, when a French vessel foundered just to the north of Cape Cod and its crew came ashore, the Indians used the wreck as an opportunity to give as they had so far received. According to one account, Indians from up and down the coast gathered together and "never left dogging and waylaying [the French] till they took opportunities to kill all but three or four, which they kept as slaves, sending them up and down, to make sport with them from one sachem to another."

Just as Epenow and other Native Americans had been shown for "wonders" in the streets of London, the Frenchmen were taken around southern New England and might have even made it as far as Nantucket. One of the Frenchmen was of a religious bent, and prior to his death in captivity had learned enough Massachusett to tell his captors that "God was angry with them for their wickedness, and would destroy them and give their country to another people." Not taking kindly to this prophecy, the sachem assembled his subjects around a nearby hill and, with the Frenchman beside him on the hilltop, demanded if "his God had so many people and [was] able to kill all those?" The Frenchman responded that he "surely would."

In 1616, the year after the Frenchman delivered his prophecy, native peoples began to die in coastal New England. Starting in Maine, where French traders seem to have introduced what may have been bubonic plague or viral hepatitis, the disease quickly worked its way south. Referred to by epidemiologists as a "virgin soil" epidemic (since the population had no prior exposure to the disease and lacked the antibodies required to defend itself), the plague raged out of control for at least three years. It is conservatively estimated that coastal communities from Maine to Narragansett Bay, where the plague stopped its southern spread (perhaps because hostilities between the neighboring Wampanoag and Narragansett reduced interaction to a minimum), suffered losses of more than ninety percent.

In the early stages of the outbreak, the Indians' traditional habit of gathering around the sick and, once a person had died, grieving for extended periods beside the open grave, only hastened the transmission of the disease. Circumstances quickly forced them to dispense with their ancient practices. Roger Williams, who witnessed the effects of a second round of diseases on the Narragansett in the 1630s, described how it had become common practice to uproot an entire village as soon as the plague appeared: "I have seen a poor house left alone in the wild woods, all being fled, the living not able to bury the dead. So terrible is the apprehension of an infectious disease, that not only persons, but the houses and the whole town, take flight."

With people dying all around them and entire villages on the run, it was only inevitable that desperate, last-ditch confrontations occurred between groups that, even in the best of times, had been uneasy neighbors. These "civil dissensions and bloody wars," combined with losses from the three-year epidemic, reduced coastal New England's once vibrant, complex native culture to a sad and terrifying ghost of its former self. More than a decade after the outbreak, the large number of unburied skeletons in the vicinity of Boston moved one English settler to describe the area as a "new found Golgotha."

One of the first Europeans to become aware of the extent of the human devastation was the explorer Thomas Dermer. With Thomas Hunt's former captive Squanto (who had made his way back to England from Spain) as his guide, he set out from Monhegan Island in an open boat on May 19, 1619. This is what he saw:

> I passed alongst the coast where I found some ancient plantations, not long since populous, now utterly void; in other places a remnant remains, but not free of sickness. Their disease the plague, for we might perceive the sores of some that had escaped, who described the spots of such as usually die. When I arrived at [Plymouth,] my savage's native country[, we found] all dead.

Dermer subsequently sailed to an unnamed island to the south of the Cape that was, in all likelihood, Nantucket. (Another account of the voyage refers to the island as "Nautican," a name later used in a deed to describe Nantucket.) If this island was Nantucket, it seems to have been unaffected by disease. Dermer reported to have "had good quarter with the savages, who likewise confirmed former reports"–a possible reference to Harlow's account of his voyage to the island eight years before. Dermer also told of finding "several places digged" on the island. Whatever those excavations were, they piqued his curiosity to the point that he sent samples of earth from the sites back to England, as well as various "commodities elsewhere found."

If Nantucket did escape exposure to the Plague of 1616-19, it was only one in a sequence of events that would make the island increasingly attractive to Indians on the mainland. In the cold autumn of 1620, the Pilgrims came.

The Pilgrims' clumsy, unnecessarily confrontational search for a settlement site was fairly typical of how they would conduct themselves over the next few years. With Miles Standish, a pugnacious
soldier of fortune, leading the way, they cruised along the north
shore of Cape Cod, rifling Native American graves and storage pits,
stumbling into a deer trap (which left William Bradford suspended
in the air by his ankle), and shooting at any Indians who dared come
within range. Disease-scorched Plymouth proved blessedly native-
free (as Thomas Dermer had reported), so it was there that they
decided to settle.

By the following spring the Pilgrims had lost half their number (of
just over a hundred) to cold, malnutrition, and diseases of their own.
If not for the eventual appearance of the English-speaking, world-trav-
eling Squanto, Plymouth Plantation might have become just another
unsuccessful attempt to establish an English foothold in America. But
with the help of Squanto, who not only acted as an interpreter but also
gave practical advice when it came to the secrets of growing crops in
America, the Pilgrims began to make some headway.

If Squanto was the key to the Pilgrims' beginnings in America,
their future, as they soon realized, depended on the Wampanoag's
supreme sachem, Massasoit, whose character emerges at this time in
the writings of several English chroniclers. According to Edward
Winslow, the sachem was "a very lusty man, in his best years, an able
body, grave of countenance, and spare of speech: in his attire little differing from the rest." Despite his physical vitality, his political power
was still suffering from the effects of the plague, and it is clear that his
eventual alliance with the English was part of a calculated strategy
that he entered into with extreme ambivalence. Later the Pilgrims
would learn that, prior to making any overtures, the Wampanoag had

assembled "in a dark and dismal swamp [and] attempted to have cursed the English."

With the English on his side, Massasoit was positioning himself to reassert some of his people's former glory relative to the Narragansett. After receiving a bright red "horseman's coat" from a small delegation of Pilgrims, the sachem launched into a "great oration." According to Edward Winslow, the sachem declared: "Was not he Massasoit, commander of the country about him, was not such a town his, and the people of it, and twenty towns more he named was his?"

Whether or not Winslow heard only what he wanted to hear, Massasoit's own people knew perfectly well that there were limits to their sachem's power in the region. Although villages throughout the region (including Cape Cod and the islands) might be obligated to pay him tribute, their leaders had no qualms about acting independently and even in open defiance of Massasoit's authority. More than a few of the depopulated and demoralized villages were reluctant to fall in line with the English. Rumblings to the north in the Massachusetts Bay region and to the east toward Cape Cod prompted the Pilgrims to insist on the signing of a new treaty. In this document, dated September 1621, hitherto refractory sachems (including the former English captive Epenow, back on Martha's Vineyard and in a position of some power) pledged allegiance to Plymouth and King James.

But it was not to last. During trading expeditions to Cape Cod led by the undiplomatic Standish, the natives made it known that they were becoming annoyed with the English interlopers. Complicating the situation was the establishment of yet another English settlement just to the north of Plymouth in Wessagusset (modern Weymouth) during the fall of 1622. When winter set in and the Wessagusset settlers stole native corn to feed themselves, Indian-English tensions in the region reached an all time high. Meanwhile a new set of diseases began to appear among the natives. Squanto, who was by now living with the English at Plymouth, died of what was described as an "Indian fever." Then Massasoit, the key to the Pilgrims' ambitions in the region, fell ill.

Edward Winslow arrived at Wampanoag headquarters to find the sachem on his deathbed, with "women rubbing him to keep heat in him." Although temporarily blinded, the sachem recognized the Englishman's voice, took him by the hand and said, "I shall never see thee again!" As luck would have it, Winslow's attempts at a cure effected a miraculous recovery. In gratitude, Massasoit told of a secret plot among the area's sachems to destroy the English. Although the Massachusett in the vicinity of Wessagusset were the ringleaders, Massasoit named six villages in and around Cape Cod, along with all the Indians of Martha's Vineyard, as part of the conspiracy. He then advised the Pilgrims to "kill them of Massachusett that were the authors."

This was just the opportunity Standish was looking for. With eight others, including an Indian named Hobbamock (who had taken over Squanto's role as an Indian-English go-between), Standish marched to Wessagusset. But instead of an insurrection, the Pilgrims found everything to be fairly calm. Unable to feed themselves, some of the English settlers had even elected to live with their Indian neighbors.

Standish decided to take matters into his own hands. Claiming that he wanted to entertain them at a feast, Standish lured four Indians, including the sachem Wituwamet, into a Wessagusset house, then proceeded to stab them with their own knives. A few hours later, the English were able to pull the same trick on another group of unsuspecting Indians. By the time they were finished, seven Indians had been killed. Upon his return to Plymouth, Standish mounted the head of Wituwamet on a pole outside the colony's fort.

The evidence suggests that, despite their supreme sachem's claims, there had been no organized plot to overthrow the English.

Motivated by a desire to consolidate his ties with Plymouth, Massasoit had found a way of playing to the Pilgrims' mounting paranoia in a way that brought about the elimination of a troublesome rival to the north.

Standish's assault on Wessagusset threw the region into chaos. Not only had the natives been attacked without provocation by the English; they had also been betrayed by their own leader. Although historians have tended to focus on the Pequot War in the 1630s and King Philip's War in the 1670s, the raid on Wessagusset had a much larger impact on the Indians of Cape Cod and the islands as fears of additional Pilgrim-led reprisals spread throughout the region. According to Edward Winslow, "this sudden and unexpected execution…hath so terrified and amazed [the Indians], as in like manner they forsook their houses, running to and fro like men distracted, living in swamps and other desert places, and so brought manifold diseases amongst themselves, whereof very many are dead."

Lost in this latest tide of disease were three Cape Cod sachems– Canacum, Aspinet, and Ianough. Winslow claimed that prior to his death Ianough (for whom Hyannis would be named) "said the God of the English was offended with [the Indians], and would destroy them in his anger." The Indians lucky enough to survive the latest outbreak of disease next had to face the prospect of starvation. According to Winslow, "they set little or no corn, which is the staff of life, and without which they cannot long preserve health and strength." Thus, because of fears unleashed across the region by the murders in Wessagusset, the order of existence on Native American Cape Cod had been permanently thrown into disarray.

The legends of the giant Maushop may speak to this new and disturbing era and how Martha's Vineyard and especially Nantucket became increasingly attractive to mainland Indians as possible safe havens. In the story of Maushop's moccasins, the slumbering giant leaps to his feet in a rage. The legend may well be describing how the incident at Wessagusset served as a terrifying wake-up call. No longer able to live peacefully on Cape Cod, the Indians began to look for a way out. By hurling his sandy shoes into the sea, Maushop creates a sanctuary for the newly dispossessed people of the mainland. Perhaps not coincidentally, the Vineyard was known at this time as Capawack, meaning "the refuge place," while Nantucket's name ("the faraway land") also suggests a place removed from immediate danger. Both names imply a mainland perspective.

There is strong evidence that an influx of mainlanders to both the Vineyard and Nantucket did, in fact, occur, and that it was not particularly appreciated by the islands' original inhabitants. According to a statement left by Matthew Mayhew of the Vineyard in 1694, there were Indian families that had been relegated to the lowest rung of island society primarily because they "were known strangers or foreigners" even though "the time of their forefathers' first inhabiting among them was beyond the memory of man." Whatever had happened, even if it was no longer clearly remembered in 1694, had not, as of then, been entirely forgiven. And in this epoch of jolting change, a mere seventy years might well have been "beyond the memory of man."

If large numbers of people did migrate from the Cape to the islands, it would have placed a mounting strain on the shellfish reserves, farmlands, and wood supplies that had once made Nantucket's Indians the healthiest and tallest in the region. And as nutrition levels declined, subsequent generations of Nantucketers would have grown to a shorter height. One of the earliest recorded Maushop legends links the giant's disappearance to exactly this scenario: "After [the Indians] grew thick around him," the tradition states, "he left them."

There is yet another legend specific to Nantucket that combines many of the same elements contained in the Maushop legends: giants, the arrival of a new group of Indians, and, at the center of it all, a whale.

According to the legend, recorded in 1829, the first people to settle on Nantucket came from Chappaquiddick, just to the east of Martha's Vineyard. Instead of Maushop, the Indians discovered two giants sharing the island—the Good Spirit and the Evil Spirit. Soon after the arrival of the Chappaquiddick Indians, the Evil Spirit rebelled against the Good Spirit over possession of Nantucket's eastern half. Although the fighting was long and drawn out, Good ultimately prevailed, with the final stand occurring amid the rolling, prairie-like plains, now known as the Moors, in the island's eastern interior. Here the Evil Spirit, a monstrous giant with many heads and arms and with hissing serpents for legs, fell with a mighty crash. Besides killing many Indians, the giant's fall created Madequecham (pronounced "MAD-a-ka-SHAM") Valley, an ancient runnel of glacial melt that runs diagonally across the eastern half of the island.

Rather than signaling the end of the monster, this cataclysm marked only the beginning of a new and terrible time. Far from dead, the Evil One was sentenced by the Good Spirit to eternal imprisonment beneath the island. Pinned by an unbearable weight of sand, the Evil One would occasionally writhe in agony, causing the island to tremble as if in the midst of an earthquake. Driven mad by pain and anger, the monster gnawed off his many legs, unleashing a horde of serpents that wriggled and squirmed their way out from underneath the island. By the time the serpents entered the waters of Nantucket Sound, they had assumed the form of whales.

A native warrior, standing on a ridge of hills that afforded a panoramic view of the island and the harbor to the north, saw a whale appear in Nantucket Sound just beyond the barrier beach of Coatue. The whale dove underwater and after a few minutes miraculously appeared within the harbor, to the south of Coatue. Diving again, it appeared this time in one of two contiguous ponds in a hollow just to the west of the Indian. This was clearly no ordinary whale.

A cry went out, and it wasn't long before a group of Indians set out in their canoes to attack the mysterious whale. When they unleashed their arrows, the monster dove into the water and then surfaced in the other pond. Only after Indians and their canoes filled both ponds were they able to kill the whale, or "pootar." To this day, the two reed-fringed ponds are called the Poot Ponds.

Does the Poot Pond legend describe the end of a golden age on Nantucket? In the beginning, the island's isolation and resources combined to nurture a significantly taller and healthier population that, as the presence of two giants may suggest, was comprised of two distinct peoples. Then a new group of Indians took up permanent residence on the island, creating an era of unprecedented upheaval and conflict that culminated in the appearance of a legendary whale. To help us follow up on this pivotal detail, we must return to the giant Maushop, this time focusing not only on his interest in whales but on his treatment of his own family.

4

THE KILLERS COME

The first Indian who came to the Vineyard was brought thither with his dog on a cake of ice. When he came to Gay Head, he found a very large man, whose name was Maushop. He had a wife and five children, four sons and one daughter; and lived in the Den. He used to catch whales, and then pluck up trees, and make a fire, and roast them. The coals of the trees, and the bones of the whales, are now to be seen. After he was tired of staying here, he told his children to go and play ball on a beach that joined Noman's Land to Gay Head. He then made a mark with his toe across the beach at each end, and so deep, that the water followed, and cut away the beach; so that his children were in fear of drowning. They took their sister up, and held her out of the water. He told them to act as if they were going to kill whales; and they were all turned into killers (a fish so called). The sister was dressed in large stripes. He gave them a strict charge always to be kind to her. His wife mourned the loss of her children so exceedingly, that he threw her away. She fell upon Sakonnet, near the rocks, where she lived some time, exacting contribution of all who passed by water. After a while she was changed into a stone….

> —as told to Benjamin Basset in 1792 by
> the Gay Head Indian Thomas Cooper,
> who learned it from his grandmother, born
> before the arrival of the English

According to William Simmons, the name Maushop derives from a proto-Algonquian word meaning "big man" or "giant," a term that the Narragansett applied to their supreme sachem Canonicus, who was also known as "Mausup." Might the Wampanoag have also referred to Massasoit as Maushop? If this is true, at least some of the Maushop legends may have provided the Indians with a way to say some fairly critical, even subversive things about the Wampanoag sachem.

Certainly the giant's strange and disturbing treatment of his family parallels Massasoit's actions relative to the Indians of the Cape and islands in 1622. Just as Maushop creates a trap for his own children before he literally throws away his wife, so were Massasoit's people on Cape Cod seemingly betrayed by their leader in connection with the Wessagusset raid, in whose aftermath many Indians were observed abandoning their villages and "running to and fro like men distracted."

In 1830 James Athearn Jones (who had grown up on the Vineyard with a Gay Head Indian nursemaid) published a Maushop legend that expanded on the account provided by Thomas Cooper in 1792. In Jones's version of the legend, the giant is not only a fickle and disturbed family man (beating his wife and overzealously punishing his children), he is a sachem whose cruel treatment of his people coincides with an increasingly unreasonable interest in whales: "He soon began to harass his subjects with new demands and querulous exactions. He now frequently demanded the half of a whale [for tribute] instead of a tenth, or took, without asking, the whole of a grampus or finback. Instead of contributing his aid to promote marriages, he was very diligent in preventing them...and created frequent wars between the different tribes on the island."

With the Maushop legends, the island's Indians may have left us with an account of how their supreme sachem underwent a transformation. Instead of acting like a traditional pre-contact sachem, who had to rule in accordance with his people's wishes or risk being "put down," Massasoit's role had changed. He seems to have become what in the language of imperialism is termed a Big Man: an indigenous leader willing to compromise the interests of his own people in order to retain his privileged position vis-à-vis the powerful invaders. The economic catalyst of Massasoit's transformation into a Big Man, or Maushop, relative to the Indians of the Cape and islands appears to have been the whale.

As the legends suggest, the whales that washed up on New

England's beaches were an important source of food for the Indians. According to Roger Williams, "The natives cut them in several parcels, and give and send them far and near, for an acceptable present or dish." The Indians also valued the whales for their bones. This seems to have been especially true on a tree-poor island such as Nantucket, where whalebone tools, such as spades and shovels, have been found. But by the 1620s, it was not only the Indians in New England who were interested in whales.

Although the English shared the Indians' enthusiasm for whalebone (specifically the flexible, plastic-like strips of baleen that grow in the right whale's mouth), they had no use for the whale as a food source. For them it was the "oyle"–obtained by boiling out the blubber–that made the right whale something more than a seasonal curiosity. New England's greasy answer to Mexico's gold, whale oil would enable Europe to illuminate and lubricate itself into the Machine Age. But transforming a live right whale into casks of oil would prove to be no easy matter.

As early as 1614 Captain John Smith unsuccessfully attempted to establish a whaling operation in Maine. Six years later, while crossing Cape Cod Bay, the Pilgrims found themselves surrounded by right whales, "playing hard by us." Although it had been their souls that had initially prompted them to sail to America, the vision of all this floating blubber immediately brought to mind their pocketbooks. Lamented Bradford, "if we had instruments and means to take them, we might have made a very rich return, which to our great grief we wanted. Our master and his mate, and others, experienced in fishing, professed we might have made three or four thousand pounds worth of oil."

It was not long, however, before the English were beginning to harvest the bounty they saw all around them. Upon his return to London, William Morrell, who came to Plymouth in 1623, would poetically report: "The mighty whale doth in these harbors lie, /

Whose oil the careful merchant dear will buy." By this point, the Dutch, based in present-day New York, had also begun to make their presence known in the region—much to the annoyance of the Pilgrims. Nantucket's isolation may have made it particularly attractive to the Dutch (who also had an interest in whaling at the east end of Long Island), enabling them to trade directly with the Indians without interference from the English. (As Elizabeth Little has pointed out, there were at least three Indian families on Nantucket with Dutch last names.) With both the Dutch and English in the market for whale oil, Massasoit may have taken a renewed interest in a whale-rich island that had previously been of relatively minor importance to him. That Nantucket's population was, if anything, increasing (as the number of Indians in the rest of his territories continued to decline) would have only added to his interest in the island.

The large number of whales that frequented Nantucket's waters at the time meant that there was no need to pursue the whales in boats; so many washed ashore or grounded on shoals that the Indians could rely on what the English called "drift" whales. To this day when whales wash up on Nantucket, they commonly do so along the southwest shore, and it was here that Massasoit seems to have established a beachhead. There is a bridge, many times rebuilt, across Long Pond in this portion of the island that is still called Massasoit Bridge.

Nantucket's emergence as an Indian whaling center may lurk behind the legend of the giant bird and the bones it left behind. Instead of human remains, it has been suggested by Elizabeth Little and Clinton Andrews that the legend really refers to whales. In 1602, Gosnold's men had seen "many huge bones and ribs of whales" on the north shore of a small island that may now be part of Chappaquiddick. Given the large number of whales that passed by Nantucket each winter, its beaches would have undoubtedly had a similar appearance. (The name Siasconset, for example, an ancient village site at the east end of the island, means "place of great bones.") Just as Maushop pursued a giant bird to an island he had never seen before, so may have Massasoit's growing interest in whale oil taken him to Nantucket, an island cluttered with bleaching bones. And just as the giant cloaked the island in smoke, so would have Massasoit's driftwhalers created their own smothering clouds as their fires boiled the blubber into oil.

What evidence we have of Indian driftwhaling on Nantucket was recorded after the first English settlers arrived in 1659. By that point, driftwhaling was a well-established industry that was conducted, almost exclusively, by Indians at the west end of the island, many of whom commuted to Nantucket on a seasonal basis from their homes on Martha's Vineyard. In 1665, Massasoit's son and heir, Metacom, or Philip, visited the island and stated that "he had no claim to the land of Nantucket; but only power, in point of government, over some Indians not belonging to the island"–an apparent reference to the Vineyard-based driftwhalers. As late as 1677, a court document refers to Massasoit's "order" as the authority still determining how Nantucket driftwhalers divided up their spoils.

Although many of these driftwhalers were Vineyarders, there were at least some of them, led by a sachem named Attapeat, who took up permanent residence on Nantucket in the vicinity of Miacomet pond. According to a tradition recorded by Zaccheus Macy in the eighteenth century, Attapeat "was call[ed] a great warrior, and got his lands by his bow," i.e., through violent means. A Maushop legend recorded by James Athearn Jones claimed that the giant created Nantucket as a gift to a young Indian on the Vineyard. Was this Attapeat? Even if Massasoit did grant him driftwhaling rights on Nantucket, Attapeat would have had to displace the Indians who already lived on the island's southwestern shore. That he did so "by his bow," is not only born out by Macy, but by yet another reference in the legends of Maushop.

One of the giant's last acts was to transform his children into killer whales. Is this a metaphoric account of how driftwhalers (whale-killers in a literal sense) were dispatched to Nantucket from the Vineyard? Perhaps this is what the Poot Pond legend is about when it describes the appearance of a strange, whale-like creature in an island pond soon after the arrival of Indians from Chappaquiddick. Then there is Maushop—a creator/benefactor turned manipulator/exploiter with an appetite for whales. If all this adds up to an account of how Massasoit's entrance into the European whale-oil market plunged Nantucket into war, it is a pattern borne out by many Native American Big Men who, according to the archaeologist Peter Thomas, "were no less guilty than some English of pursuing self-aggrandizement at the ultimate expense of other members of their own society." In any event, there are at least three more legends that tell of a time when two groups fought it out on Nantucket with the guile and savagery of killer whales.

Just to the west of Nantucket is the island of Tuckernuck. For Vineyard Indians looking to move into the western half of Nantucket, Tuckernuck was the perfect staging area for an attack. There is a legend that may describe the unsuccessful beginning of the Vineyard invasion. Recorded by the historian Obed Macy in 1842 and told to him by William Worth, whose grandfather maintained close relations with many of the island's Indians, this is an oral tradition with an unusually good pedigree.

According to Worth's account, the Indians on Tuckernuck had been looking for an opportunity to attack the Indians based on Nantucket's western extreme at Madaket for quite some time. That this was something more than a blood feud is indicated by Macy's mention that the Tuckernuck Indians planned to secure "an unconditional surrender of all their rights and privileges," especially when it came, no doubt, to driftwhaling. Whereas Madequecham Valley served as the boundary between Nantucket's eastern and western peoples, Madaket Harbor seems to have been the western equivalent, with Indians from Nantucket and Tuckernuck using it to fish while maintaining "a reasonable distance from each other."

One day, however, an old man and his son from Madaket drifted too close to Tuckernuck and found themselves surrounded by hostile Indians. Although the old man was killed, his son was spared "on the condition that he would join them in subduing their enemy." Described as "unusually intelligent and active," the young man outwardly agreed to join the Tuckernuck Indians but secretly determined to do everything he could to avenge his father's death.

Time passed and the young man from Madaket soon won the confidence of his captors. It wasn't long before the Tuckernuck Indians revealed the full extent of their plan: "to land at Madaket in the night and surround the wigwams of their enemies and massacre them all." Having learned of "every part of the conspiracy," the young man "privately crossed to Nantucket," alerted his former people of the impending attack, and returned to Tuckernuck without being detected.

The next night, the Tuckernuck Indians and their guide paddled quietly to a rise of land along the shores of Madaket Harbor. After dragging their canoes up above the tide line, the Tuckernuckers crept "around the hill not suspecting that their enemies were watching every movement." Approaching from the other side of the hill, the Madaket Indians hid the paddles of the Tuckernuck canoes, then went in pursuit of their supposed attackers.

As soon as they realized that their presence was known, the Tuckernuck Indians rushed back to the landing area, only to discover that their paddles were gone. "Availing themselves of their confusion," the Madaket Indians attacked and "cut them off to a man; not one escaped."

Madaket was not the only battle zone on Nantucket. A number of legends refer to battles fought between the eastern and western Indians in Madequecham Valley, a natural divide that the Poot Pond legend attributed to the fall of an evil giant. Whether it was in the vicinity of Madequecham or on the beaches of Madaket, Nantucket's Indians fought very differently from the Europeans. According to Roger Williams,

> Their wars are far less bloody and devouring than the cruel wars of Europe, and seldom twenty slain in a pitched battle; partly because when they fight in a wood, every tree is a buckler. When they fight in a plain, they fight with leaping and dancing, that seldom an arrow hits; and when a man is wounded, unless that shot follows up on the wounded, they soon retire and save the wounded. And yet, having no swords nor guns, all that are slain, are commonly slain with great valor and courage; for the conqueror ventures onto the thickets, and brings away the head of his enemy.

Williams even described how the natives cut off a head: "tearing his head a little aside by his lock, they in the twinkling of an eye, fetch off his head, though with a sorry knife." He also reported that "they are much delighted after battle, to hang up the hands and heads of their enemies."

Physical evidence has been found—from bashed-in skulls to severed body parts—indicating that violence had long been a fact of life on Nantucket. However, if a legend apparently told in 1830 by Benjamin Franklin Folger (antiquarian and friend to Abram Quary) is to be believed, Nantucket experienced a kind of brutal watershed in the seventeenth century that the island's Indians would later look to as the beginning of the end.

On a hill in the southeastern portion of the island lived the sachem of Nantucket's "eastern tribe" with his wife, his daughter, and his only son Roqua. According to the story told by Folger, all was happiness until war broke out with the Indians to the west. Taking up their bows and arrows and "the ponderous war club," the two peoples fought it out, presumably in the vicinity of Madequecham Valley, with the easterners ultimately being forced from the field of battle. Before their defeated and humiliated enemies had a chance to regroup, the westerners attacked the defenseless eastern village, killing all the women, children, and old men: "The scalps being torn from the bleeding temples, their bodies were thrown among the blazing ruins of their village." One nameless western warrior distinguished himself that day, murdering no less than twenty people, including the parents and sister of Roqua who alone of his family survived the slaughter.

Eventually, the victorious western tribe returned home, "loaded with spoils," while the defeated easterners staggered back to their village to find it in ruins. As his fellow braves "mourned over their fallen fortunes," Roqua silently steeled himself for revenge. As soon as darkness came, he took his weapons in hand and slipped away unnoticed.

With each step toward the enemy village, along paths that were no wider than a modern-day horse trail, he heard a voice "floating on the wind." It was his dead father, urging revenge.

By the time he had reached the rival village, Roqua could feel a truly supernatural strength coursing through him. Led by the spirit of his father, he found the wigwam of the brave who had killed his family. He entered the wigwam, carefully approached the brave's sleeping platform, and without hesitation buried his club in the murderer's head.

Next he grabbed a stick from the smoldering fire in the center of the wigwam and touched it to the dried grasses of the dwelling's sides. As flames shot up through the wigwam's smoke hole, Roqua ran throughout the village, methodically spreading the fire from wigwam to wigwam. And then, as people began to pour out in panic, Roqua killed Indian after Indian. Backlit by the burning village, Roqua paused to find his next victim when an arrow pierced him in the chest.

Although his club dropped out of his hand, Roqua still stood proudly before the assembled westerners and, according to Folger, proclaimed, "Behold, a tempest approaches from the north—the canoes of the white men with spreading sails shall descend upon your shores. Victors and vanquished shall perish alike and one promiscuous grave shall bury all. For approaching death…gives…." And with that, Roqua fell down dead to the ground.

Even if the legend of Roqua comes to us embellished by nineteenth-century Romantic flourishes, the events it describes fit with what we have already heard. Whether it was the fall of an evil giant that split Nantucket in half or young men avenging their families, Nantucket was an island where no one could be trusted.

The tale of Roqua seems to suggest that this climate of violence and betrayal finally reached a point where it could go no further. In the early eighteenth century, Experience Mayhew spoke of the Indians on the Vineyard and Nantucket having been "wasted by" internecine conflict not long before the arrival of the English. Hector St. John de Crèvecoeur, who visited Nantucket prior to the Revolution, claimed that this state of "perpetual war" ultimately reached the point that the island's two peoples "became so thin and depopulated" that they were in danger of becoming "totally extinct."

Crèvecoeur reported that peace finally arrived through the introduction "some years before the Europeans came" of a "partition line which should divide the island from north to south"—an apparent reference to the use of Madequecham Valley as a kind of demilitarized zone: "the people of the west agreed not to kill those of the east; except [if] they were found transgressing over the western part of the line; those of the last entered into a reciprocal agreement. By these simple means, peace was established among them.... This happy settlement put a stop to their sanguinary depredations; none fell afterward but a few rash, imprudent individuals; on the contrary, they multiplied greatly." Although peace had come to the island, tensions remained high. One step on the wrong side of Madequecham Valley, Crèvecoeur seems to imply, and there was trouble.

For an understanding of what life was like on Nantucket during this period of uneasy coexistence, we have a remarkable source: a deed relating to claims made by two minor western sachems who were in "partnership" with Attapeat. Recorded in 1678, the deed describes events that occurred "a long time ago" when Massasoit was the Wampanoag's supreme sachem—actually some time between about 1620 and 1659. Since it was taboo to use the name of the dead, all the sachems whose names appear in the deed are referred to in terms of their descendants, as, for example, "Harry's father" and "Spotso's father."

The one exception is Wanackmamack, who was Nantucket's senior sachem when the English arrived in 1659 and whose bounds in the southeastern section of the island included the territory inhabited by Roqua and his people. To Wanackmamack's north was the other eastern sachem, the father of Nickanoose, whose village was located beside a pond at Wannasquam (known today as Squam). The deed includes the testimonies of twelve Indians and provides a fascinating glimpse into the complexities of Native American life on Nantucket in the first half of the seventeenth century.

The first event described in the deed is a "great meeting" that included sachems from both the eastern and western portions of the island. During the meeting, Nickanoose's father (from the east) "did give to Spotso's father and...Harry's father" (from the west) the two areas along the southern shore of Nantucket Harbor known today as Pocomo and Shawkemo, an area that may have been a contested holdover from the war years.

But if land allotments on Nantucket were made at the behest of the eastern sachems, a different dynamic took over when trouble broke out on the island. The deed tells us that soon after they were awarded their lands bordering the harbor, Harry's father and Spotso's father "went to do some murder." That it involved eastern Indians is suggested by the fact that Wanackmamack and Nickanoose's father were moved to appeal to off-island authorities at "Mount Hope"– specifically the Wampanoag's supreme sachem Massasoit. Wanackmamack explained to Massasoit that "he desired... that...Spotso's father and Harry's father should have that land no longer but desired that Wanackmamack might have it." The deed records that Massasoit "was willing."

Soon after, yet another Nantucket Indian, "Nanasoket's father," took the opportunity to ask Wanackmamack if *he* could have the land that had once belonged to the two western sachems, but Wanackmamack, in the dignified, austere manner that was expected of a sachem, "Saith nothing to him."

Then came, according to the deed, "a great hunting meeting at Manna and a great many Indians were there." Manna, which means "at the place of the deep well," is an approximately twenty-acre section in the vicinity of the present-day airport, just to the west of Madequecham Valley.

Although Harry's father was not present at this meeting, Spotso's father was, and he took the opportunity to ask that he be given back "the land that he had before." This request seems to have been made within a wigwam, and it was only after the "great men...went out to smoke...and come in again" that it was announced that the decision had been made in favor of Spotso's father.

Here we see evidence of the progress that had been made with the establishment of the "happy settlement" described by Crèvecoeur. Although they were clearly two distinct peoples, they were now negotiating with, rather than annihilating, each other. And if the eastern sachems had reasserted their seniority on the island, tensions between the east and west remained high enough that it was to the benefit of both factions to involve Mount Hope in any decisions involving an out-of-the-ordinary event. Given the relative placidity of the times (not to mention the diplomacy required to maintain it), it is only appropriate that our knowledge of this era comes, not from a legend, but from a document in Nantucket Town's Registry of Deeds.

One source claims that this uneasy truce began around 1630, which happens to coincide with the Puritans' arrival in Boston. With the Puritans came a new round of diseases on the mainland. Smallpox, probably transported to America by Puritan children, began to kill with a fury reminiscent of the plague of 1616-19. According to William Bradford in Plymouth, writing in 1633, the Indians "die like rotten sheep."

A year later, Massachusetts Governor John Winthrop recorded in his journal the experiences of an Englishman with close ties to the Indians, John Oldham. Ultimately, Oldham's death at the hands of Indians from Block Island would spark the Pequot War, but in 1634 his small trading vessel, the *Rebekka*, arrived safely in Boston loaded with 500 bushels of native-grown corn. Besides reporting on the many shoals he was forced to navigate during his voyage, he told of an island "about ten leagues in length east and west called

Nantucket." Instead of being repulsed by arrows as Harlow had been, Oldham was apparently made welcome on the island. No longer a place of war and death, this was an island whose inhabitants were flourishing. In the fall of 1634, Winthrop recorded Oldham's assessment: "Nantucket is an island full of Indians."

That very same year, William Wood published *New England's Prospect*, in which he provided detailed information concerning the region's Native Americans. Wood tells of a game played by rival Indian villages that would have made excellent use of Nantucket's beaches. First, two goals were set up as much as a mile apart on a beach "as even as a board." As the women and children watched and sang, the men (who decorated themselves in war paint) kicked a ball ("no bigger than a handball") back and forth, sometimes "flouncing into the water," sometimes breaking into "lubberlike wrestling." Perhaps it was with a contest such as this, which lasted for several days and was followed by a feast, that the eastern and western Indians perpetuated their traditional differences without subjecting the island to the claustrophobic terrors of another war.

Whatever the case may be, Nantucket would remain an island full of Indians for another twenty-five years.

5

The Black Book

When the Christian religion took place in the island, [Maushop] told [the Indians], as light had come among them, and he belonged to the kingdom of darkness, he must take his leave; which to their great sorrow, he accordingly did; and has never been heard of since.

–William Baylies, after a visit to Gay Head in 1786

"I once traveled to an island of the wildest in our parts...." So begins Roger Williams' account of a significant religious experience he had while visiting an island somewhere off the New England coast prior to 1643. "I was alone, having traveled from my bark [perhaps in a canoe], the wind being contrary; and little could I speak to [the Indians] to their understanding, especially because of the change of their dialect or manner of speech."

Could this have been Nantucket? According to several sources, Indians from both the Vineyard and Nantucket spoke a distinct dialect of Massachusett that would have been difficult for Williams to understand, given his familiarity with the mainland Wampanoag and Narragansett. Remote, shoal-guarded, and "full of Indians," Nantucket would have certainly qualified as the wildest island in New England throughout the first half of the seventeenth century.

During Williams's first night on the island, one of the Indians "had a vision or dream of the sun, whom they worship for a God, darting a beam into his breast; which he conceived to be the messenger of his death." This prompted the Indian to call together all his friends and neighbors whom he treated to a feast. In the meantime, Williams reported, this "poor native...kept waking and fasting, in great humiliations and invocations, for ten days and nights."

Although at first unable to make himself understood, Williams was finally able to break through the communication barrier: "through the help of God, I did speak, of the true and living only wise God, of the creation of man and his fall from God, etc., that at my parting, many burst forth 'Oh, when will you come again, to bring us some more news of this God?'"

Whether or not Williams visited Nantucket, this story suggests that despite their profound cultural differences, the Indians and English shared an intense interest in spiritual matters. But before we can examine the unique and complex role that Christianity would eventually play on Nantucket, we must do as we did when it came to tracing the legendary life of Maushop—we must look to Martha's Vineyard. It was here, almost twenty years before the first English settlers came to Nantucket, that news of the Puritans' deity was once again heard.

In 1641 Thomas Mayhew, a forty-eight-year-old textile trader and landowner from Watertown, Massachusetts, began to negotiate with a representative from the Earl of Stirling for the purchase of an island. But instead of Martha's Vineyard, Mayhew was originally interested in Nantucket and the small islands just to the west of it. A title was drawn up, and according to the Vineyard historian Lloyd Hare, Mayhew or "someone in his behalf" (perhaps his twenty-year-old son, Thomas Junior) sailed to Nantucket to secure "Indian rights."

Negotiations did not go as planned. We do not know what happened on Nantucket in September 1641. It may have become clear to Mayhew that with two different native factions on the island, it was going to be difficult to gain rights to all of Nantucket. He may have even encountered some hostility on this island where peace was still, relatively speaking, a late-breaking event. Whatever occurred,

Mayhew became convinced that he needed another island for his settlement site.

Ten days after putting together the first document, the earl's agent drew up an additional title that included Martha's Vineyard and the Elizabeth Islands. Feeling confident that with this much land to work with (Martha's Vineyard is more than twice the size of Nantucket) he would be assured "of obtaining from the Indians gradually what could not at once be procured," Mayhew began to make plans for a settlement on the eastern end of the Vineyard.

Initially these plans were carried out by his well-educated and highly religious son, who would live on the island for two years before he was joined by his father. Although European explorers had been told that the island was called Capawack, Thomas Junior, who served as his community's minister, quickly learned that the Indians, including those on Nantucket, referred to the island as Noepe (pronounced "NO ep AY," meaning "amid the waters"), which the English said as Noop or Nope.

There were four sachemships on Noepe: Chappaquiddick, an island to the east, and Aquinnah (later Gay Head) to the west, with the main part of the island divided into Nunnepog (Edgartown) and Takemmy (Tisbury). The English settlement at Edgartown was still in its infancy when in 1643 an Indian named Hiacoomes came under the notice of Thomas Junior. Having heard some of the English speak about the spiritual means "for the attaining of the blessings of health and life," Hiacoomes began to visit the English in their homes and even started attending church services. Soon Hiacoomes was spending every Sunday night at the house of Thomas Junior. Both in their early twenties and, in their own ways, quietly purposeful, Hiacoomes and the younger Mayhew seem to have established a special bond.

Although Hiacoomes was the one being inculcated, this was clearly a two-way "discourse," and Thomas Junior learned much about the natives' spiritual beliefs. Like any good seventeenth-century Puritan he was horrified by the fact that the Indians had more than one god (thirty-seven, to be precise) and that many of those "feigned deities" took the shape of what Roger Williams described as "creatures"–from the sun to the moon to the sea to fire. First and foremost was the god they regarded as their creator, Kiehtan (known as Cautantowwit by the Narragansett) who, according to Edward Winslow, "dwelleth above in the heavens, whither all good men go when they die, to see their friends, and have their fill of all things." Also known as "the great south west God," according to Roger Williams, "from whom came their corn and beans," Kiehtan was the god upon whom the sachems depended for support.

On the opposite end of the spectrum was Hobbamock, a sinister god of darkness who appeared at night and in swamps and assumed a variety of disturbing forms (and for whom, it may be remembered, Standish's Indian accomplice in the Wessagusset raid was named). As far as the Puritans were concerned, Hobbamock was none other than the Devil himself. Worst of all, from the English perspective, the native equivalent of a minister, a powwow (not to be confused with the ceremonial gathering of the same name), worked hand-in-glove with Hobbamock. Instead of the sober mien expected of a Puritan divine, a powwow worked his "sorcery" in a distressingly physical manner, healing the sick or casting spells or seeing into the future by means of "horrible outcries, hollow bleatings, painful wrestlings, and smiting their own bodies."

Although Roger Williams was so disturbed by the powwows' "strange antic gestures" that he refused to bear witness to their ceremonies, he appreciated, as did Mayhew, the Native Americans' inherent spirituality: "I must acknowledge I have received in my converse with them many confirmations of those two great points…1. That God is. 2. That he is a rewarder of all them that diligently seek him." Concerning the Indians' habit of crying out

"Manitto" (which means, "It is a god") whenever they saw an example of "any excellency in men, women, birds, beasts, fish, etc." Williams recognized a "strong conviction natural in the soul of man, that God is filling all things, and that all excellencies dwell in God, and proceed from him, and that they only are blessed who have the Jehovah for their portion."

Although Mayhew is the source of most of what we know about his own missionary efforts on Martha's Vineyard, it is likely that he did not record many of the initial difficulties he encountered, especially when the Massachusett language was still new to him. It could well be that Mayhew found himself the butt of Native American humor of the sort experienced by the Canadian missionary Father Pierre Biard, who discovered that some of the Indians had "palmed off on us indecent words, which we went about innocently preaching for beautiful sentences from the Gospels."

We do know, however, that in the early stages of Mayhew's missionary efforts, Hiacoomes was something of a liability. From the lowest rung of Indian society and hardly a commanding presence ("not at all accounted of," Mayhew admitted), it was relatively easy for other Indians to dismiss and mock him, calling out "Here comes the *English man.*" Then, in 1644, fate stepped in and provided Mayhew with the entrée he had been looking for.

One night the Chappaquiddick sachem, Pakeponesso was entertaining a group of friends in his wigwam. Pakeponesso seems to have been one of Maushop's killer whales, with claim to a piece of land at the west end of Nantucket. He had also publicly ridiculed Hiacoomes and even punched him in the face. That night it started to rain, and as Pakeponesso and another Indian stood up on one of the sleeping platforms to place a grass mat over their wigwam's smoke hole, a bolt of lightning blasted them, knocking Pakeponesso unconscious and killing the other Indian. Although the Chappaquiddick sachem survived, he badly burned his leg in the wigwam's fire, and more than a few island natives began to wonder whether this might have been a warning from Hiacoomes's new god.

The following year disease struck the island's Indians. Although the illness killed people throughout the Vineyard, a pattern appeared to emerge: Most traditional households were ravaged, but those Indians who had expressed some interest in Christianity "did not taste so deeply of it," while Hiacoomes and his family were completely untouched by the disease. This prompted one Vineyard sachem, Towanquatick (who appears to have been the son of Epenow, the Indian who traveled to England and back), to ask Hiacoomes to "show his heart unto them, how it stood toward God, and what they must do."

By this point Hiacoomes had undergone a transformation. No longer judged a "harmless man among them," he had developed into an eloquent and forceful speaker. According to Mayhew, the Indians "wondered that he which had nothing to say in all their meetings formerly, is now become the teacher of them all." Instead of a liability, Mayhew's first convert had become a living emblem of the new religion's potential to effect powerful positive change. It had also provided a man with few-to-no options for advancement within his traditional society to perform a kind of end run to personal fulfillment—a maneuver that would change forever the native culture of Martha's Vineyard.

During his talks with Towanquatick's people, Hiacoomes explained about God, Jesus Christ, and "Adam's transgression and the misery of the world by it." For the Puritans, this was the essential point: that the Indians understand the concept of sin. Mayhew reported that "Hiacoomes told me himself that this was the first time that ever he saw the Indians sensible of their sins; formerly they did but hear it as a new thing, but not so nearly concerning them, for they were exceeding thankful saying, also *now we have seen our sins*."

Although this Calvinist view of the universe was a long way from

Fig. 21
An extremely unreliable engraving depicting Bartholomew Gosnold trading with the Indians on Martha's Vineyard in 1602, especially given the fact that Gosnold's expedition included only one ocean-going vessel, the *Concord*. By Theodor de Bry. *Photo courtesy of Edward E. Ayer Collection, The Newberry Library, Chicago.*

Fig. 22

Gosnold's men claimed to have been "ravished" by the beauty of what they saw in and around their settlement site on Cuttyhunk Island, and looking at this painting by Albert Bierstadt, one can see why. Dwarfed by the surrounding landscape, the English and Indians are shown meeting on a slender strand of beach between the *Concord* at anchor on the left and the newly constructed fort in the center of the painting. *Old Dartmouth Historical Society-New Bedford Whaling Museum.*

Fig. 23

Across Long Pond, at the west end of Nantucket, is what is called Massasoit Bridge, shown here in the fall of 1997. The bridge, many times rebuilt, may date to a time when the Wampanoag sachem oversaw the creation of a driftwhaling operation on the southwest shore of the island. *Photo by Nathaniel Philbrick.*

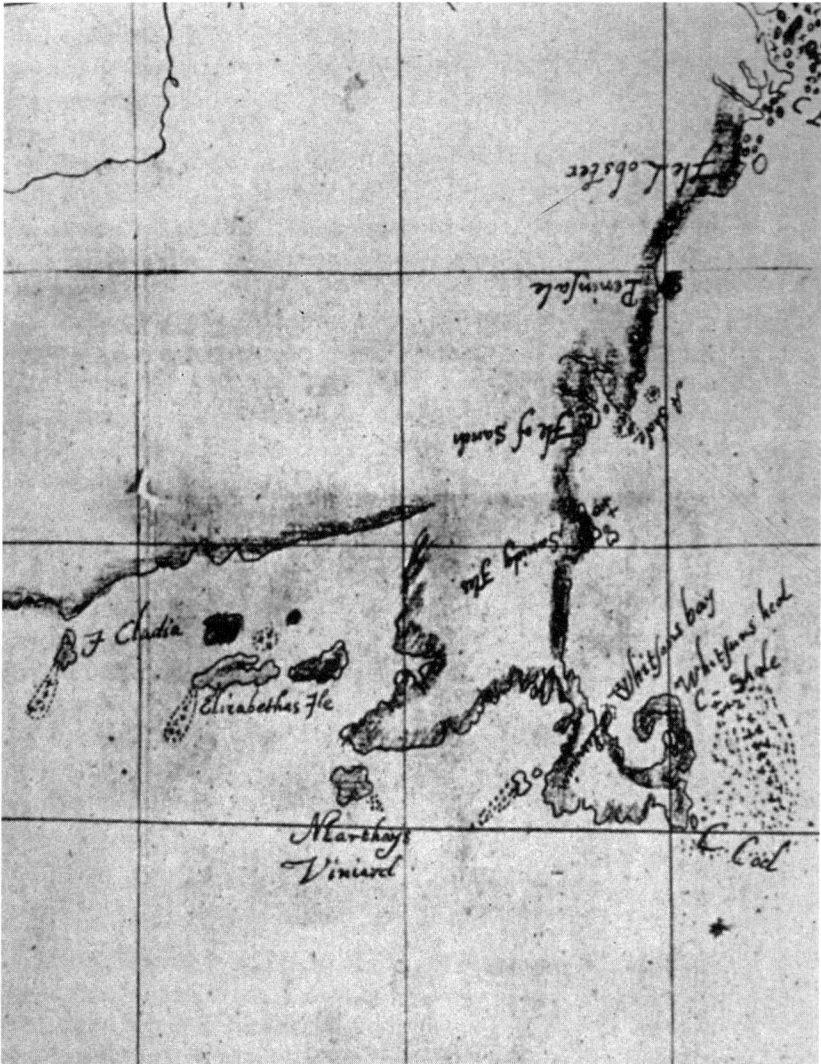

Fig. 24
The so-called Velasco Map (1610), thought to have been based on information provided by Bartholomew Gosnold and perhaps others. Note the clear and surprisingly accurate renderings of Cape Cod, Martha's Vineyard, and the Elizabeth Islands. Nantucket, however, is nowhere to be seen. *Archivo General, Simancas, Spain.*

Fig. 25

The first Nantucket Indian to be documented by Europeans? According to tradition, a native Nantucketer was the model for the Indian portrayed on the Seal of the Governor and Company of the Massachusetts Bay, drawn in England in 1629. This may have been an Indian named Sakaweston, who in 1611 was abducted from an island that was in all probability Nantucket and taken to England. According to Captain John Smith, Sakaweston lived "many years in England" before leaving to fight in the Thirty Years War in Bohemia. Note that the Indian is saying, "Come over and help us." *Courtesy of Massachusetts Archives.*

Fig. 26

This bronze sculpture of Massasoit, supreme sachem of the Wampanoag, stands on Coles Hill across from Plymouth Rock. Although the Pilgrims were enthusiastic supporters of Massasoit, native Nantucketers seem to have had a more ambivalent relationship with their sachem, who may have engineered an invasion of the island by Vineyard driftwhalers during the first half of the seventeenth century. *Photo by Alicja Mann, courtesy of Word Studio.*

Fig. 27
When the Pilgrim William Bradford met the sachem Ianough in the Barnstable area of Cape Cod in 1621, he described him as "a man not exceeding twenty-six years of age, but very personable, gentle, courteous and fair conditioned." In a few short years, however, Ianough, along with several other Cape Cod sachems, would be dead, victims of the chaotic aftermath of the Pilgrim's raid on Indians at Wessagusset in the vicinity of what is now Weymouth. This bronze statue of Ianough is on Main Street, Hyannis, a town named for the sachem. *Photo by Martin Booker.*

Figs. 28 and 29

Two fanciful late sixteenth-century views of native whaling. In the top print, by Theodor de Bry and set on Santa Maria Island, the Europeans look on approvingly as natives do the difficult and dangerous work of capturing and landing whales; in the second engraving by Hans Bol, supposedly depicting Basque whaling in Newfoundland, natives and whites man the whaleboats as coopers work on the beach. Although there is no evidence that Nantucket Indians pursued whales in boats prior to the arrival of the first English settlers in 1659, there is indirect evidence of a native driftwhaling operation at the west end of the island that may have catered to both the English and Dutch. *The Kendall Whaling Museum, Sharon, Massachusetts* (top), *and Old Dartmouth Historical Society-New Bedford Whaling Museum.*

Fig. 30

At the National Cathedral in Washington, D.C., is this History of Baptism window showing, in the lower right, Thomas Mayhew baptizing Hiacoomes, the first Vineyard Indian to accept the Christian faith. Hiacoomes's son Joel would later attend Harvard College, only to be killed by Nantucket Indians on the north shore of Coatue just a few months before he would have received his degree in 1665. The window was created by Wilbur H. Burnham, Jr., and installed in 1954. *Courtesy of the Washington National Cathedral.*

Fig. 31
This early painting by an unknown artist depicts Richard Bourne preaching to the Mashpee Indians in the seventeenth century. (The white, toga-like robes worn by some of the Indians seem to have been added for reasons of propriety.) Gatherings similar to this undoubtedly occurred on Nantucket when the Vineyard missionary Thomas Mayhew visited the island. *Photo by Alicja Mann, courtesy of Word Studio. Mashpee Wampanoag Indian Museum.*

Fig. 32
Nantucket's equivalent of Maushop's den. Looking to the west toward the clay-streaked cliffs along the north shore of the island. This was the area where the legendary shaman Mudturtle was reputed to have lived in a cave. *Photo by Melissa D. Philbrick.*

the natives' notions of Kiehtan and Hobbamock, it must be realized that the Native Americans' world had radically changed over the last three decades. For its part, Puritanism had emerged out of an England beset by many of the same pressures that the Indians were now experiencing: killing plagues and wrenching social and economic turmoil. Just as Puritanism had provided its English converts with a disciplined alternative to a world of terrifying loss, so did the belief in sin, guilt, and the need for redemption through Christ hold out hope for a native people whose society had suffered what William Simmons has called "massive erosion and change." Mayhew reported that the sachem Towanquatick told him: "That a long time ago they had wise men, which in a grave manner taught the people knowledge; but they are dead, and their wisdom is buried with them.... He told me that...he hoped the time of knowledge was now come."

Having witnessed firsthand the fragility of their own oral traditions, the Indians were in a position to appreciate the staying power of the written word, particularly when it came to the Puritans' omnipresent black book, the Bible. According to Roger Williams, the Narragansett sachem Maitunnomu once admitted that he was inclined to believe the English claims concerning heaven and hell because it was written down in a book "which God himself made concerning men's souls." Maitunnomu went so far as to say that since his people had no written records and took "all upon trust from our forefathers," the English "may well know more" than the Indians.

As early as 1643 Hiacoomes had expressed a desire to learn how to read, so the English provided him with a child's primer that he was still carrying around with him seven years later. By 1651, Mayhew had established an Indian school with more than thirty children in attendance.

Along with the written word came the concept of prayer. The Indians traditionally relied upon visions, often induced through physical hardship and, on occasion, the pokeweed that seems to have been so readily available on Nantucket, for enlightenment. For their part, the Puritans depended on a form of devotional meditation so rigorous that it imparted what one historian has called an "almost sensual joy." As strenuous, intense, and ritualized in its own internalized way as the powwows' more outwardly demonstrative ceremonies, the Puritan approach to prayer may have been easier for a Native American in the seventeenth century to relate to than it is for many of us today. As James Ronda has speculated, Indian spiritual traditions such as the vision quest, in which a young man privately searched for "personal identity, special powers, and a guardian spirit," evolved into solitary praying rituals on the Vineyard. Meanwhile, the Indians' oral traditions—most commonly communicated through the ritualized performances of the natives' elders—were transmogrified into the European forms of gospel and sermon.

But what Simmons has termed "the most profound social conversion to occur anywhere in New England" did not always proceed smoothly. For their part, the powwows, whom Mayhew called "the strongest cord that binds [the Indians] to their own way," were not about to surrender without a fight.

On a dark night in 1647, Towanquatick, who had been the first sachem to welcome the establishment of a Christian meeting for his people, felt the vengeance of the Vineyard's traditional faction. He was alseep on the ground near a fishing weir with several other Indians and one Englishman when out of the darkness emerged an Indian who, "being about six or eight paces from [Towanquatick], let fly a broad headed arrow." Instead of killing the sachem, the arrow ricocheted off his eyebrow and "slit the top of the nose to the bottom." Although there was quite a bit of bleeding, the sachem's wounds proved treatable. The next morning Mayhew visited with Towanquatick and was so impressed by his unshaken belief in God that he claimed the sachem "bears in his brow the marks of the Lord Jesus."

In 1649, by which time increasing numbers of Indians had begun to attend Hiacoomes's Sunday services, a powwow angrily stormed in at the end of a meeting. According to Mayhew, he shouted, "I know the meeting Indians are liars; you say you care not for the pow-wows." After singling out three of the worshipers and "railing at them," he claimed that the powwows "could kill all the meeting Indians if they did set about it." Although one of the Indians spoke in defiance of the powwow, it was Hiacoomes who carried the day. According to Mayhew, he issued a challenge: that he would stand in the midst of "all the powwows of the island...and when they did their worst by their witchcrafts to kill him, he would without fear set himself against them, by remembering Jehovah." Then, with a dramatic flourish, he pointed to his foot and said he would "put all the pow-wows under his heel."

Not long after this confrontation, which left the powwow with "nothing to say," Hiacoomes's faith was challenged from another, more personal front when his newborn son died after only five days. Up until this time, not a single member of the Indian meeting had succumbed to disease. Instead of blackening their faces with charcoal and wailing in grief beside their son's grave in the traditional manner, Hiacoomes and his wife displayed the "patient resigning" expected of a good Englishman. According to Mayhew, who attended the grave-side ceremony, "as we were going away one of the Indians told me he was much refreshed in being freed from their old customs, as also to hear of the resurrection of good men and their children to be with God."

About this time, two powwows came before the Indian meeting with their "joints shaking, and their bowels trembling, their spirits troubled," to disavow their old ways. For the Indians this was an astonishing turn of events, since the powwows had traditionally been the ones to instill the fear and trembling. Whether or not it was the appearance of new diseases or, as one of the powwows maintained, the arrival of the "word of God," they both admitted to having "been much foiled in their devilish tasks, and that instead of curing have rather killed many."

By 1652 Hiacoomes and the converted Indians, now numbering nearly three hundred (including eight former powwows), requested that Mayhew help them create a government compatible with their new-found religion. Less than ten years after they had begun, Mayhew's missionary efforts on Martha's Vineyard had resulted in the creation of a self-sufficient community with not only a church but a state.

Although the first to begin missionary work in New England, Mayhew was by no means the only one. John Eliot would be the most famous "apostle to the Indians," overseeing the creation of "Praying Towns" throughout the Massachusetts Bay region in which the Indians were encouraged to abandon all vestiges of their traditional beliefs and practices. On Cape Cod, Richard Bourne began preaching in the Mashpee area as early as 1653, with Thomas Tupper starting soon after in Sandwich.

About this time the Puritans' London-based missionary arm, the New England Company, began to offer financial assistance to these various missionary efforts. The company's 1654 outlay to Mayhew included £8 for a boat "for the safe passage of yourself and Indians betwixt the island and the main," and required that the boat be "carefully preserved and employed only for the service intended, and not at the pleasure of the Indians etc. upon other occasions." It may have been with the acquisition of this boat that Mayhew and

Hiacoomes began their missionary efforts on the neighboring island of Nantucket.

By 1656 Mayhew was being assisted by the forty-one-year-old Peter Folger, who seems to have shared the young missionary's enthusiasm for scholarship and god. Described as "the English schoolmaster that teacheth the Indians and instructs them on Lord's Day," Folger may have made it possible for Mayhew to devote more time and energy to his missionary efforts on Nantucket, where we know he and Hiacoomes made regular visits.

In many ways, Mayhew was the quintessential missionary. Modest and in possession of a "sweet affable way of conversation," he made a point of winning an Indian's trust before he brought up the subject of religion. According to his descendant Matthew Mayhew, "as he [grew] in their acquaintance and affection, he proceed[ed] to express his great concern and pity for their immortal souls."

He was also tireless, willing to spend days and nights in the natives' wigwams discussing "all their scruples and objections." On Sundays, he talked with the Indians long after the service had ended: "generally he spent more time after sermon in reasoning with them than in sermon; whereby...it came to pass that their religion was as well in *head* as *heart*."

Although missionaries such as John Eliot were just as indefatigable, Mayhew had one distinct advantage: the island environment. Self-contained and isolated, Martha's Vineyard and especially Nantucket provided a sense of focus and community that were much more difficult to achieve amid "the wilds" of the mainland. The islands also contained a much higher ratio of natives to English than was true on the disease-ravaged mainland. (Not until the 1720s would the whites begin to outnumber the Indians on Martha's Vineyard and Nantucket.)

These demographics encouraged a much more culturally permissive environment within the Mayhew mission. Instead of demanding that his converts adhere to a rigid code of conduct (Eliot insisted that the Natick Indians not only dress like the English but also dispense with such traditional habits as picking and eating lice), what were known as Praying Indians on Martha's Vineyard maintained a much firmer attachment to their native ways. Hiacoomes, for example, never adopted a Christian name (as was required in Natick), and wigwams, instead of English-style houses, remained the preferred mode of native habitation on the Vineyard well into the following century.

Whereas Mayhew looked to the conversion of the Native American religious leaders, the powwows, as the linchpin for winning the natives' souls, Eliot focused his attention on the political authority of the sachems, many of whom had a vested material interest in maintaining the status quo. While Eliot complained of the sachems' sinfulness, and did everything he could to undermine their power, Mayhew was perfectly willing to leave the secular side of native society intact, assuring the Vineyard sachems "that religion and government were distinct things." Matthew Mayhew recounted how Thomas Mayhew Senior explained to the Indians that while his god was "in power above any of the Indian monarchs," he was also "a great lover of justice: that therefore he would in no measure invade their jurisdictions; but on the contrary, assist them as need requires.... [I]n no long time they conceived no ill opinion of the Christian religion." Given that natives on both the Vineyard and Nantucket were, at least to some degree, under the political sway of Massasoit (who remained steadfast in his refusal to accept Christianity), this proved an extremely shrewd strategy.

In 1657 Thomas Mayhew, Jr.'s fifteen-year missionary effort was put to the ultimate test. Up until this point the farthest he had ventured from the island was Boston, but even during those relatively brief absences it was said that he was "sore missed" by the Praying Indians. Eventually a lingering desire to give "the English people a better idea of the progress of missionary work in America" (along with the need to resolve a problem surrounding his wife's inheritance) led him to make plans for sailing to London.

According to tradition, Mayhew took leave of the island in fine style. First he conducted a service at the west end of the island and then collected, Pied Piper fashion, Indians at the various meeting sites throughout the island until there were hundreds gathered by the time he turned to them for his farewell address. It was reported that once Mayhew had departed the Indians left stones where their minister had last spoken to them.

Mayhew traveled with his brother-in-law and a young Indian boy to Boston, from where they set sail in November in a vessel full of some of New England's brightest intellectual stars. The ship was never heard from again. Thomas Mayhew, Jr., was thirty-six years old.

As late as August of the following year, his father was holding out hope that he might still somehow be alive, writing, "I cannot yet give my son over." Wrote John Eliot, "The Lord has given us this amazing blow." The commissioners for the New England Company called the loss "almost irreparable." For years to come, it was said, the Indians of Martha's Vineyard could not speak Mayhew's name without openly weeping. The spot where Mayhew had given his farewell address (today marked by a plaque) became heaped with stones.

But Mayhew's legacy would prove something more than a cult of personality. Whereas Eliot's Praying Towns would quickly fall into disarray soon after his death in 1690, Mayhew's more culturally tolerant system would not only last well into the next century, but leapfrog to another island. According to the contemporary historian William Hubbard, the Vineyard was a place "where civility and Christianity hath taken a deeper root than in any other plantation of the Indians." But if Mayhew had also laid the seeds for the growth of Christianity among the Indians of Nantucket, things would always be a little different on that faraway island.

For more than a decade after Martha's Vineyard became the scene of the most successful missionary effort in New England, Nantucket remained relatively free of European influence. While the Mayhews certainly made inroads among some of Nantucket's Indians, it was still an island where native beliefs and practices had a better chance of survival than almost anywhere else in the region. For those Vineyard powwows who refused to come under the sway of the Mayhews, Nantucket may have become a haven of last resort. Let us now turn to the story of a Nantucket Indian shaman named Mudturtle that may reflect how subsequent generations of Praying Indians came to disparage and even mock the memory of those who dared to resist the rising tide of Christianity.

Whether or not he had come from the Vineyard, Mudturtle was an outsider on Nantucket. Instead of a wigwam, he lived in his own version of Maushop's crater-like den, a shoreside cave to the west of Brant Point. Today, if you walk to the edge of the conservation land known as the Tupancy Links, you can still see the rocks that mark the remnants of Mudturtle's cave. It was within this steep, mud-ooz-ing cliff that Mudturtle eked out a meager living as a fortune teller and dealer in "rat-skins, smoked snakes, [and] pokeweed."

Like any good ogre, Mudturtle was hideously deformed. His feet splayed out in contrary angles. One knee curved in, the other curved out; and he walked with a hulking, zigzag gait. The palm of his right hand faced upward; the palm of his left hand contained a curled thumb. His left arm was a foot longer than his right arm. His elbows were jointed in such a way that he could twirl his forearms in oppo-site directions like propeller blades. He had no ears. His eyes (one brown, the other yellow) were so far apart that he looked at the world the way a bird does, his head twitching back and forth. His face was speckled with green spots, giving his reddish skin the look of oxidized copper. His hair reached skyward in a crazy, quivering mess. His backside went from a rounded hump to a long bony tail that was said to be the source of his evil powers.

Mudturtle's personality was as twisted as his body. His demented, capricious, and cruel sense of humor made him feared by all the Indians on Nantucket. But Mudturtle was not content with inflicting himself on just the western Indians among whom he lived. He also made it his business to interfere, as best he could, with the affairs of the Indians to the east.

One day he learned that the daughter of an eastern sachem had recently been married. Mudturtle, who had always lusted after this beautiful young woman, decided to kidnap the girl and take her back to his cave.

At sunset he launched his dugout canoe and began the long paddle up harbor to the eastern village of Squam. With the tide against him, it was midnight before he beached his canoe and began to approach the unguarded village. Hobbling into the wigwam of the newlyweds, Mudturtle opened a large sack made out of squirrel and rat skins and quickly drew it over the bride's head. Muffling her cries with the sack, Mudturtle carried her back to the canoe and set off for his cave.

It wasn't long before the girl had pulled off the suffocating sack and alerted the village with her panicked cries. Even without any ears, Mudturtle could hear the shouts of the warriors as canoe after canoe set out after him in hot pursuit. Exultant, Mudturtle filled the air with his own shrieks.

And so, beneath a luminous moon, the monster from the west paddled for home, only to discover that his pursuers were rapidly gaining on him. As he approached Coatue's First Point, he realized that drastic action was called for, and he tossed the captive princess overboard. As the easterners veered off to save the girl, Mudturtle made good his escape, losing himself in the shadows along Brant Point.

It was then that the enormity of what he had done caught up with Mudturtle. During his frantic paddle down the harbor he had dislocated both an elbow and an ankle, and he took the injuries as an omen of horrible consequences to come. In agony and despair, Mudturtle paddled out into Nantucket Sound and threw himself into the sea.

The next morning a well-armed contingent of eastern Indians arrived at the western village of Miacomet, demanding the head of Mudturtle. If it were not provided to them within two days, there would be war. But, of course, Mudturtle was nowhere to be found. After a day and a half in front of the powwow's cave, pleading with him to come out, the western sachem and his braves resigned themselves to the inevitable.

The battle was fought where these east-west confrontations traditionally occurred–the wooded and swampy terrain of Madequecham Valley–and many westerners fell that day. Not long after, a violent storm washed Mudturtle's body onto Brant Point. Although he was buried below the tide line as quickly as possible, Mudturtle's body washed up again the following day. Three times Mudturtle's body was buried only to resurface each time. Finally it was determined that his tail, thought to contain his supernatural powers, should be cut off, and he was buried face-down with a conch shell in each hand. This time he remained interred. The tail was eventually sent as a peace offering to the eastern sachem, who wore it ever after as a charm against nightmares.

Mudturtle is Maushop come full circle in his transformation from benevolent creator to a creature of discord whose only legacy is of desperate and senseless violence. For Nantucket's native people, he may have embodied the weird and unnerving cultural turbulence that the island experienced as a consequence of its proximity to both the Vineyard and the mainland. For this island full of Indians, the 1640s and '50s may have been a particularly harrowing time as Nantucket became a kind of refugee camp buffeted by the contrary forces of tradition and change. While the powwows led the call to keep the white man and his jealous god away, the sachems, having seen how well their counterparts fared on the Vineyard, inevitably began to think seriously about letting the English in.

Whether or not the legend of Mudturtle depicts how, after much resistance, the island's political leadership finally brought the powwows in line, by 1659 there was at least one eastern sachem who was prepared to open the floodgates.

6

FEDERATED ALONG ONE KEEL

They were nearly all Islanders in the Pequod, Isolatoes *too, I call such, not acknowledging the common continent of men, but each* Isolato *living on a separate continent of his own. Yet now, federated along one keel, what a set these* Isolatoes *were!*

–Herman Melville, Moby-Dick

He was the right man at the right time: an Indian with a flair for controversy and a talent for brinkmanship. He was a political animal, and in keeping with the opportunistic streak that would serve him well all his life, his name of Nickanoose meant to "suck the foreteat." But the eastern sachem Nickanoose had something more than his own interests at heart. If he was bold enough to reach out and grab the golden ring, he would also do everything in his power to ensure that his people shared in that good fortune for as long as possible.

To Nantucket's first English settlers in 1659, the island appeared to have great economic potential. Nantucket was an island without wolves, and nowhere else in coastal New England was as well suited for sheep raising–especially since Nantucket was not, as of yet, under any effective colonial jurisdiction. Here was a place where a group of Englishmen could create a self-supporting community well removed from, but not out of touch with, the rest of Puritan New England. And the English were prepared to pay for these advantages. If you were one of the ruling sachems on this fourteen-mile-long island, here was a development opportunity whose time had come.

Certainly Nickanoose owed his ancestors a debt of gratitude. Because of their aggression, the island had been deemed uninhabitable by the white man, a message forcibly delivered to Harlow back in 1611 and reinforced when Mayhew first came to Nantucket in 1641. But by 1659, things had changed on the volatile little island. In Nickanoose, Nantucket now had a sachem with the savvy to present a united front (well, at least the illusion of a united front) to the English, and the wherewithal to insist that Native American demands be attended to over the long haul. A Big Man on a small island, Nickanoose had had a unique opportunity to observe the English from a distance prior to the creation of the bicultural pressure cooker that would become Nantucket.

A child of the post-contact era, Nickanoose came of age in the violent decades after Wessagusset. Although Nantucket was without a permanent English settlement throughout the first half of the seventeenth century, the island's Indians inevitably encountered their share of white people—not only from the Vineyard but from traders in search of Indian corn and, of course, whale oil. Nickanoose lived in the woodsy, swampy, and fertile northeastern corner of the island known as Wannasquam, or Squam for short. To the east was the sea, to the north the harbor, with Great Point, which the Indians called Nauma, reaching out toward Cape Cod. Not surprisingly, his people maintained close ties with the mainland; two of his children would eventually move to Harwich.

Nickanoose shared the eastern end of Nantucket with Wanackmamack, the sachem to the south whose winter quarters were nestled amid the rounded hills and swamps at Occawa in the center of the island. If Wanackmamack was the senior of the two (and formally regarded as the "Chief Sachem of Nantucket"), Nickanoose would take the more active role when it came to the eastern Indians' relations with the English.

Publicly he was a conciliator (his sign was a broken arrow), but privately Nickanoose led what seems to have been a fairly turbulent life. After his first wife bore him two sons and a daughter, the sachem "turned away his proper wife, and took another woman" with whom he would have four more sons and at least one more daughter. Nickanoose's conduct so angered Jethro, one of his children from his first marriage, that the son moved off the island to Cape Cod.

Even though peace had come to the island with the establishment of the border at Madequecham, relations had remained edgy between the two groups. (A people could not tell and retell the legend of Roqua–based on events that had occurred within memory of many Nantucketers–without maintaining a certain bitterness.) There was also a cultural divide. The easterners, even if their numbers had been recently augmented by refugees from the mainland, had a long-standing relationship with their lands, which were the finest on the island. The westerners, on the other hand, might possess Nantucket's best driftwhaling beaches but were, relatively speaking, land poor. Indeed, it is no accident that the name Madaket means, according to Henry Worth, "bad land." (Even today, the island's dump is located in Madaket, while the sewage-treatment plant is not far from Attapeat's stronghold in Miacomet.)

The driftwhalers' itinerant ways–moving back and forth from the Vineyard on a seasonal basis, and then, once on Nantucket, arguing with each other over whose piece of whale meat was whose–were not the ways of Nickanoose's people. With access to a wide range of natural resources–from the land as well as the sea–the easterners may have viewed the westerners as decidedly lower class: impertinent and violent late arrivals who, much like the "washashores" of the twentieth century, had helped to ruin what had been (at least when transformed by the myth-making machinery of memory) a golden age. They were not the people a proud eastern sachem wanted his daughter to marry into.

Two traditions have been passed down to us describing a love affair and marriage between a young couple from opposite sides of Madequecham Valley. Although one version (recorded in a ballad written in 1876 "in the spirit of Longfellow's Hiawatha") calls them Wonoma and Autopscot (a variant of Attapeat), Elizabeth Little has suggested that this legend is actually talking about Nickanoose's daughter Askammapoo and the minor western sachem Spotso. What follows is a possible scenario, based not only on tradition but what few relevant documents are available to us.

It started with a sudden outbreak of sickness in Attapeat's village at Miacomet. With their close attachment to the Vineyard and European whaling markets on the mainland, the western Indians, referred to as the Tomokommoths in the records of a 1665 town meeting, may have been the ones to introduce foreign diseases to the island. When all the remedies his people had available to them failed, Attapeat, having heard that Nickanoose's daughter Askammapoo had a talent for healing the sick, appealed to the easterners for help.

Indians used a wide variety of plants, from cranberries to skunk cabbage, to treat almost every conceivable complaint. (Besides being a substitute for tobacco, pokeweed was used to treat poison ivy, rheumatism, and hemorrhoids.) Since many of these remedies remained well-kept secrets, passed down among the women within a single village and even family, this would have meant that Askammapoo and the easterners, with their long-standing knowledge of the island's resources relative to the upstart driftwhalers to the west, were at a distinct advantage when it came to the art of healing. The plant- and herb-rich forests and swamps at their end of the island would only have added to the eastern Indians' advantage in this regard.

For whatever reason, Nickanoose allowed his daughter to travel to the Tomokommoth village to attempt a cure. It may have been that the sachem recognized that on an island as small as Nantucket, it was in everyone's best interests to nip a potential epidemic in the bud.

Askammapoo's mission proved a complete success. Although we don't know what it was she used to treat the disease, we do know that Indians commonly used boiled cedar needles and twigs to treat fevers, which is how the ballad describes the illness. Whether or not this was part of Askammapoo's cure, she also worked a different kind of magic on a young sachem named Spotso, and the two fell in love. However, knowing the history of conflict between their two peoples, the couple decided to keep the relationship a secret.

It was not long before east-west relations had once again begun to deteriorate. According to the ballad, a squabble over possession of "the land that lay between them"—perhaps the fertile southern edge of the harbor mentioned in the 1678 Indian deed—was the cause of the diplomatic breakdown. In any event, the eastern Indians began to make preparations for war.

When she heard of the plans, Askammapoo decided to alert Spotso. Although the ballad claims that she paddled a canoe down the harbor to Spotso's village to the west, an earlier version of the legend describes how the lover ran along the beach at the island's south shore, being careful to remain below the tideline so that the waves washed away all traces of footprints. After alerting the Tomokommoths, Askammapoo returned undetected to Squam.

Instead of a massacre at Madaket, everything turned out for the best: Once the easterners realized that their enemies were on to them, they decided against launching an attack. Soon after, Spotso appeared at Nickanoose's door and confessed his love for the sachem's daughter. Reluctantly, Nickanoose agreed to the marriage, and from that day forward Nantucket's east-west battles were a thing of the past.

Perhaps contributing to the eastern sachem's willingness to agree to the match was the realization that the marriage made possible an interesting tactical move. With a Tomokommoth for a son-in-law, Nickanoose was now positioned to broker a real estate deal that would not only benefit himself and his fellow eastern sachem Wanackmamack, but would also help to undermine their old rivals to

HISTORICAL INDIAN LOCATIONS AT NANTUCKET, "The Faraway Land"

1. Abnecount's Island
2. Abram's Point, Home of Abram Quary, Nantucket's "Last Indian"
3. Acamy, also Tawtemeo–now Hummock Pond
4. Altar Rock
5. Cain's Hill
6. Cain's Pond
7. Canoopache Swamp
8. Cappamet Harbor, later Capaum Pond– Home of the Japhets
9. Chappomiss Valley
10. Cheegin's Island

MUSKEGET ISLAND

37

GRAVELLY ISLAND

TUCKERNUCK ISLAND

76

42

11. Coatue, "At the Pine Woods"
12. Coboahcommoh, Site of Whale Station
13. Codspannett Field
14. Consue
15. Coskata Pond
16. Cotockta
17. Eat Fire Spring
18. Flat Root Pond
19. Gibbs Pond, named for the Indian John Gibbs, or Assassamough
20. Gibbs Swamp
21. Great Mioxes Pond
22. Hot House Spring
23. Jude Island
24. Little Mioxes Pond
25. Long Joseph's Point
26. Long Pond
27. Madaket Ditch
28. Madaket, "Bad Land"
29. Madaquecham Pond
30. Madaquecham Valley
31. Massasoit Bridge
32. Maxcy's Pond

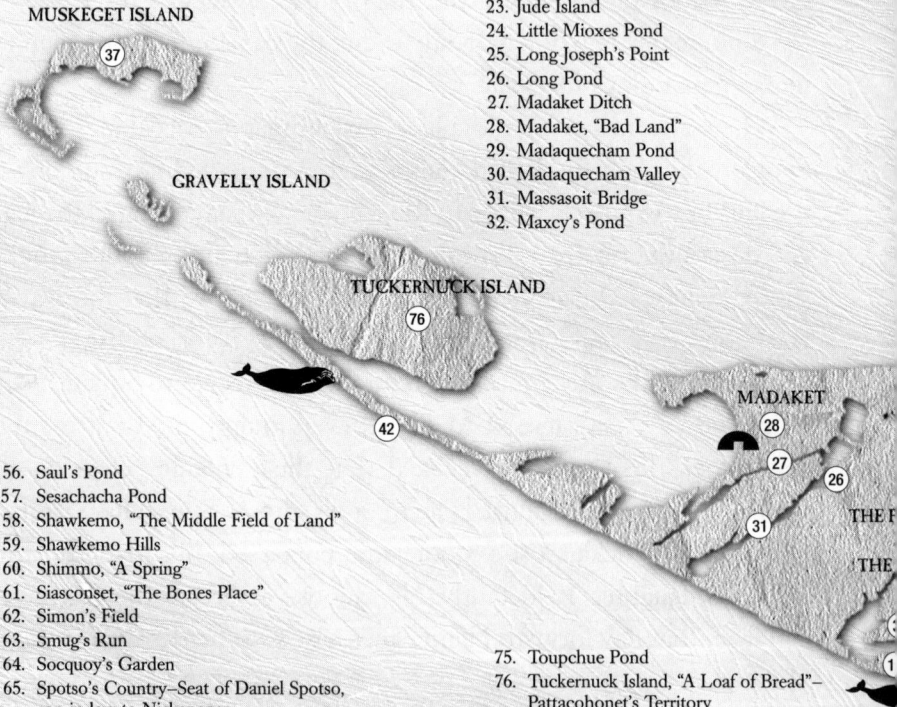

MADAKET

28
27
26
31

THE F
THE

56. Saul's Pond
57. Sesachacha Pond
58. Shawkemo, "The Middle Field of Land"
59. Shawkemo Hills
60. Shimmo, "A Spring"
61. Siasconset, "The Bones Place"
62. Simon's Field
63. Smug's Run
64. Socquoy's Garden
65. Spotso's Country–Seat of Daniel Spotso, son-in-law to Nickanoose
66. Squam, originally Wannasquam, "At the Top of the Rock"–Seat of Nickanoose
67. Squatesit, location of Indian Church
68. Swain's Neck or Nashayte
69. Tashama's Island
70. Taupawsha's Swamp
71. Tetaukimmo
72. The Cliff
73. The Woods, also The Long Trees
74. Tom Nevers Pond

75. Toupchue Pond
76. Tuckernuck Island, "A Loaf of Bread"– Pattacohonet's Territory
77. Wammasquid, location of Indian Church
78. Wannacomet, "The Pond Field"–Home of the H
79. Waquitaquab Pond
80. Washamon's Island
81. Watt's Run
82. Wauwinet, son of Nickanoose
83. Weecodnoy
84. Wesco, "The White Stone"
85. Weweeder, "A Pair of Horns"
86. Wigwam Ponds

33. Miacomet Pond
34. Miacomet, "A Meeting Place"–Seat of Attapeat
35. Manna, "At the Place of the Deep Well"
36. Moudowe Creeks
37. Muskeget Island, "Westernmost of the Sturgeon Islands"–Seiknout's Territory
38. Nanahuma's Neck
39. Nauma, now Great Point
40. No–Bottom Pond
41. Nobadeer Pond
42. Nopque, "The Landing Place," now Smith's Point
43. Occawa, "Where the Church Meets" (also called Sakedan)–Seat of Wanackmamack
44. Philip Quaab's Run
45. Pochick
46. Pocomo
47. Pocoy
48. Polpis, "Branching Harbor or Cove"
49. Poot ("Whale") Ponds
50. Popsquatchet Hills
51. Quaise or Masquetuck, "The Reed Land"
52. Quanaty, "The Long Hill"
53. Quidnet
54. Sankaty Head, or Naphchecoy, "Round the Head"
55. Saul's Hills

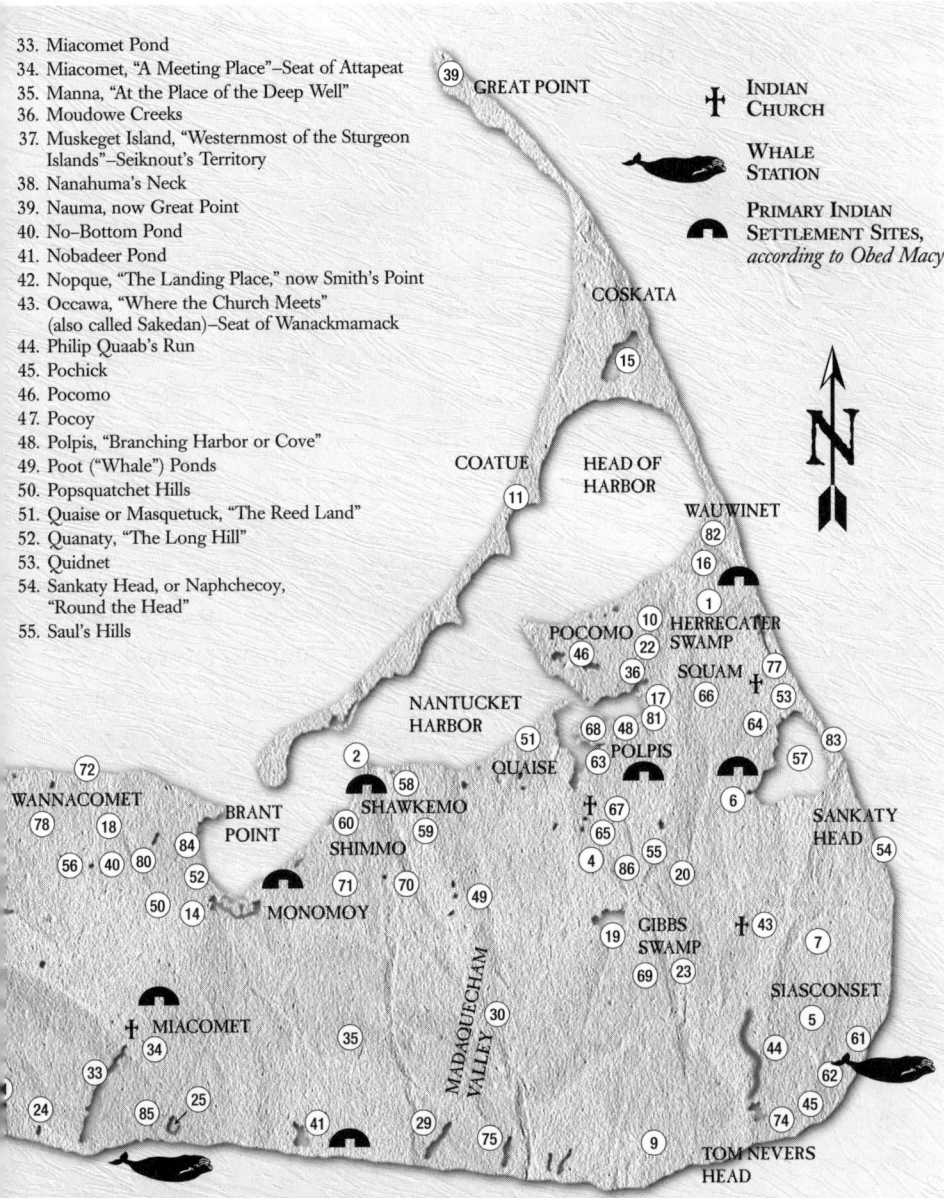

Nantucket's Native American legacy lives on in its place-names. Combining the names recorded on the 1869 Ewer map with locations identified by Elizabeth Little, this map provides an overview of the island's native place-names. The translations are from either Zaccheus Macy or Henry Worth and, in many cases, are no better than best guesses. *Map by Frederick Swartz.*

the west–particularly Attapeat. Nickanoose would sell the west end of the island (of which he and Wanackmamack had, at best, an extremely tenuous claim) to the English.

On June 12, 1659, the confusion began. Perhaps confusion is too strong a word. Mayhew certainly knew what he was getting himself into, and to a certain extent, so did the Indians. By signing a document in which the Indians agreed to sell the west end of the island to Mayhew, the two parties agreed to begin a process of negotiation rather than, as might be assumed in today's world of "done deals," conclude a specific transaction.

In the deed, Nickanoose and a minor sachem from the west named Nanahuma, sold "the plain at the west end of Nantucket" to Mayhew in exchange for £12, to be paid in the form of wampum (an indication that Nantucket's Indians were not, as some traditions claim, completely unfamiliar with this form of beaded currency). The deed included a crude map that designated that the "Plain Country" began to the west of Hummock Pond (referred to as Acamy) and included a series of ponds, generically referred to as "Long Pond" (a name that has stuck), "Another Pond," and "Salt Pond." Then on July second, for the price of £30 and two beaver hats (for himself and his wife), Mayhew signed the deed over to a group of settlers and investors from the mainland north of Boston, one of whom was Mayhew's cousin Thomas Macy. Of interest is that Mayhew specifically reserved an area for himself well to the east of the English territory on Nantucket, in a prime stretch of land known as Quaise.

One might assume that the English had, by this point, "bought" the west end of the island. That not only the Indians but also the English assumed otherwise is indicated by yet another deed signed almost a year later that extended the English-Indian property line from Waquitaquab Pond (not far from the Head of Hummock Pond) over to a pond in Monomoy at the southwest corner of the harbor, so as to include the area of today's town known as Wesco. The deed, signed by Nickanoose and Wanackmamack, stipulated that the English pay another £14.

In a pattern that would persist throughout the century, the English implicitly recognized that the Indians had an entirely different understanding of what it meant to sell a piece of land. For the Indians, the concept of ownership was ludicrous. Everyone knew that people were a part of the land, that the most anyone could do was to borrow the use of it. As far as the Indians were concerned, they had simply granted the English the right to share it with them—a right that could be maintained only through the payment of tribute on a fairly regular basis. In turn, the English would, in some instances, pay more than once for a piece of land. They would also, in other instances, allow the Indians to remain on lands that were technically English.

Instead of a completed transaction, a land deal was regarded by the Indians as the beginning of a long and mutually rewarding relationship, providing them with ready access to a wide range of European goods without dramatically affecting their ability to enjoy the island's resources. And since they would be outnumbered by their Indian neighbors well into the next century, the English had no choice but to keep their native co-inhabitants, if not happy, at least not fighting mad.

Although white historians have focused on (and inevitably heroicized) the arrival of Nantucket's first English settlers—Thomas Macy and his family, along with Edward Starbuck and a handful of others—in the fall of 1659, it would have been, from a Native American perspective, nothing special. English settlers from the Vineyard had begun grazing their sheep on the west end of Nantucket as early as 1654, and given Mayhew's many missionary trips there, a few English living in temporary structures at Warren's Landing on Madaket Harbor and Head of Long Pond a few miles into the interior would have prompted only mild interest.

For the English, however, it was a strange new world. When a large group of Indians began to assemble near the harbor, then proceeded to work "themselves up into a great fury, singing and dancing with all their might," Macy became convinced that they were on the verge of an attack. Edward Starbuck was called for, and "being a bold man," he "sallied forth upon the astonished natives," brandishing his cane and issuing a series of oaths. After the Indians had dispersed, the English discovered that they had interrupted nothing more than a powwow (the ceremony rather than the religious leader) calling for rain.

The Indians do not seem to have held Macy's and Starbuck's ignorance against them. Starbuck, who would take the time to learn Massachusett, became such a favorite of Nickanoose's and Wanackmamack's that in January of 1661, they gave him, with their "free and voluntary wills," all of Coatue.

After the first winter, the English began to carve out twenty-acre house lots in the vicinity of a small harbor, actually a pond connected to the sea, called Cappamet and, later, Capaum, along the north shore. From this harbor (well to the west of today's town), the lots extended out in two directions–to the south toward a narrow forest contained within U-shaped Hummock Pond (referred to as the "Long Trees" in Mayhew's Indian deed), and to the east toward Wesco, beside what the English called the Great Harbor. Over the next few years, approximately thirty English families would make Nantucket their home. In 1663, Peter Folger, the Vineyard's schoolmaster to the Indians, moved permanently to the island to act as, among other things, the town's Indian interpreter.

The eastern sachems had to be extremely pleased with the island's new English residents. Not only had they paid twice for the privilege of settling on the island's worst lands (lands that Mayhew had known enough to avoid), but they had paid Nickanoose and Wanackmamack for lands that may have not even been technically theirs to sell. One wonders if Nanahuma, the westerner who had signed on as a Nantucket sachem with Nickanoose in the first deed to Mayhew, had done so only after receiving some pressure (or some promises) from the conniving eastern sachem.

Eventually Nanahuma, and a number of other Tomokommoths, would claim that their territories had been sold out from underneath them. But by that point it was too late. The English had already begun to settle on the island, and although the westerners would be compensated in a variety of ways, not only by the English but also by Nickanoose and Wanackmamack, they had, in effect, lost control of their lands.

In the meantime, the eastern Indians remained insulated from the English by the territories of Attapeat and several other minor Tomokommoth sachems (including Askammapoo's new husband Spotso). This meant that those westerners who had not lost their lands found themselves with some new neighbors who had some extremely unsavory habits. Not only did the English almost immediately begin to cut down an alarming number of trees for their timber-frame houses, they also brought with them animals–pigs, cattle, and especially sheep–with a voracious appetite for grass and, of course, Indian corn. And since Nickanoose and Wanackmamack had given the English not only the west end of the island but the right to graze their animals over *the entire island* from fall until spring, Attapeat and company had better get used to living with sheep. (Given that the Indians considered white animals to be bad luck, the development may have been something more than a mere annoyance for the Tomokommoths.)

In the short term, it was a triumph for Nickanoose. He and Wanackmamack had been paid a significant sum by a tenant whose presence would not bother them in the least. That he had, in the process, made life a little more miserable for Attapeat and the Vineyard transients may have made the deal all the sweeter. And with his new son-in-law to help smooth whatever ruffled feathers he had caused among the Tomokommoths, the likelihood of stirring up any real trouble among the western Indians had been effectively minimized.

During this early and relatively innocent period, the English may have made possible a brief flush of prosperity in the villages of both the eastern and western Indians. The English plows, tradition tells us, were especially appreciated: "The Indians would with delight, for whole days together, follow the traces of the plowshare; and they earnestly entreated the English to plow their land for them." They were equally "astonished" by the English guns, "by which more birds could be killed in a day, than they could destroy with their arrows in a month." The white man's iron fishhooks would have had a similar impact on Indian fishing, meaning that it was now possible to grow, catch, and hunt significantly more corn, fish, and birds in a shorter period of time. The economic transformation wrought by these changes raised the question of whether the Native Americans would in time become dependent on the English.

But Nickanoose, who was well aware of what had happened on Cape Cod and the Vineyard–particularly when it came to the English lust for land–knew enough to leave nothing to chance. Realizing that the English honored not the spoken word but the written word, he did an extraordinary thing. To cover himself and especially his children, Nickanoose had his own deeds written up–some of which even predated the arrival of English settlers. Thanks to almost twenty years of contact with Puritan missionaries and schoolteachers on the Vineyard, there were Indians on Nantucket who could not only read but write, and Nickanoose put them to work.

We have only an English copy of a deed that seems to have been originally written in Massachusett "before the English came unto Nantucket to dwell." In the deed Nickanoose declares that his eldest son Wauwinet will be the one who eventually takes over his sachem right and, of course, his lands: "none else can dispose or divide this land if not willing...to the disposing of it forever." Given his complex family situation, Nickanoose felt it necessary to add a postscript: "afterwards to all his children, Nickanoose, only Wauwinet great, and nobody else."

Then, of course, there was the matter of his daughter's marriage to a western sachem. In August 1660, with the English just beginning to arrive on the island, Nickanoose called an Indian named Adam to his wigwam. Not only could Adam write Massachusett he could write English, and he drafted a deed in which Nickanoose gave his daughter half his lands. The document begins and ends with the statement "I AM Nickanoose." A man of great personal force, the sachem wills himself into the future. If Wauwinet is his heir apparent, Askammapoo and her husband Spotso have also been granted a significant portion of the sachem's property. And as it would turn out, Askammapoo–not her older brother Wauwinet–would be the one whose children would carry on her father's legacy into the next century.

Nickanoose may have begun to lay the groundwork for this future even before the arrival of the English, but it would not always go as planned.

In the winter of 1665, a bark left Martha's Vineyard bound for Boston. On board the vessel was an Indian named Joel Hiacoomes, son of the island's leading Christian Indian. Joel was a young man of exceptional promise. Along with a handful of other Native Americans, he had spent several years studying at Harvard College and had mastered

Latin and Greek to the point that he was on the verge of gaining his bachelor's degree. But Joel would never make it back to Cambridge.

It was probably the Nantucket Bar that got them. Heavily loaded with goods, the bark may have grounded on the shoal in a rapidly building winter gale from the north, then washed up onto Coatue. Instead of providing aid, the first Indians to arrive on the scene started killing the passengers who were still alive so that they could claim the wreck as their own. Whether or not Joel had the opportunity to admonish them in the name of his Christian god, the Nantucket Indians killed everyone aboard before they got down to the business of stripping the bark of goods.

What ultimately made these murders such an outrage was not the death of Joel but that Indians had killed white people. The murders also bore a disturbing resemblance to the incident that had helped spark the Pequot War almost thirty years before when John Oldham (who had traded for corn on Nantucket in 1634) was found dead just off Block Island in his own vessel with several Indians on board.

News of the Nantucket murders spread up and down the coast. In Plymouth an order was issued that "Mr. Hinckley" on Cape Cod "take care that those people about the southern parts or South Sea [Nantucket Sound], where [the murderers] were lately known to be," report what information they might have, and that "if the Nantucket Indians suspected for murder be…found within this government, that search may be made by the magistrates…."

On Nantucket, it was Nickanoose who was in the hotseat, since it had been Indians from his territory who had committed the crime. Only a trip to Wampanoag headquarters in Mount Hope, where Massasoit's son Metacom (better known to history as King Philip) had taken over as supreme sachem, could set things right.

For some reason, Nickanoose felt he needed an intermediary in his dealings with King Philip. According to a deed recorded by William Worth, "being accused of being privy to a murder committed by the

Indians on English men at Coatue and being in great fear he hired or otherwise got Quaquachwinnit to go with him to Plymouth in the winter to ask council of Nickanoose's head sachem." Nickanoose's "great fear" was such that he went so far as to give Quaquachwinnit a sizable chunk of land (hence the deed reference) in exchange for accompanying him to the mainland.

Did Nickanoose, a sachem from one of the Wampanoag's more distant territories, simply feel he needed someone else to back him up? Perhaps his role in the English settlement of the island had so soured his relations with Attapeat and the Tomokommoths (commonly known on the island as "Philip's men") that Nickanoose dreaded having to appear before their chief sachem. Then why Quaquachwinnit? Perhaps his oratorical skills made him the Native American equivalent of a high-priced defense attorney. We will, of course, never know. Thanks to the seventeenth-century deed recorded by William Worth, we do know, however, that some time after Nickanoose's and Quaquachwinnit's visit to Philip, "Indians were hanged on Nantucket."

Whether or not it was to attend these executions, we also know that Philip traveled to Nantucket in October of 1665–an event that would have been, in its own way, as momentous as the murders. But instead of heightening tensions (at least during this visit), Philip seems to have helped to strengthen Indian-English relations on Nantucket. During a meeting of the town, Attapeat and his people declared themselves "subject to the English government in Nantucket.... This was done in the presence of [King Philip]." Although it has been generally accepted by historians that the Tomokommoths were, in effect, spurning their supreme sachem, this was probably not the case. Philip himself had already made a similar proclamation in Plymouth only a few years before. If anything, by formally witnessing the Tomokommoths' loyalty oath (which also included "King Charles the Second"), Philip was lending his support to the oath. (Remember, this was a decade before the outbreak of King Philip's War.)

Once again, Nickanoose had demonstrated an extraordinary talent for diplomacy. By doing everything in his power to ensure that the Indian murderers were brought to justice, he had turned what might have been a catastrophe into an opportunity for bolstering Nantucket's fragile Indian-English alliance. Whatever it was that occurred during his meeting with Philip at Mount Hope, the supreme sachem came to Nantucket seemingly predisposed to act as a concil-iator, and may have even helped to smooth some of the rough edges created by the sale of the western end of the island to the English.

It had taken a marriage, some murders, some hangings, and now a loyalty oath, but by the end of that October meeting in 1665, east had finally begun to meet west when it came to Nantucket's long-stand-ing Indian divide. Whether or not Nickanoose could be properly termed the architect of this brave new world on Nantucket, he had been largely responsible for the arrival of the English, and it had been their presence that had made possible the gradual groping toward coexistence. But if it had all started with a real estate deal, it was a deal that included some hidden and very long-term costs for the island's Native Americans—costs that both the eastern and western Indians had only begun to pay.

7

THE SHARK POOL

"Queequeg no care what god made him shark," said the savage, agonizingly lifting his hand up and down; "weder Fejee god or Nantucket god; but de god wat made shark must be one dam Ingin."

—Herman Melville, Moby-Dick

According to several estimates, there were approximately 3,000 Indians on Nantucket when the English arrived in 1659. For an island of only fifty square miles, it is an astonishing number. This would have meant that Nantucket had a population density that was, according to one historian, the equivalent of western Europe's and more than *ten times* what it had been anywhere else in New England *before* the plagues of 1616-19.

Although some have argued that the island's pre-1659 population was closer to 1,500 (still a tremendous number), it would have probably been difficult to affix a specific figure to Nantucket's Indian population as Tomokommoth driftwhalers moved back and forth from the Vineyard and the flow of refugees from the mainland ebbed and surged. Whatever the case may be, there is little doubt that there were more Native Americans per square mile on Nantucket than anywhere else in New England.

Even without the arrival of the English and their diseases, a native population of this magnitude probably would have been only a temporary phenomenon. The Indians may have begun to experience some serious shortages of food and firewood even before the English arrived—a factor that may have contributed to Nickanoose's and Wanackmamack's decision to accommodate the more technological-

115

ly advanced English. As it was, it would take almost a century for the island's English population to reach the Indians' pre-English settlement level of 3,000.

We have almost no information on the diseases that ravaged the island's Native Americans during the next forty years. Crèvecoeur claimed that "when the Europeans came, [the Indians] caught the smallpox, and their improper treatment of that disorder swept away great numbers." Although it is difficult to conceive of what would have constituted "proper" treatment given that this amounted to a virgin soil epidemic and no effective medical measures existed, Crèvecoeur may be referring to the various rituals used by the powwows.

Whatever its cause, the tidal wave of death that would sweep across the island had already become a kind of foregone conclusion elsewhere in New England. But Nantucket was demographically prepared for the onslaught. Its Indian population swollen to extraordinary numbers, Nantucket remained one of the region's largest Native American communities even after it sustained a seventy-five-percent population drop in a period of only forty years. This meant that despite disease and death, Nantucket continued to be a profoundly native place well into the eighteenth century.

Whereas Nickanoose's diplomatic maneuverings resulted in a paper trail that leads from Nantucket to Boston and back again, his Tomokommoth counterpart, Attapeat, is virtually absent from the documented record. When it came to the daily realities of life on Nantucket in the 1660s, however, Attapeat and his people were very much in the thick of it. Far from being pawns in a game of diplomatic chess between the English and Nickanoose, Attapeat and company (who had a history of using their bows) demanded the respect and attention of the English. Not only did they have close ties to

Wampanoag headquarters in Mount Hope, they were also Nantucket's chief driftwhalers—a fishery in which English Nantucketers could not help but take a financial interest. (In 1668 a committee was delegated to "make a bargain...concerning all whales that shall come on shore on the island on the town's behalf.") Then, of course, there was the unavoidable fact of the western Indians' geographic proximity to the English.

Instead of a neat and tidy division between white and native worlds, the embryonic English settlement found itself contained within a portion of the island that was still very much the western Indians' domain. And these Indians were in no hurry to leave. In 1662 the English issued the order that any Indians who stayed "on the land and made use of the same after the 14 day of October 1662 shall pay to the English 5s per week." But by 1665, the Indians were still there. Growing increasingly resigned to their presence, the English proposed that the Indians help them dig a trench (still in existence) connecting Long Pond to Hither Creek "for taking fish and also for making of meadow." The Indians would get half the fish "so long as they attend the weir carefully."

Four years later, in 1669, there were enough Indians still living at the west end of the island to warrant a town order "forbidding any Indian...dwelling on Madaket from hunting or driving the cattle from that land." To the east, but well within the English bounds, was a swampy area in the vicinity of No-Bottom Pond. Here, on a rise of land that would be named for him, lived the Indian Jacob Washamon, husband to Wannataquanmow, "squaw sachem of half Nope." Not until 1676 would Washamon, who was a weaver, sell his English-style house and move out to Nickanoose's lands at Squam. Almost a century later, in 1763, eight Indians were still living at the west end of the island.

Whether they liked it or not, the English were going to have to share their portion of the island with the Tomokommoths—an extremely Indian concept of landownership that would persist on Nantucket for quite some time. The English might pass laws that threatened expulsion, but they knew enough not to push it too hard. Vastly outnumbered on an island where there were several different native factions that might, in Thomas Macy's words to the New York governor, "take offense," the English had to be very, very careful.

The inherent delicacy of Indian-English relations on Nantucket– not to mention the tormented complexity of the east-west relation- ship–would become agonizingly, even terrifyingly clear to all when, in a surprise appearance, Metacom returned to the island. Instead of witnessing a Tomokommoth loyalty oath, the Wampanoag sachem had an entirely different agenda. This time he came to Nantucket not to pacify but to kill.

Names were extremely important to the Indians. When a person experienced a significant change, it was common to take on a new name. In 1660, soon after the death of his father, Metacom's older brother Wamsutta formally requested that the Plymouth authorities "change his name…according to the custom of the natives." The English granted the Wampanoag sachem his wish, and Wamsutta and Metacom became Alexander and Philip, respectively.

As we have already seen in transcriptions of deeds on Nantucket, it was taboo to speak the name of the dead, especially if he had been, according to Obed Macy, "a distinguished person." At some point after the hangings on Nantucket, a local Indian from Wanackmamack's bounds made the mistake of speaking the name of Philip's dead father. For the Wampanoag this was as serious a crime as the killings on Coatue, and it wasn't long before Philip and a party of war canoes had set out for the island on a mission to bring the Nantucket Indian to justice.

The local Indian's name was Assassamough. His English name of John Gibbs also happened to be that of Peter Folger's maternal grandfather, suggesting that Gibbs had a particularly close relationship with the island's Indian interpreter. To this day, a kettlehole bordering the cranberry bogs is called Gibbs Pond; before it became a bog, this marshy section of the island was known as Gibbs Swamp.

According to one account, the sachem and his men arrived at the west end of the island, probably at Nopque, today's Smith Point. Since Gibbs lived at the east end of the island, Philip intended to "travel along shore under the bank...so as not to be discovered." Given that the south shore of the island is typified by a wide beach and a relatively steep bank, this would have provided Philip with excellent cover for a quick, across-the-island strike.

But on an island as densely populated as Nantucket, it was extremely difficult to maintain secrecy. Before Philip and his men could find him, word had reached Gibbs that he was a wanted man, and in no time Gibbs had disappeared into the swamps. Whether or not he was assisted in any way by the island's Indians, Philip eventually found Gibbs and began to make preparations to put the transgressor to death.

On a high hill overlooking Gibbs Pond is an unusual rock that, according to tradition, was used by the Indians as a site for putting to death not only people but, in later years, sheep. Now known as Altar Rock, this highly visible spot provides the locus for a breathtakingly beautiful, panoramic view of the eastern end of the island and would have been a natural place for Philip to conduct the execution, especially given its proximity to Gibbs Swamp.

At some point, however, the English appeared on the scene and offered to ransom Gibbs's life. Although Zaccheus Macy claims that Philip agreed to the proposal and that "it took all the money they could muster to satisfy the said King," his kinsman Obed Macy offers a slightly more interesting account of the "parley."

In order to collect the money, the English had to return to their settlement at the west end of the island. Philip and his warriors seem to have accompanied them and, once in English territory, "taken possession of one or two houses, to the great terror of the inmates." Like it or not, the island's white population found itself in the middle of what had started out as a purely internal Indian matter.

After passing the hat, the English came up with the sum of £11– well below the figure Philip had originally named. When presented with the money, the Wampanoag sachem became indignant and with "threatening language, pronounced with an emphasis which foreboded no good," demanded that he receive the full amount.

Given the extent to which Philip was willing to push an extremely dangerous situation, one can only wonder if there was something personal about his expedition to Nantucket. Gibbs was what the English called a Praying Indian and would eventually become the island's first minister with a congregation to the east of Gibbs Swamp at Occawa. Philip, on the other hand, resolutely refused to convert to Christianity, just as had Massasoit before him. At one point Philip even pointed to a button on the coat of the missionary John Eliot and claimed that he had about as much respect for the white man's god as he had for Eliot's button. And yet, despite his scorn for Christianity, the Mount Hope sachem seems to have had, at one time, a close relationship with an Indian much like Gibbs–John Sassamon, a converted Indian who served as Philip's interpreter. Philip's relationship with Sassamon would eventually sour, however; it would be Sassamon's alleged murder by Philip's henchmen in January 1675 that would help instigate what became known as King Philip's War. Thus, ten years before the death of Sassamon, Philip had a run-in with a Praying Indian on Nantucket.

The pressures on Attapeat, the Nantucket sachem with the closest ties to Philip, must have been particularly intense during this confrontation. There is no evidence, however, that he and the

Tomokommoths played any role whatsoever in the incident. Indeed, Attapeat, a grizzled war veteran who had won his lands back in the days when Nantucket was a bloody battlefield, may have viewed Philip, who was not yet thirty years old, as something of a light-weight—especially compared to his legendary predecessor Massasoit.

Philip, Obed tells us, finally pushed the English to the point that they refused to back down: "they told him, that if he did not immediately leave the island, they would rally the inhabitants, and fall upon him and cut him off to a man." Although Obed claims that Philip was unaware of the "defenseless condition" of the English, it may have been a little more complicated than that. Philip may have come to realize that he was not only angering the English; he was also straining his relations with the Tomokommoths. So, with the £11 in hand, Philip "happily took the alarm, and left the island as soon as possible." Gibbs was a free man.

As far as we know, King Philip never returned to the island. In August 1675, as war raged on the mainland, the western Tomokommoths appeared in court to "disown Philip," reaffirming their allegiance to the English king and voluntarily turning over "some arms [three guns and a bow]...as a testimony of their fidelity to the English." With this oath, Nantucket's Native Americans officially cut a tie with Mount Hope that had begun to unravel almost a decade earlier.

By this point, the legends of Maushop may have evolved to reflect the native Nantucketers' uneasy relationship with their supreme sachem. From the giant's tormented and unpredictable actions relative to his wife and children to the virtual tantrum that causes him to hurl his moccasins into the sea, these were stories to which the Indians of Nantucket, forced once again to reinvent their relationship to the world beyond their island, could relate. Whether they constituted what one scholar has called "folklore as sedition," the legends of Maushop may have provided a metaphoric framework with which to understand not only the Wampanoag sachem's belligerent appearance on Nantucket but the desperate and disturbing series of events that would one day be known as King Philip's War.

There is a paradox at the heart of Indian-English interaction on Nantucket in the seventeenth century. While many, if not most, white settlers came to the island to escape the intrusive influence of Puritanism, Nantucket's Indians were already on their way to becoming god-fearing Congregationalists even before the settlers' arrival. In September 1664, at the urging of John Eliot, Thomas Mayhew sent the Vineyard sachem Wampamog (also known as Samuel) to Nantucket for the purposes of spreading the word of God. Whether or not he was, as Eliot maintained, "called by the Nantucket Indians to teach them," Wampamog met with great success on his adopted island. By 1671, Mayhew was directing a quarter of the funds provided to him by the London-based missionary society to Nantucket, not only to help support the efforts of Wampamog (who would remain on the island until his death in 1689) but also to John Gibbs (the Indian who had been nearly killed by King Philip) and several unnamed "sachems from Nantucket."

As on Martha's Vineyard, the political hierarchy of the Nantucket Indians, the sachems, took an active role in the promulgation of Christianity. Also as on the Vineyard, this undoubtedly created a rift between the sachems and the powwows, which may help to explain Mudturtle's image as a difficult and ultimately destructive shaman. By the end of the century, John Gardner would write, "I may now say there is not known a powwow among them;...yet amongst the now praying Indians, there is an increase. God raising up even of themselves preachers...."

In 1674, it was reported that John Gibbs presided over Nantucket's first church, not far from the swamp where he had once hid from Philip. There were about twenty men and ten women in "full communion in the church," and about forty children who had been baptized. In addition to Gibbs's congregation in Occawa, there were groups of Indians gathering for services in two other locations: Squatesit, to the northwest of Altar Rock (the future site of what became known as "Spotso's Meetinghouse"), and Wammasquid, believed to be in Nickanoose's territory between the ponds of Sesachacha and Squam. Besides Gibbs, there were three other Indians–Wampamog, Joseph, and Caleb–engaged not only in spreading the gospel but in teaching school.

Altogether, there were approximately "three hundred Indians, young and old, who pray to God and keep the Sabbath upon that island." By 1678 Mayhew was able to report to the missionary society that "for Nantucket, things are in a very comfortable way. I sent four understanding Indians thither purposely, whose going was very useful in several respects too long to recite."

As Mayhew made clear in his 1678 report, it was he, not the English settlers of Nantucket, who supervised the growth of Christianity on Nantucket. In fact, those white Nantucketers who were Baptists (which included Thomas Macy and the interpreter, Peter Folger) seem to have not entirely approved of the Congregational practices of Nantucket's Indians. In 1674 the Vineyard minister John Cotton claimed that "the English upon that island, who are about twenty-seven families, and many of them Anabaptists, did at first seek to hinder [the Indians] from administering baptism to infants; but now they are quiet, and meddle not with them."

Without the supervision of an on-island English minister, Nantucket's Indians were free to worship in their own way. The result was an Indian church service that was essentially Congregational but which included rituals that dated back to before contact. According to Zaccheus Macy (who reported that an Indian minister was called a "coutaumuchary"): "And when the meeting was done, they would take their tinder-box and strike fire and light their pipes, and, may be, would draw three or four whiffs and swallow the smoke, and then blow it out of their noses, and so hand their pipes to their next neighbor. And one pipe of tobacco would serve ten or a dozen of them. And they would say 'tawpoot,' which is, 'I thank ye.' It seemed to be done in a way of kindness to each other." Just as Maushop had marked his discovery of Nantucket with a smoke, so, too, did the island's Praying Indians integrate the ritual into their adaptation of a Congregational service.

The intimate and long-standing connection between Nantucket's Indian churches and the Mayhew mission on the Vineyard, combined with the English Nantucketers' unwillingness to establish their own Congregational church, created a strange and fascinating dynamic on the island. While hundreds of Nantucket Indians went to church every Sunday–many of them clutching their own copies of Eliot's translation of the Bible into Massachusett, *Mamusse Wanneetupanatamwe Up-Biblum God*–white Nantucketers were under no commitment to attend a place of worship. From a Puritan perspective, Nantucket's English settlers were the savages, while the Indians, despite their naturally savage state, were the civilized ones. As late as 1720, the Congregational minister Samuel Danforth would describe Nantucket as a frontier "bordering upon or near to the place where Satan hath his throne." In Danforth's view it was not Nantucket's large Indian population that made the island a godless frontier but the lax religious practices of the white community.

Instead of listening to sermons, a significant number of English Nantucketers seem to have used the Sabbath to go on what might be described as the white man's walkabout: a casual jaunt around the island without any specific destination in mind that came to be known as a "rantum scoot." By 1680 there were apparently so many people wandering around the island on a typical Sunday that the

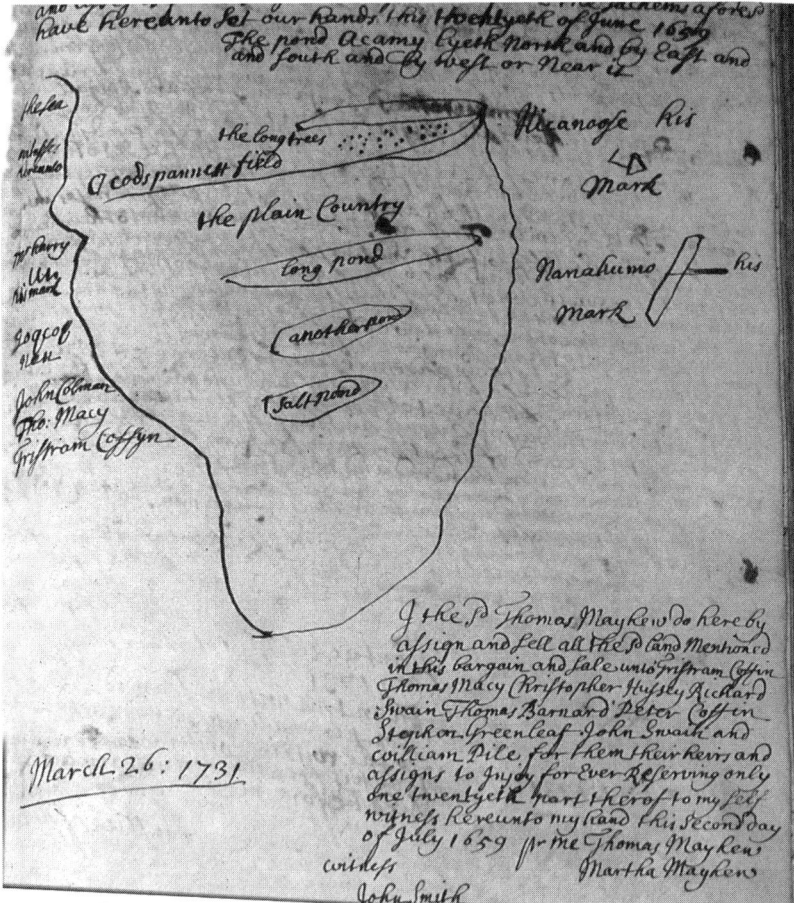

Fig. 33

This eighteenth-century copy of Mayhew's 1659 Indian deed contains a crude map of the lands purchased by the English at the west end of Nantucket (north is to the left). At the top (east) of the map is the hook-shaped pond referred to as Acamy in the deed but today known as Hummock Pond (and divided into two ponds by erosion). The dots surrounded by the pond are referred to as "the long trees," while the land to the left is "Codspannett Field." Below the pond is "the plain Country," indicating that this area of the island was relatively treeless. Beneath this title are "long pond," "another pond," and "salt pond." To the right of the map, the document contains the marks of Nickanoose and Nanahuma. To the left are the names of the witnesses, including John Coleman, Thomas Macy, Tristram Coffin, and several Indians. In the text in the lower right, Mayhew signs over the deed to Nantucket's First Purchasers. *Photo by James McIntosh. Registry of Deeds, Town of Nantucket, Massachusetts.*

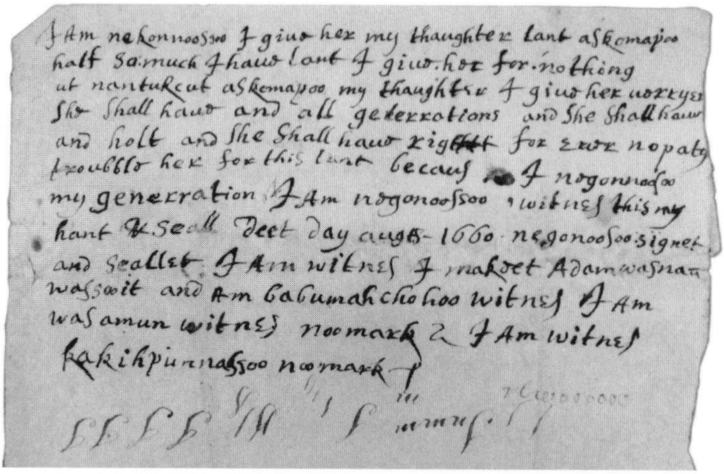
I Am nekonnoossoo I giue her my thaughter lant askomapoo
half sa much I haue lant I giue her for nothing
at nantukcut askomapoo my thaughter I giue her worryes
she shall haue and all geterrations and she shall haue
and holt and she shall haue right for ever no paty
troubblo her for this lant becaus I nogonnoossoo
my generration I Am nogonoossoo witnes this my
hant & seall deet day augst-1660 negonoossoo signet
and seallet I Am witnes I maket Adamwasnan
wassoit and Am Cabumahchohoo witnes I Am
wasamun witnes noomark I Am witnes
kakihpunnassoo noomark

Fig. 34
The deed, apparently drafted by an Indian named Adam, with which the eastern sachem Nickanoose (alternately spelled "Nekonoossoo" and "Nogonoossoo" in the deed) gave his daughter, Askammapoo, half his lands in August 1660 "for nothing." *Photo by Terry Pommett. Courtesy of the Nantucket Historical Association.*

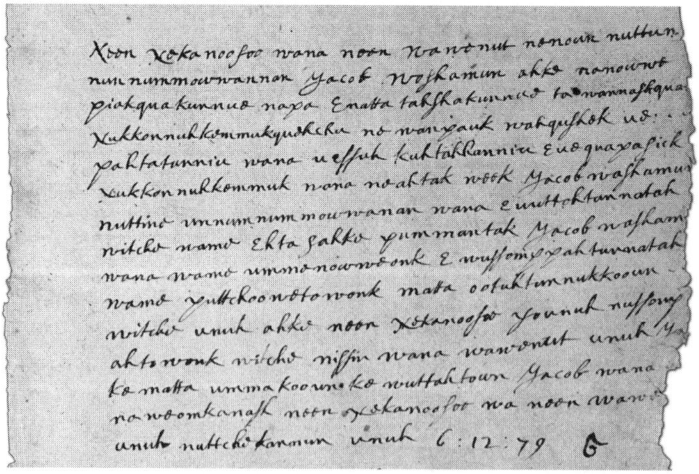

Fig. 35
A copy of a 1679 deed written in the Massachusett language involving the Nantucket Indian weaver Jacob Washamon. The phonetic version of the language had been created by the missionary John Eliot in 1663 when he translated the entire Bible into Massachusett. *Photo by James McIntosh. Registry of Deeds, Town of Nantucket, Massachusetts.*

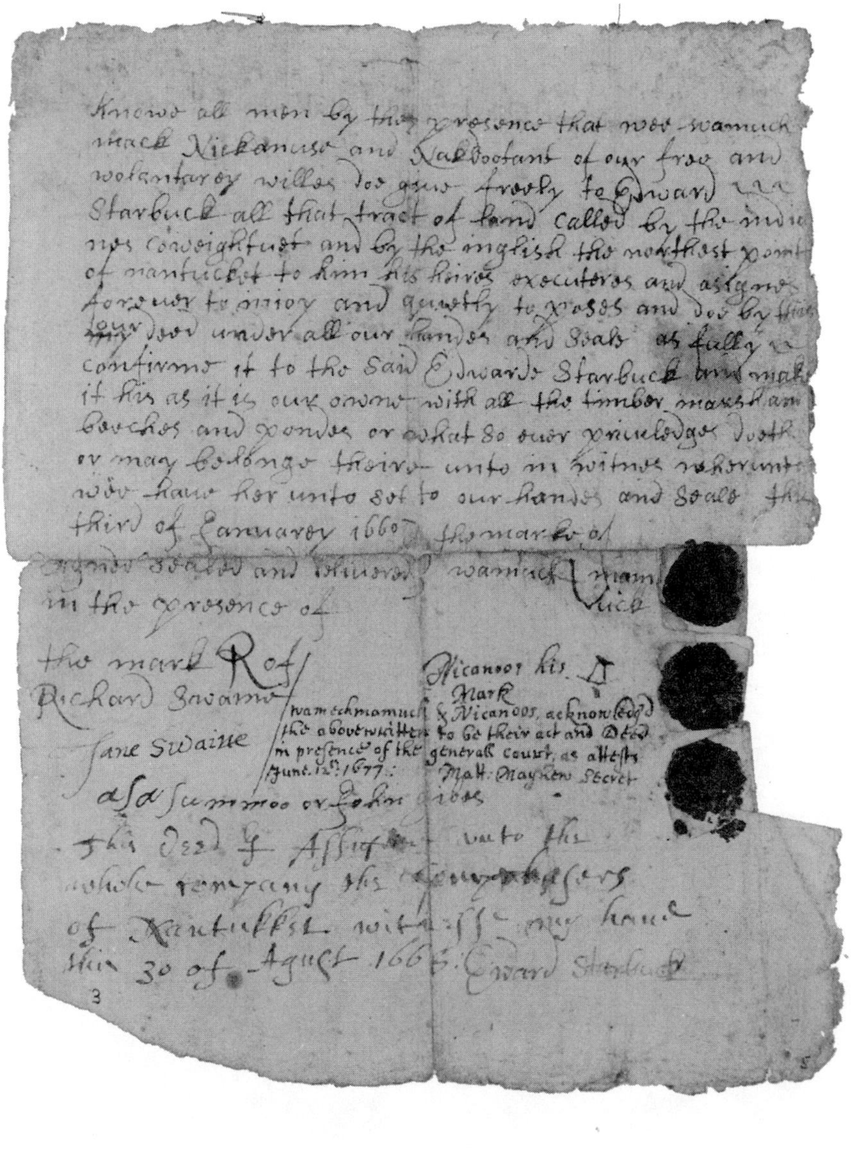

Fig. 36
The deed with which Wanackmamack and Nickanoose gave Coatue (referred to as
"Cohuoightuet") to Edward Starbuck. Note that one of the witnesses is "Asasummoo or
John Gibbs," the Indian who would become Nantucket's first native minister. *Courtesy of
the Nantucket Historical Association.*

Fig. 37
In 1665 it was proposed that a group of Indians and English dig a trench from Long Pond to Madaket Harbor "for taking fish and also for making of meadow." Today, what is known as the Madaket Ditch still exists. This photograph was taken from Madaket Road looking toward Hither Creek. *Photo by Nathaniel Philbrick.*

PHILIP. *KING* of Mount Hope.

Fig. 38

It may be a caricature, but this 1772 engraving of King Philip by Paul Revere is nonetheless based on a firsthand description of the "royalties" worn by the Wampanoag sachem around the time of his death in 1676: two powder horns, a red cloth blanket, and a nine-inch-wide, black-and-white wampum belt depicting "flowers and pictures of many birds and beasts," along with a smaller belt worn "upon his head" with "two flags on the back part" that hung down across his back, and a third "small belt with a star upon the end of it" hung across his chest–all visible in Revere's engraving. Although Philip, or Metacom, visited the island well before the outbreak of King Philip's War, it is possible that he wore at least some of these pieces during his appearance at a town meeting on Nantucket in October of 1665. *M. & M. Karolik Fund, Courtesy of the Museum of Fine Arts, Boston.*

Fig. 39
In the 1660s King Philip traveled to Nantucket to punish the Indian John Gibbs for speaking the name of Philip's dead father–taboo in Wampanoag culture. In this 1992 painting by Rodney Charman, the sachem stands with his prisoner at Altar Rock as the English offer to ransom the Nantucket Indian's life. *Photo by Margaret S. Moore. Collection of the Egan Foundation.*

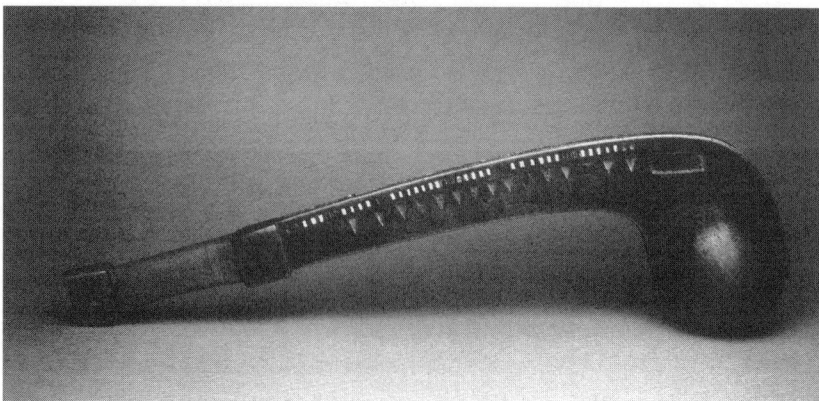

Fig. 40
Purported to be King Philip's war club, made of solid maple. It is possible that this weapon accompanied the Wampanoag sachem on his punitive raid to Nantucket. *Collection of the Fruitlands Museum, Harvard, Massachusetts.*

Fig. 41

The Eastern Niantic sachem Ninigret II, shown here in 1681, was approximately the same age as sachem Nickanoose's son Wauwinet and Wanackmamack's son Jephtha. This painting by Charles Osgood (a copy after the original) is one of the few reliable existing representations of a native New Englander from the seventeenth century. *Courtesy of the Massachusetts Historical Society.*

MANNER OF INSTRUCTING THE INDIANS.

Fig. 42

Although from a different era and place, this engraving from William Apess's *Indian Nullification of the Unconstitutional Laws of Massachusetts Relative to the Mashpee Tribe* (1835) speaks to an issue that influenced English-Indian relations on Nantucket from the very beginning: the use of alcohol. As the native population plummeted and the labor needs of the English escalated, liquor increasingly became the means by which white Nantucketers drew the island's Indians into debt and a life of servitude. *Courtesy of the American Antiquarian Society.*

Fig. 43

The Old Indian Meeting House in Mashpee before being restored in the 1960s. There were at least four timber-frame Indian churches on Nantucket that were probably similar in appearance to this structure. Nantucket's oldest surviving meeting-house, the Old North Vestry, was built well after the first Indian timber-frame church was constructed at the end of the seventeenth century. *Courtesy of the Mashpee Historical Commission.*

town felt it necessary to pass the following law: "For the prevention of such misdemeanors which some take occasion to practice on the Lord's Day by reason of absence of most people from their habitations and such temptations as vagrant persons are exposed to, thereby the court orders that no person present in Lord's Day to be absent from their houses or usual places of abode."

Rather than attend church, white Nantucketers were *required by law* to stay at home on a Sunday, a more civilized alternative, it seems, than walking around like a "vagrant" person–exactly the kind of conduct that was usually, and disparagingly, attributed to the peripatetic lifestyle of traditional Indians. Thus, on this island in the middle of nowhere, Indians had the opportunity to turn to Christianity on their own terms while the English could not help but be influenced by a native population that had them literally surrounded.

One of the reasons Christianity was so tremendously successful among the Nantucket Indians may have been that they were increasingly hard pressed to support themselves on this overcrowded island. In 1675, the Puritan minister Daniel Gookin said as much: "The truth is, the Indians, both upon the Vineyard and Nantucket are poor; and, according as the scriptures saith, do more readily receive the gospel and become religious." The introduction of the plow and the gun may have resulted in a momentary increase in productivity, but the long-term consequences of these "innovations" on the ecology of the island would be disastrous. Pigs rooted up the Indians' clam beds and sheep ate up what remaining browse was left for the deer (if, in fact, there were any deer left) while the livestock's hooves devegetated and churned up the sandy ground, dramatically increasing the exhaustion of the soil.

Instead of fishing and hunting at home, a significant number of Nantucket Indians were, by the 1670s, regularly traveling to the mainland to work among the English. According to Gookin, "usually every summer [the island's Indians] come up to our parts about

Boston and the towns adjacent, to work in harvest labor and other employ." Meanwhile, back on Nantucket, the Indians were, by necessity, increasingly doing things the English way. In addition to providing the English with cod and feathers, the Indians had, according to Gookin, begun to "sow English as well as Indian corn, spin and knit stockings, and are more industrious than many other Indians." Well before the advent of whaling, Nantucket Indians had begun to come within the economic orbit of the English.

But if Christianity had made the Nantucket Indians commendably "diligent and industrious," there were other forces out there that had the opposite effect, forces that worked from both within and without the island microcosm. Nantucket's isolation made it an easy place for off-islanders to provide Indians with alcohol. A petition filed at the end of the seventeenth century complains of "much drunkenness among the Indians, which often occasions disturbance not only to the sober Indians who complain thereof but likewise to the English and may prove an occasion of discord by outrages committed by the Indians." The petition, which sought measures to forbid the sale of alcohol to the island Indians, claimed that there were two sources of "cider and other strong drink": "other Indians from Rhode Island and the mainland," who apparently used nearby Tuckernuck Island as a kind of raucous base camp, and English "vessels coming into the harbor or going near the shores of said islands."

Not mentioned in the petition was a third source of alcohol: the English settlers themselves. Colonial New Englanders, by and large, liked to drink. (According to a modern estimate, the average colonist in 1770 was drinking the equivalent of seven shots a day!) Tristram and Dionis Coffin, the island's most prominent first settlers, had been tavern keepers prior to moving to Nantucket.

There is evidence that during public gatherings on the island–from weddings to houseraisings–English and Indians drank side-by-side. By 1695, Stephen Hussey had moved to the Shimmo portion of the island where he held a celebration for the wedding of his daughter. In addition to "a great number of friends," there was, according to Obed Macy, "a large concourse of Indians gathered to the festivities." At one point, Stephen's wife Martha was informed that her plum porridge had been ruined when "an Indian who was standing over the porridgepot accidentally let his bottle of rum fall against the side of the pot," sprinkling shards of glass and, of course, rum into the mixture. On an island where the boundaries between the Indians and English were not always well defined, and where rum was an accepted part of most public occasions, Indians clearly had more than a few potential sources of alcohol.

The use of alcohol on Nantucket was not limited to social gatherings. It very quickly became a part of the workplace, as English Nantucketers used it to ensure a ready and willing labor supply. In 1675 Thomas Macy reported that Captain John Gardner offered his Indian workers a dram of rum each morning before they went out codfishing. If a local tradition is to be believed, John Gardner's daughter Mary experienced firsthand the potential dangers associated with providing the Indians with alcohol. Around the year 1693, Mary, her husband Jethro Coffin, and their two young children were living in a newly constructed home on Sunset Hill now known as Nantucket's "Oldest House." Early one morning, soon after Jethro left to go whaling, Mary was reawakened by sounds in the attic. Suddenly an Indian, falling through a hole in the unfinished attic floor, landed in a room adjoining Mary's bedroom. Whetting his knife and threatening to kill her, the Indian approached the terrified young mother who quite sensibly jumped up from the bed and ran to a neighbor's house for help. The Indian was eventually apprehended, his basket and a bottle of rum still outside the front door.

Although English Nantucketers regularly complained of the drinking habits of the Indians (Macy claimed that it made them act "like wild bears and wolves in the wilderness"), the fact of the matter was that the English undoubtedly consumed much more alcohol, on average, than the Indians. It was *the way* the two peoples drank that differed.

For the Indians, alcohol provided a quick and easy pathway to the kind of altered state of consciousness previously achieved either through ceremonies involving extreme physical hardship or the use of hallucinogens, such as pokeweed. They may not have liked the taste of what an Indian in the St. Lawrence Valley called "the water that takes away one's wits," but they enjoyed what it did for them. This meant that even though alcohol had a devastating cumulative effect on the Indians, many of them chose to drink, according to the historian Peter Mancall, "voluntarily and for positive results." Some Indians may have used it ritualistically to achieve a sense of "heightened powers." For others it undoubtedly provided a temporary means of escaping the despair and frustrations of a world in which the loss of friends and family to disease was becoming an almost daily occurrence.

There is also evidence that drinking binges provided the context in which Indians articulated their mounting unhappiness with the direction life on Nantucket had begun to take a decade or so after the arrival of the English. Just as the British blamed the taverns in and around Boston for the rise of political unrest in the years prior to the outbreak of the Revolution, so did English Nantucketers claim that the Indians caused trouble only when "they were in some degree intoxicated."

Whether or not they were aggravated by rum, by 1675 some serious cracks had begun to appear in the Indian-English alliance. Nickanoose, for one, was not happy. And unlike King Philip on the mainland, he had the demographics to make the English listen.

Not even the English could believe how quickly they had begun to use up the island's resources. Even though they had access to all the grass at the west end of the island and the use of the grass throughout the island during the seasons when the Indians were not growing corn, it took only five or so years before they realized that their sheep and cows were on the verge of transforming Nantucket into a windblown wasteland. In addition, the English were also harvesting marsh grass, or Spartina, for hay. As long as it was green and edible, English livestock were going to eat it.

Part of the problem was the growing popularity of horses, which consume tremendous amounts of grass. By 1667, the Vineyarders were told to remove their horses from Nantucket and the Proprietors restricted themselves to one horse per family. But that was just the beginning. By 1669, a complex set of rules (known as "stinting rights") was established to keep horses and other livestock from gobbling up all the grass. By then the English settlement included twenty "full-share" men (the original owners) and fourteen "half-share" men (people like Peter Folger and John Gardner who had been brought in to practice a specific trade) for a total of twenty-seven shares. A whole share permitted grazing of forty cattle and forty sheep, with a horse equaling two cows.

All that would have worked just fine if the Indians had kept to their traditional practices. But it soon became clear that, like many young people, Nickanoose's and Wanackmamack's sons Wauwinet and Jephtha, were not content with the old ways. They wanted horses of their own. And as indulgent parents throughout the ages have tended to do, Nickanoose and Wanackmamack each purchased for their sons what seems to have been the seventeenth-century equivalent of a Jeep Wrangler—a horse.

The problem was that even though the two eastern sachems still owned their ancestral lands, they had sold the rights to the grass from fall to spring. This meant that when the Indians grazed their horses on their own lands, the English felt legally justified in confiscating the animals, which from the Indians' point of view was shockingly unfair. (Thirty years later the governor of Massachusetts would also see it their way, labeling the grass clause in the original Nantucket deed a "circumvention and fraud.") Although Wanackmamack seems to have taken the development in stride, Nickanoose was not about to let the English get away with it.

And it wasn't just the question of horses. There was also the matter of dogs. For centuries, native dogs had held an important, even sacred place in Indian culture. Relatively small and sharp-muzzled, the dogs provided assistance in hunting and, in times of hardship, even acted as a source of food. But native dogs and sheep did not mix. The dogs that had once helped to pursue the island's deer took to running down, and occasionally killing, English sheep. As early as 1663, the English began passing laws requiring that the Indians destroy all their dogs. Committees were even formed (composed of both English and Indians) to implement the law. In 1670 the town was visited by a particularly troublesome dog that, given the Indians' association of the color white with bad luck, may have been viewed as the canine incarnation of Nickanoose's wrath. The town record reads: "whosoever shall kill the wild dog—a white dog having been seen several times about the town, shall be paid thirty shillings."

Right about that time, in 1671, Nantucket officially came under the jurisdiction of New York, whose governor required proof of the Indian deeds. A copy of the appropriate deed was written out; Wanackmamack signed it but Nickanoose refused. Even though Nantucket's native population had declined to around 1,500, the English were still outnumbered by more than fifteen to one and had no choice but to compromise on the issue of grazing rights.

In 1672, the town granted Nickanoose's and Wanackmamack's sons the right to own horses. They also threw two or three more horses into the bargain as long as the eastern sachems agreed to keep no more horses.

But Nickanoose was just getting started. Now that he understood the full extent of the white man's acquisitive nature (which had taken even a man of his considerable ingenuity and experience by surprise), he proceeded to beat the English at their own game. He began to write more deeds.

In August 1675 he drew his line in the sand. He enlisted the Indian Tehas to draft a deed granting his (Nickanoose's) brother Judah the right to keep six cattle on his land as long as Judah continued to pay him "pennies all the year in victuals and cloths." In words that he hoped both the Indians and the English would understand, Nickanoose let it be known that it was his land and therefore up to him to determine how it would ultimately be used. If the English wanted to fine him and impound his animals, well then, he would, in words reported by John Gardner, "not forbear but must fight."

Just as Nickanoose mounted his campaign to win back control of his own lands, two events–one regional, the other local–helped to put into focus why it behooved the English to take the Indian seriously. The first was the outbreak of King Philip's War. As much of New England burned, and several off-island full-share men (such as Tristram Coffin's eldest son Peter) sought temporary refuge for their families on Nantucket, the English settlement was provided with vivid and terrifying proof of what Nickanoose and his people were capable of if they were compelled to fight.

Whether or not it was because of growing tensions on the mainland, Nickanoose's son Jethro, who had relocated to Cape Cod in reaction to his father's second marriage, temporarily returned to Nantucket in 1675. Jethro soon discovered that he was no longer a part of his father's plans and, in keeping with family tradition, took Nickanoose to court. Out-Nickanoosed by his own son, the old sachem, with perhaps grudging respect, acknowledged "in open court" that after his death Jethro should share "equally with Wauwinet."

Just as King Philip's War rocked the mainland, English Nantucketers found themselves embroiled in their own little conflict. Perhaps inspired by Nickanoose's game of subversion and recalcitrance, the half-share men mounted a campaign to win for themselves a stake in future divisions of land, even though this was not a part of their original agreement with the full-share men. Led by Tristram Coffin and Thomas Mayhew (who had maintained a stake in the island), the island's full-share establishment thus found itself besieged on two fronts as the Indians and the half-share men united forces in an all-out campaign to reinvent local government.

By aligning themselves with the half-share men, the Indians gained a voice that reached all the way to New York. John Gardner (in a letter delivered to the governor by a Nantucket Indian) wrote to express his belief that the deed Nickanoose refused to sign was a forgery foisted on them by the full-share men and "might be the occasion of involving us in blood" with the Indians. Gardner's alliance with the Indians seems to have been based on something more than a sense of justice. Even though alcohol proved difficult to come by after the outbreak of the war, Gardner was able to secure sixteen gallons of rum that were summarily "carried to the Indians," according to the disapproving Thomas Macy.

When half-share man (and Gardner's confidant) Peter Folger was thrown into jail for failing to hand over the town's court records, Folger took pen to paper to inform the governor of how his treatment had "set a fire to the whole island, for I, having lived thirty years upon this island and the Vineyard, was so well known and so well beloved of English and Indians (whether deserved or not) that the Indians inquired what the cause of my imprisonment." According to Folger, it greatly disturbed the Indians to see a man of Folger's age (sixty) treated in such a way, while relatively young men, such as the recently arrived Peter Coffin (thirty-eight), took over the reins of town government: "They cannot believe that young men, especially such men, can understand things like old men, and they are always in doubt whether they have justice or no."

By then the English were not the only ones with access to the courts. Modeling their system on what had already been created among the Indians of Long Island, Nantucketers had appointed constables among the Indians who were equipped with "staves with the King's arms upon them, the better to keep their people in awe and good order." But by 1677, anything but good order characterized both English and Indian courts. While a host of half-share men and women were either fined or disenfranchised for "contemptuous carriage," the minor western sachem Obadiah burst into the Indian court at one point and "using reviling speeches and speaking opprobrious words" attempted to rescue an Indian who had been sentenced to a whipping.

Instead of physical intimidation, it was a Nickanoose-drafted land-use deed that ultimately forced a compromise. In a deed allowing his brothers Keatthohquen and Wohwaninwat to use his lands, Nickanoose reasserted his complete and absolute control over everything on those lands, including "roots or trees or grass and all that is therein aye and the stones...and if the whale shall happen to come [a]shore that shall be theirs also. . . ." Seven days after filing this deed with the General Court in June 1677, Nickanoose finally agreed to attach his signature to the older, contested deed.

Having won that round, Nickanoose was ready to strike a compromise. After the English resolved their own internal dispute (by granting the half-share men a stake in future divisions of land as long as they turned over all privately purchased Indian deeds), a committee was appointed to lay to rest the issue of horses and grass.

The ultimate result was the creation of what became known as a horse common, which granted the right to pasture a horse. A total of eighty-seven horse commons were divided among four sachems: Nickanoose and his son-in-law Spotso, Wanackmamack's son

Jephtha, and, finally, Attapeat's son Musaquat, who in 1678 was for the first time officially granted status equivalent to the two eastern sachems. Just as the English half-share men had won themselves a piece of the action, so had the Indians negotiated their way to a settlement that enabled them a right to graze their animals on the Nantucket commons.

Nickanoose would die soon after the agreement was reached in 1682, having kept his own ancestral lands intact. His son Wauwinet would survive him by only a little more than a decade. By 1695 Spotso and Askammapoo's son Daniel Spotso had taken over the sachemship, heralding an era that would see the sale of almost all his grandfather's lands to the English. The horse commons compromise would prove a very short-term solution when yet another controversy over grass rights emerged at the turn of the century.

By that time, however, the island had developed a new economic focus. By 1690, it was no longer grass that most interested the English; it was whales. And just as the English had looked to Indian lands to sustain their livestock, so would they turn to their native neighbors—not for their resources, but for their labor.

8

THE WHALE

Tashtego's long, lean sable hair, his high cheek bones, and black rounding eyes–for an Indian Oriental in their largeness, but Antarctic in their glittering expression–all this sufficiently proclaimed him an inheritor of the unvitiated blood of those proud warrior hunters, who, in quest of the great New England moose, had scoured, bow in hand, the aboriginal forests of the main. But no longer snuffing in the trail of the wild beasts of the woodland, Tashtego now hunted in the wake of the great whales of the sea....

–Herman Melville, Moby-Dick

For years the Indians had told how a whale miraculously appeared in the Poot Ponds. By 1672 the English were telling a strikingly similar story, but instead of an inland kettlehole, the whale swam into the sea-connected pond called Cappamet Harbor. And unlike the Indians, who immediately went about trying to kill their whale, the English were not sure what to do with this huge spouting beast. Until that time, the only whales anyone on Nantucket had regularly dealt with were already dead.

Finally, after three days of watching the whale swim around the placid confines of the harbor, the English got up the courage to try to kill it. First, "measures" were taken to keep the whale from escaping (perhaps several boats were stationed at the entrance) even as an iron harpoon was, according to Obed Macy, "invented" and then forged.

Since a dugout canoe would remain the boat of choice on Nantucket almost to the end of the century, it is more than likely that the island's second known whale hunt was conducted in an Indian canoe. It is also likely that even if an Englishman was the one to hurl the newly wrought harpoon, it was a handful of Indian paddlers who brought the whale within the white man's reach. Thus may have begun a tradition of multicultural whale killing that would dominate the island for the next hundred years.

Killing a whale in a harbor (or a pond) is one thing. To do it in the open ocean in February is quite another. Not even the Indians–whose boat-handling skills had been astounding the English since their arrival–had dared kill whales on any kind of organized basis. If this island of English sheepherders and Indian driftwhalers was going to learn how to whale "alongshore," they were going to have to look elsewhere for instruction.

At the eastern tip of Long Island, Englishmen and Indians had been pursuing right whales from the beach for several decades, and in 1672 the Nantucketers attempted to lure one James Loper to the island. Although Loper initially accepted the town's offer to "carry on a design of whale catching on the Island of Nantucket," his love for a hometown girl ultimately persuaded him to remain on Long Island.

It was not until 1690, by which time the English had put both the Half-Share Revolt and their negotiations with Nickanoose behind them, that a professional whaleman from Cape Cod named Ichabod Paddack came to Nantucket. From the standpoint of the English, it was well timed. As the town records from the 1680s and '90s amply demonstrate, thirty years of plowing the sandy soil, grazing animals, and indiscriminately cutting down trees were beginning to disastrously affect the island's environment. (Account-book records reveal that by the early eighteenth century even the slender poles used to build the Indians' wigwams had to be imported to the island.) If Nantucket was ever going to be something more than a fishing and sheep-herding backwater, there was a desperate need to find a way to survive and flourish that did not depend on the island's rapidly diminishing resources.

Even though the island's ecosystem had been seriously compromised, the English had accrued certain advantages in waiting so long before turning to whaling. By 1690, the Indian population had begun to stabilize at around eight hundred–still a significant number, but on a different (and more "tractable") order from what it had been in the early days of the English settlement. Furthermore, the Indians were by now full-fledged participants in what was increasingly becoming an island-wide economy.

Since cash was hard to come by in colonial New England, a system involving barter and the extension of credit became an accepted means of doing business. Although some English and Indians kept their own account books (a small pocketbook attributed to the Indian weaver Netowa still exists), many, if not most Nantucketers of both races relied on less formal methods of keeping accounts. In 1834 Obed Macy left this description of how his colonial ancestors conducted business:

> The farmers, the fishermen and mechanics, exchanged their commodities with each other without keeping regular accounts. Their natural dependence and common wants led them to be obliging and accommodating. A piece of chalk and the inside of a door frequently supplied the place of pen and day-book; indeed, many of their business transactions were trusted wholly to memory. If the farmer happened to be out of certain articles, which he expected to reap from his land in proper season of gathering, he would borrow of his neighbor, who would lend without reluctance. These were debts of the highest responsibility, and were always carefully paid.

This flexible, yet highly conscientious method of exchange shared some undeniable similarities with what typified Indian village life on Nantucket in the seventeenth century. From the beginning, when the English complied with the Indians' requests to plow their fields, the

Indians treated their obligations in a manner very much in keeping with Macy's description. According to one account, "The Indians were religiously punctual in rewarding [the English] for their labor. The first portion of corn collected in the autumn was laid by in baskets, to pay the English for their plowing; another parcel was reserved for seed. Neither of these portions would they touch in winter, however severe the famine might be; so honest and careful were they at that period."

Thus, even though they approached each other from different directions, English and Indian Nantucketers had more in common than one might think. Borrowing and adapting each other's practices and technologies, even as they jettisoned some of their own traditional methods, the two groups established what the historian Richard White has called in another context a "middle ground."

Take, for example, the store run by Mary and Nathaniel Starbuck, whose "Account Book with the Indians" is in the collection of the Nantucket Historical Association. When an Indian entered the English economic world of debts and credits via the Starbucks, he did not necessarily lose touch with traditional practices. Just as he had once paid tribute to his sachem in the form of corn or fish, now he could have a portion of the goods he traded to Mary Starbuck credited toward the account of his sachem as a part of his traditional obligation. The result was that sachems such as Attapeat's son Musaquat and Wanackmamack's grandson Abel tended to be, in the words of Elizabeth Little, "consumers, not producers of wealth"—at least when it came to the kinds of European goods available through the Starbucks. Thus, what has been called the "Starbuck Company Store" also functioned as an English-owned collection agency working on behalf of Indian leaders.

Yet another, potentially darker, reality of such an economic middle ground was the use of servitude to pay off a debt, and in this Nantucket was no different from the rest of colonial New England. In

1672 the General Court on Martha's Vineyard passed a law stating that a person without the ability to pay a debt or a court-ordered fine "shall be sold for satisfaction, but neither out of the county nor to any other but the English nations, neither shall he be transported out of the county unless by his own consent." Indicating that by 1672 debt servitude was already a fact of life on Nantucket, and that it applied almost exclusively to Indians, is this 1670 town law: "if any person English or Indian shall at any time carry in any vessel any Indian servant...off the island without orders from his master he shall be fined twenty shillings."

Although instituted by the English, the practice was yet another development that would have not been altogether alien to the Indians. Whereas the English had masters and servants, the Indians possessed social distinctions of their own that may have been refined and expanded as increasing numbers of predominantly poor, dispossessed Indians from the mainland moved out to the islands. According to the Vineyarder Matthew Mayhew, there were Indian families who were "not privileged with common right, but in some measure subject to the yeomanry." It was only natural, therefore, that high-ranking Indians would, along with white Nantucketers, be awarded Indian servants by the courts. In 1687 the court assigned the services of Eleazer Kosasome to Wauwinet's son Isaac; in 1689 the Indian Finch was ordered to serve the weaver Netowa; and in 1727 Esther Tauch began a five-year stint as the servant of the Indian John Diamond. The fact remains, however, that rarely, if ever, were debt judgments entered against whites on the behalf of Native Americans.

With both the Indians and the English already knit together in a complex web of economic and legal relations, Nantucket was well prepared for the arrival of Ichabod Paddack in 1690. And just as they had adapted the English ledger book to their own traditional practices, so would the Nantucket Indians take to whaling—at least in the beginning—from a position of cultural strength.

Whereas the English and their livestock had quickly spread out across the interior of the island, the beaches–particularly along the south shore–had remained the almost exclusive domain of Indian driftwhalers. When Peter Folger's son Eleazer claimed a driftwhale that the Tomokommoth sachem Musaquat considered his, Musaquat took Folger to court. After admitting that he had acquired the whale "in controversy," Folger was told to pay Musaquat "£4 in goods at the usual price in trading." If Nantucket's winter grass had been claimed by the English, its winter whales were still the Indians'.

Rather than undermining the Indians' claims, the English courts acted to formalize and refine driftwhaling rights first established by Massasoit. In 1673 the beach along the southwest shore of the island (described as "upon the plains") was divided into eight "shares." Three years later it was determined that "no rack whale that come ashore in any sachem's bounds shall be cut up until all the masters of the shares that belong to that whale do come together." And since many of the Tomokommoth driftwhalers were also residents of the Vineyard, it was determined that "if any master be off the island and leave no man to act for him, he is to lose his share."

One of the itinerant driftwhalers was Washamon, who in 1676 was awarded the baleen-rich "head of the drift whale for his share." It was Washamon's son Jacob who lived among the English in the vicinity of No-Bottom Pond. Given its proximity to his father's driftwhaling territory, it is possible that Jacob's property, containing an English-style house on ten acres of land known as Washamon's Island, acted as a base camp for the family driftwhaling business. For the English, who shipped the oil to market, having an Indian driftwhaling clan in their midst would have helped to bolster their claims that it was Indian, not English, oil and therefore exempt from the taxes normally levied on what were considered "royal fish."

With the arrival of Ichabod Paddack, however, the beaches that had once been an all-Indian domain were soon to become but a stepping-stone to a whole new level of prosperity. Many years later, white Nantucketers would tell the story of how in the very same year that Paddack came to Nantucket, some people were standing on a shoreside hill watching whales "spouting and sporting with each other." Sensing that new things were about to come to the island, one of the Nantucketers pointed toward the sea and said, "There is a green pasture where our children's grandchildren will go for bread."

If the sea had become a green pasture (this was an image to which almost all on this grass-obsessed island could relate), then the south shore of the island was the gateway to that new land of opportunity. And if the English were to control the gateway, they had better own it.

So, between 1691 and 1692, the town's proprietors bought up strips of shoreside land that more than thirty years of driftwhaling (or at least the observation of Indian driftwhaling) had taught them were prime spots for sighting whales. From Wanackmamack's son Jephtha they purchased the bluff at Siasconset; from Spotso's son Daniel they bought land at Madequecham; and from Attapeat's son Musaquat they purchased a section of land located in a cove on the eastern edge of Hummock Pond known as Coboacommoh. At these three locations, plus a fourth on land already owned by the English at the western tip of Smith's Point (just to the south of Tuckernuck), they created what were known as whale stations: seasonal outposts of whalemen housed in simple, wigwam-like shacks.

The whaleboats that Paddack directed the Nantucketers to build were almost precisely the same length as the Indians' dugout canoes (twenty feet) but were much lighter due to their cedar clapboard construction. (According to one account it took only two men to "conveniently carry" a whaleboat.) Although the town had recently prohibited the cutting of trees on Coatue, an exception was made in 1694 for those looking for materials to make whaleboats.

Even before the advent of whaling, the English had depended on the Indians' boat-handling skills when it came to negotiating the local waters in their dugout canoes. Standard operating procedure was to include at least one Indian to handle the boat when traveling beyond the island. For example, we know that in 1669 four white Nantucketers and an Indian voyaged to the Vineyard to purchase a plowshare and some furniture. That the overloaded canoe capsized on the way back (drowning all but one Englishman) is an indication of just how dangerous canoe travel could be.

Not surprisingly, then, the English turned to their resident experts, the Indians, when it came to manning their whaleboats. An Englishman might own the boat and hold the steering oar, but in the majority of Nantucket whaleboats in the early days of whaling, five out of six crewmembers were Native American. And since all six men were paid not according to the English system of wages but in a manner in keeping with what had been used for driftwhaling, the Indians knew exactly where they stood at the end of the day.

On a Nantucket whaleboat in the early days of alongshore whaling, what became known as the "lay" system worked out this way: the owner of the boat and the gear required for whaling (known as "whale craft") received half the proceeds. The other half was divided among the crew into eighths, with the two "endsmen," the captain and the harpooner, receiving double shares and the four oarsmen each receiving a single share.

The potential returns were significant. If a single whaleboat crew was lucky enough to bring home a good-sized whale, even an oarsman stood to make the equivalent of a half-year's wages on land according to the estimates of the historian Daniel Vickers. In most cases, however, two, sometimes three boats chose to combine forces, which not only increased the chances of killing the animal but greatly reduced the amount of time required to process the blubber. Unfortunately, it also reduced the amount each man was paid, and there were the long stretches during which there were no whales to be had. Over-all, alongshore whaling provided both English and Indian Nantucketers with a way to bring in some money at a time of the year (from the late fall to early spring) when farmers and sheep-herders have relatively little else to do.

For the Indians, it was more than a matter of pounds, shillings, and pence. For a people whose forefathers had once been proud warriors and deer hunters, whaling–which has been described as the ultimate hunt–seems to have had an especially strong appeal, particularly when compared to spinning English wool or carting dung. According to Obed Macy, "the Indians showed a readiness to join in and were preferred to the whites in some parts of the business. They were a stout, strong race of people and...never gave back but [were] always ready to go forward where they were sent by the captain." Although most captains were English, a few Nantucket Indians commanded their own whaleboats, which meant that if a whaleboat wasn't all Indian, it was, at the very least, five-sixths Indian. However, in a boat with an English captain, the total share allotted to the Native American crewmembers amounted to just over a fifth of the take. Even if this was the equivalent of a good wage for the Indians, it still left the whites with eighty percent of the profits.

The demographics of the island at this time–approximately 300 English and 800 Indians–suggest the large number of Indian whale-men was as much by necessity as by design. Elizabeth Little has calculated that in 1700 just about every adult male on the island–Indian and white–would have been required to man an estimated thirty whaleboats.

Given the Indians' superiority, both in numbers and in terms of boating and hunting experience, it was inevitable that they largely defined the cultural context–a seasonal village of whalehunters on a beach–that would create the archetypal figure of the Nantucket whaleman.

A whalehunt began when a lookout, either perched atop a shore-mounted mast or simply standing on a southern-facing bluff such as Tom Nevers Head (named, according to tradition, for the Indian who was once stationed there), shouted the words, "Awaite Pawana," meaning, "Here is a whale." The whalemen—some perhaps dozing in their houses, others mending their equipment—would stop what they were doing and listen for the lookout to repeat, "Pawana"—a whale.

Then, much as a fire company bursts into activity at the sound of an alarm, the whale station would become alive with movement. Most of the available information about whaling on Nantucket in the early eighteenth century comes from account books and town records, but alongshore whaling was conducted off Long Island into the first part of the twentieth century. From narratives left by those whalemen (who, with a few exceptions, used the very same technology prevalent on Nantucket two hundred years before), it is possible to appreciate the excitement, danger, and drudgery of whaling off a beach.

One of the first things a Nantucket Indian would have done on hearing the cry of "Pawana," is dress himself for the chase—probably in clothing made from the wool of Nantucket sheep. On Long Island, standard dress included "heavy woolens underneath," an old coat, and, most important of all when rowing in February, wool mittens that were first dipped in salt water—a process that "fulled up" the yarn and, if it was cold enough, created a coat of ice that kept the whale-man's hands "warm though wet."

Once the boat and the crew were assembled at the water's edge, it was time to negotiate the surf. Since codfishing stations had been organized on the eastern extreme of the island as early as the 1670s, there were Nantucketers who were already expert surfmen by the time whaling began to take off at the end of the century. With the captain calling the shots, the whaleboat would punch its way through the breakers into the open ocean.

These twenty-foot whaleboats were significantly lighter than the thirty-foot behemoths that would become standard-issue in the nineteenth century, and they were able to accelerate up to speed in no time at all–the five Indians pulling at the oars as the lone white Nantucketer steered them toward their prey. The whalemen were immediately on the lookout for a mother and her baby since it was common knowledge that a "dam" never abandoned her young. Rowing as swiftly as possible, but in utter silence in hopes of catching their prey by surprise, the whalemen approached the calf. After carefully shipping his oar, the Indian harpooner would take up his weapon and when within a range of fifteen feet or less, hurl the harpoon.

Nantucket whaleboats of the time were equipped with drogues– fourteen-inch-square boards attached to the harpoon line that acted as sea anchors, significantly slowing the whale and eventually tiring it out. With the baby fastened to a drogue, but still alive, the whalemen now turned their attention to the mother, whose unwillingness to leave the calf made her an easy target.

Although Nantucket whalers may have begun by using drogues instead of leaving the end of the harpoon line attached to the boat, at some point the islanders established the tradition known as a "Nantucket Sleigh Ride," in which the whale towed the boat along in a cloud of spray at up to twenty-five knots. At this stage the harpooner and the captain switched places–not an easy maneuver on an equipment-crammed whaleboat being tossed about by a fifty-five foot whale.

Needless to say, it was an exciting, even terrifying experience–so much so that the tension was enough to make even a seasoned whaleman vomit in the midst of the chase. Now came the most difficult and brutal part, repeatedly stabbing the whale with a razor-sharp lance until the victim began to "spout great quantities of blood."

This often resulted in the entire crew becoming drenched in a gory bath that must have been almost scaldingly warm on a frosty February afternoon. And remember, given the division of duties on a Nantucket whaleboat, it was the lone Englishman who was responsible for "finding the life" of the whale, stabbing it with his lance as many as a dozen times before the whale went into its final, tail-lashing "flurry." Then, of course, it was time for the calf. After a year of suckling, it often yielded more oil than the mother.

Depending on how long it took to finally kill the whales, the tow back could take as many as twelve hours, especially if it was against a stiff northerly headwind. Towing a whale was such laborious work (requiring a painfully slow stroke), that the whalemen were often unable to keep themselves warm as the day turned to darkness, and frostbitten extremities were a constant threat.

Once they reached shore, the whalemen knew all too well that their work had just begun. But instead of the terrifying excitement of the whalehunt, the process of cutting up the blubber and trying out the oil (known as "saving the whale") was, according to the memories of Long Island whalemen, "a picnic." But it was a long, foul-smelling picnic as the whalemen began the around-the-clock work of transforming the blubber and baleen into marketable products–staving off the boredom with stories, songs, and, of course, rum.

Although it took the Long Island whalemen as long as two to three days to strip off all the whale's blubber, Nantucketers in the early eighteenth century had more available manpower and a slight technological advantage–principally a beach-mounted capstan, known as a crab, that assisted in the removal of the blubber. Once the whale's lips had been cut off, the mouth yielded as much as 750 pounds of whiskery black baleen. Then the blubber was carted to the tryworks. In the beginning, most whaleboat owners had tryworks located near their homes; however, one Nantucketer from the nine-teenth century remembered seeing the brick ruins of the Hummock

Pond tryworks as a boy, indicating that blubber was also tried out on the premises of the whale stations. Trying out the oil for a single whale (the fire fueled by the whale's own blubber) could take as much as a week, sending out a noxious black cloud that had been a winter ritual on Nantucket since the days of Indian driftwhaling.

As whaling took over the island, the whale stations appear to have consolidated into two primary locations: Hummock Pond, which may have contained as many as sixteen whalehouses (enough to house close to a hundred men), and, a few miles to the east, Weweeder, with approximately eight whalehouses. This meant that Indians at the village of Miacomet, situated precisely between those two locations, and the English, who were just a few miles to the north, were within easy reach of the whale stations.

With their wives and children just a few miles away, Nantucket's alongshore whalemen may have been relatively well behaved, particularly compared to those at more isolated whale stations on Cape Cod, where archaeological digs at Great Island have revealed evidence of a veritable den of iniquity, complete with a tavern and perhaps a brothel. On Nantucket, alongshore whaling involved the entire island community–not only the able-bodied men, but also their families, who undoubtedly made frequent appearances on the beach.

Although from a different era, there is an engraving of the scene at the codfishing station at Siasconset about 1791 that corresponds closely to what it must have been like at the Hummock Pond whale station on a sunny afternoon in 1726, the peak year of alongshore whaling. In the engraving, a crowd of people, some in horse-drawn carts and carriages, some on foot, makes its way down to the haphazard collection of fishing shacks that now make up the village of Siasconset. Smoke curls out the chimneys as in the distance the fleet of boats spreads out across the ocean.

Whereas it was almost exclusively white Nantucketers who were making the trip to Siasconset in 1791, the scene at the Hummock

Pond whale station in 1726 (when a total of eighty-six whales were taken—eleven in a single day!) would have been as Indian as it was English. It would have also had a more industrial flavor than the cod-fishing operation at 'Sconset: a soot-blackened and foul-smelling brick tryworks, perhaps a whale carcass or two wallowing in the waves as children took turns crawling up the telephone-pole-sized lookout mast for a glimpse at the action out on the water.

A kind of shore-based amphitheater, the whale station brought the skills of Nantucket's whalemen before the entire island. And it was not just English whaleboat captains such as John Swain, Jonathan Coffin, Paul Paddack (a relative of Ichabod), Abishai Folger, and Ebenezer Gardner that people remarked on. People also talked about the Indian crewmembers, many of whom were men of considerable standing in the Native American community: Schutquade, who lived near Sesachacha Pond and whose great-grandson would be Abram Quary; John Diamond, the son-in-law of the Tomokommoth sachem Peter Musaquat; Ben Abel, great grandson of the eastern sachem Wanackmamack, who whaled alongshore throughout the 1720s and '30s; and many others. Then there was the whaleboat captained in 1726 by Staples, an Indian whose crewmember James Pock would enter his share of the whale they took that year in the Starbucks' account book.

Staples was, by no means, Nantucket's only Indian alongshore whaling captain. In 1730 and '31, Eben Smugg captained a whaleboat out of the Weweeder whale station whose crew included, among others, Obed Japhet, Tom Poney (who would keep an account with the Starbucks over a record span of thirty-two years!), and Isaac Wooso. In 1742 the Indian Jonathan Micah captained a boat owned by Richard Mitchell that included as crew the Indian John Tashama, Jr. In 1754 John's brother Isaac Tashama went alongshore whaling with the Indian captain Eben Corduda. Additional Indian captains included Stubb, Diamond, and others whose names will never be known.

The greatest challenge faced by the English was not killing whales, it was finding enough Indians to man their whaleboats. Inevitably, the same economic system that had provided the basis for a middle ground became increasingly one-sided. By extending credit to a group of at least five able-bodied Indians, an English whaleboat owner possessed a way to ensure that those Indians would whale for him. Thus, each whaleboat owner had his own book of what were referred to as "Indian debts"–in effect a book of financial obligations requiring a group of Indians to work for that specific owner. For example, in 1719 Jonathan Bunker's will divided "all my whaling and fishing craft with all my Indian debts" among his four sons.

Since, as Obed Macy indicated, most business was conducted informally on Nantucket, surviving account books and court records provide, at best, only a partial indication of the importance of Indian debt to Nantucket's whaling economy. Probate records, on the other hand, are somewhat more helpful since it was common to list the amount of "Indian debts" credited to a person's estate. Daniel Vickers has noted that of the eight white Nantucketers whose estates contained whaling gear between 1700 and 1730, six possessed Indian debts. In 1721 Thomas Bunker's estate was valued at more than £511, with Indian debts accounting for £112 of it, or a fifth of his net worth.

Just because an Indian owed money to a white whaleboat owner did not mean that he was being victimized by that owner. What the anthropologist Kathleen Bragdon has called "patron-client relationships" developed between more than a few whaling merchants and Indians–particularly when an Indian had a marketable skill. Consider, for example, the case of Eben Smugg, who was apparently a man of many talents. Not only did he rise to the rank of whaleboat captain, he was a capable joiner and carpenter. In order to keep Smugg in his fold, Nathaniel Starbuck, Jr., gave the Indian considerable latitude when it came to the collection of the money he owed. As Bragdon has pointed out, Smugg's account with the Starbuck store regularly ran more than £40 overdue each year. If the extension of credit restricted an Indian's options, it also gave him the opportunity to develop a long-term relationship with an employer based on mutual trust and respect. Under ideal circumstances, an Indian whaleman on Nantucket had, according to the estimates of Elizabeth Little, the potential of earning as much as four times the annual wage of a white seaman in Boston.

But abuses were inevitable in a business as dependent on the use of debt as the Nantucket whale fishery–especially when alcohol was thrown into the mix. According to Obed Macy, "some of the English were so wicked as to take the advantage, and would trade with them for their baskets, fish, corn, and vegetables, and pay them in spiritu-ous liquors, and frequently get them in debt, and cause them to go a whaling to pay their 'masters,' as they called them. This kept them in a low, degraded state." For every Eben Smugg, there was an Abraham Monkey, an Indian whose predilection for rum and trou-ble meant that he spent most of his life whaling for a series of court-appointed masters.

For a Native American, a master's book of Indian debts had the potential of becoming what a bill of sale was for a slave: the docu-ment that tied him to a life of servitude. In 1732, three Indians were accused of stealing John Pinkham's "pocket book" in an attempt to destroy the evidence of debt that he held over them. Pinkham took them to court, and two of the Indians, Simon Tanah and Deborah Nosson, had their tenures of servitude lengthened by more than four and five years, respectively.

For some Nantucket Indians the term of servitude was so long that they were, for all intents and purposes, enslaved. From 1706 through 1753 six Indians (as opposed to "Indian debts") were listed in the estates of white Nantucketers, ranging in value from Thomas Bunker's "Indian girl Dorcas" (£10 in 1721) to Daniel Folger's unnamed "Indian servant" (£60 in 1748). The listings are virtually identical in form to those documenting African-American slaves, of which there were twelve during the same period. Of particular interest is a court case from 1735 in which an Indian named Jesse was accused of stealing more than £22 worth of goods from a freed black man named Jonas. Instead of making an African American a master, the court sentenced Jesse to three years of servitude to "Jonas' attorney," John Gardner. Clearly, the line between Indian servitude and African slavery on Nantucket was a fine one.

As early as 1716 the Indian John Punker petitioned the General Court in Boston concerning English exploitation of Indian whalemen on Nantucket. According to Punker, it was impossible for an Indian to get a fair hearing since virtually everyone in the island's white community was related: "If the Indians sue the English, the judges, jury, sheriff and clerk are the defendants." Eventually, a committee was sent to the island to investigate Punker's charges. The result was the passage of a bill in June 1718 that outlined in disturbing detail just the kinds of actions described by both Punker and (a hundred years later) Obed Macy: "a great wrong and injury happens to said Indians…by reason of their being drawn in by small gifts, or for small debts, when they are in drink, and out of capacity for trade, to sign unreasonable bills or bonds for debts, which are soon sued, and great charge brought upon them, when they have no way to pay the same but by servitude."

Although the bill prescribed measures for controlling the abuses, the informality and insularity of Nantucket's island environment meant that the English continued, for the most part, to do as they pleased. For example, the account book of the carpenter-whaleman Richard Macy includes several drafts of an agreement with the Indian Ephraim that most certainly never saw the light of an island courtroom: "Ephraim having taken the money forty shillings he doth engage to bring the money in two months and bind his two young sons for fishing...till they are of twenty-one years of age."

Although in at least one instance an Indian successfully sued for an "abatement" in his term of servitude, most agreements such as the one between Ephraim and Macy were negotiated (and, inevitably, renegotiated) face-to-face—whether it was on the beach, in a whalehouse, or in front of the Indian's wigwam. According to Daniel Vickers, "Insults, threats, sulking, and brute force were all part of a bargaining idiom in which both parties tried to obtain the best terms possible."

As might be expected, whale merchants, often aided and abetted by rum, tended to get the upper hand in the negotiations. The Indians, however, quickly developed strategies for, in the words of one observer, "torment[ing] the ship or share owner with [their] indecision and demands." According to Edward Kendall, who witnessed such an interchange on the Vineyard: "First, [the Indian] agrees to go [on a whaling voyage], and accordingly receives some stipulated part of his outfit; then he 'thinks he won't go'; unless such and such articles are supplied; and these articles he often names at random for the sake of inducing a refusal. One Indian...mentioned to me that he thought he would not go unless five pounds of soap were given him; and another thought the same unless he received seven hats."

The English might have dominated the island's economy, but the fact remained there were large portions of life on this bicultural island that no one controlled. If the Indians began to dress and act more and more like the English, the English were just as profoundly influenced by their contact with the Indians. And as observers from Crèvecoeur to Benjamin Franklin (whose grandfather, Peter Folger, had been Nantucket's first Indian interpreter) had commented, American colonists rarely escaped unscathed from what the ethnohistorian James Axtell has called "the extraordinary drawing power of Indian culture." But how far were English Nantucketers drawn into the Indians' world?

Axtell has examined how the captivity experience created what he calls "white Indians." Although not as sudden or traumatic, the often violent, all-consuming, communitywide obsession known as alongshore whaling provided English Nantucketers with an exposure to Indian culture that was without parallel in eighteenth-century New England. And just as French fur traders and American frontiersmen inevitably felt the effects of "Indianization" (Crèvecoeur's term), so did white Nantucketers have more in common with their native coinhabitants than they probably would have cared to admit.

As late as 1791, white Nantucket children were being brought up in a manner that betrayed a strong native influence. According to Walter Folger, "The boys, as soon as they can talk, will make use of the common phrases, as 'townor,' which is an Indian word, and signifies that they have seen the whale twice; and as soon as they are some years older, they are seen rowing in boats for diversion, which makes them expert oarsmen, a thing that is requisite in taking the whale."

But it was not simply the way a Nantucket whaleman talked. He possessed a "peculiar" physicality that was different from all other sailors. According to Crèvecoeur, "A man born here is distinguishable by his gait from among a hundred other men, so remarkable are they for a pliability of sinews and a peculiar agility, which attends them to old age." Suggesting that this "agility" may have been a learned behavior is Henry David Thoreau's description of an Indian moose hunter in the Maine woods: "He proceeded rapidly...with a peculiar, elastic, noiseless, and stealthy tread...in a way no white man does." One wonders if Thoreau would have modified his assessment if he had seen a Nantucket whaleman in the eighteenth century.

Although Quakerism is generally given credit for nurturing the strong and independent women required to sustain a whaling port, Nantucket's Indian women had been tending crops, raising their children, and gathering shellfish for thousands of years before anyone heard of George Fox. Indeed, the gender roles typical of Native Americans in southern New England (it was the man's responsibility to hunt, fish, and fight) are essentially those that white Nantucketers would practice throughout the eighteenth and nineteenth centuries.

Perhaps it was the whalehouse that best symbolized the complex interweaving of cultures that occurred on Nantucket in the early days of whaling. It might have been sided with boards instead of grass mats, but the framing of a whalehouse was almost as light as that of a wigwam. Instead of the high peaked roof of a traditional English cottage, a whalehouse roof was relatively squat, as if in angular imitation of a rounded wigwam. The whalehouse could also be moved easily—whether dragged on ash rollers, floated on a raft, or taken apart and rebuilt—to take advantage of the latest trends in fishing. Inside these dirt-floor houses, Indians and English ate their fish and told their stories around brick fireplaces whose masonry merged into blackened board flues that occupied an architectural limbo between a wigwam's smokehole and an English chimney.

Whether or not it was within the musky confines of a whalehouse, everyone on Nantucket was moving toward a future that would be forever shaped by long days and nights on an eroding beach—the violence and camaraderie of the hunt tempered by a bloodless obsession with financial matters to create the uneasy mixture of concern and callousness that would define Indian-English relations on Nantucket in the eighteenth century.

In years to come, the English would look back to alongshore whaling (which came to a halt around 1760) as a golden time of communal prosperity, a time when even the weather conspired to make what was otherwise a very hazardous occupation almost magically safe. According to Obed Macy, writing in 1835, "It has often been remarked by the aged, that the winters were not so windy and boisterous at that time as at present though quite as cold; and that it would sometimes continue calm a week or even a fortnight."

Although there are several recorded whaling deaths on Cape Cod Bay, tradition has it that not a single *white* person was killed in all the years of alongshore whaling on Nantucket. The racial qualification suggests that the island's Indian whalemen may not have been so lucky, although no one seemed inclined to record how many (let alone who) had been lost.

Yet another English tradition indicates that Nantucket's alongshore whaling fleet did, in fact, experience its share of boisterous weather, and that when things turned bad, it was the Indians, not the English, who tended to suffer. In 1792 Zaccheus Macy recorded what amounts to a kind of insider's alongshore whaling joke, with the punch line based on the fact that almost all Nantucket whaleboats had only one Englishman aboard and five Indians.

> But it happened once, when there were about thirty boats about six miles from the shore, that the wind came round to the northward, and blew with great violence, attended with snow. The men all rowed hard, but made but little head way. In one of the boats there were four Indians and two white men. An old Indian in the head of the boat, perceiving that the crew began to be disheartened, spake out loud in his own tongue and said, "Momadichchator auqua sarshkee sarnkee pinchee eyoo sememoochjkee chaquanks wihchee pinchee eyoo": which in English is, "Pull ahead with courage: do not be disheartened: we shall not be lost now: there are too many Englishmen to be lost now." His speaking in this

manner gave the crew new courage. They soon perceived that they made head way; and after long rowing, they all got safe on shore.

Although some have described this as a "touching" story, that is
missing the point of the old Indian's joke. By saying that there are
"too many Englishmen to be lost now," the old man is implying that
two different standards existed for English and Indian Nantucketers.
Indian whalemen died; English whalemen didn't; and given that this
particular whaleboat had double the usual complement of white men,
then the four Indians had nothing to worry about.

If this anecdote is any indication, the Indians were bitterly aware
of their ultimate role in Nantucket's rapidly expanding whaling economy. They might provide the back-breaking labor; they might have
served as the unrecognized role models upon which an island of
farmers and sheepherders learned how to become whalemen; but, in
the end, they were expendable—invisible casualties in a beach-based
war against the whale that the English would nostalgically remember
as a time of wonderful weather and unmatched security.

But all that was about to change.

9

THE LIGHT

For a pious man, especially for a Quaker, [Bildad] was certainly rather hard-hearted, to say the least. He never used to swear, though, at his men, they said; but somehow he got an inordinate quantity of cruel, unmitigated hard work out of them.... His own person was the exact embodiment of his utilitarian character. On his long, gaunt body, he carried no spare flesh, no superfluous beard, his chin having a soft, economical nap to it, like the worn nap of his broad-brimmed hat.

–Herman Melville, Moby-Dick

Although it would ultimately lead them to what was called "the deep," and from there to virtually all the oceans of the world, Nantucket's sperm-whale fishery began as a throwback to an earlier era. Sometime before 1712, a strange whale with a bulbous head and a long lower jaw equipped with teeth instead of baleen washed up in the vicinity of the Hummock Pond whale station.

The Indians were the first to find it, but hearing of the discovery from his Indian servant Gregory, Richard Macy became the first white man on the scene. A carpenter by trade and a bully by disposition, Macy, well over six feet, used a sledge to remove the whale's teeth and, assuming them to be of "great value," hid them in a convenient place.

It was not long before a large crowd had assembled around this unusual whale. The Indians, undoubtedly assuming that their ancestral driftwhaling rights were still in effect, claimed it as theirs. The English, however, were not about to surrender such a unique and potentially profitable find, and utilizing the legal double-talk that

165

they would develop into an art form in the century ahead, claimed the whale "by a right comprehended...in the purchase of the island."

Meanwhile a town official appeared on the scene and claimed the whale in the name of the king. A heated debate ensued, during which Macy threatened to "take the whole company one by one and handle them as a woman would her child" if he was not allowed to keep the teeth. Whether or not Macy's forcefulness had anything to do with it, it was ultimately determined that the whale should go—not to the King nor the Indians—but to "the white inhabitants who first found the whale."

Thus, the appearance of a dead sperm whale ushered in a new era on the island. By 1712, Nantucketers were sailing whaleboat-equipped sloops out to the edges of the Gulf Stream in pursuit of a whale whose oil burned with a much brighter and cleaner light than that of the right whale. In the meantime, a light of a different sort—the "Inner Light"—had begun to take over the religious life of the island as white Nantucketers (including Richard Macy) turned increasingly to Quakerism. But as the anecdote concerning the discovery of the first sperm whale might suggest, the appearance of these new lights, both literal and spiritual, would ultimately cast a shadow across the lives of Nantucket's Native Americans.

A few years after the sperm whale washed up on the south shore, a storm battered the north side of the island, ultimately throwing up a sandbar across the entrance of Cappamet Harbor that transformed it into Capaum Pond. It was time for the town of Sherburne, for that is what English Nantucketers had called their settlement since the 1670s, to up and move, Indian-like, to another location.

They went to Wesco, named for a white, quartz-flecked boulder on the western shore of what we now call Nantucket Harbor. New houses were built; old houses were moved from the west to the east; and, in 1723, the same man who had bullied his way to a whale, Richard Macy, built the island's first solid-fill wharf. They called it Straight Wharf because it extended out straight from the road that would eventually be known as Main Street. But in establishing this monument to Nantucket's ever-increasing commercial prosperity, Macy effectively erased what had been an important Native American landmark. Buried beneath the rip-rap and gigantic beams of Straight Wharf was the white rock that had given the area its name; it hasn't been seen since.

With Straight Wharf in place, the town of Sherburne became a community altogether different from what it had once been. Instead of a rambling settlement that extended across the western end of the island (with seasonal offshoots to the south and east), the town began to look more and more like a little city, its focus directed toward the wharf-equipped waterfront on the harbor. Fences were erected around the peripheries of town, and anyone entering or exiting to the east passed through the Newtown Gate, in the vicinity of today's central traffic rotary.

That shift in settlement pattern profoundly influenced how English and Indian Nantucketers interacted. Instead of the cross-cultural village of the whale station, Nantucketers were increasingly bound by separate Indian and English spheres. Although Indians would live in areas of Madaket for many years to come, the west end of the island, particularly when it came to the Wesco area, was English. There might be pockets of white settlement to the east (the Husseys lived in Shimmo, the Swains in Polpis, and the Bunkers in Squam), but the eastern end of the island was, in essence, "Indian territory." With the English and Indian populations reaching a momentary state of parity some time during the 1720s (at about 800 each), Nantucket's legendary east-west divide had been reestablished. This time it was not the eastern Indians and the Tomokommoths; it was Indians and English.

In place of the dividing line at Madequecham, the English, who still depended on Indian labor, instituted a curfew. Indians were permitted on Straight Wharf during the day (a whaling sloop's crew of thirteen typically had between four and eight Indians), but once it became dark, it was time for them to leave. In order to clear the town of Indians each night, the selectmen established a constable's watch intended "for suppressing disorders" caused by "Indians, Negroes, and other suspected persons." Any Indians "found upon the wharf and about town after nine of the clock at night" were to be "taken up and carried before a justice."

It was not just work that brought the Indians to town. It was also the readily available supplies of liquor. And since the Indians were expelled each night from town, English Nantucketers saved themselves from direct contact with the disturbing consequences of what Thomas Macy had once called the "drunken trade." According to his descendant Obed: "When [the Indians] were furnished with strong drink, they would leave town at night, and proceed toward their home, until the effect of the poison would cause them to drop by the way, exposed to the inclemency of the weather. It often happened in these cases that they were found dead, and not much care was taken to carry them to any particular burying ground, but were interred where they were found, which sometimes happened several days afterwards." Testifying to the truth of Macy's words is a court case from 1744 describing an incident in which "several Indians came to town and bought rum of the English and got drunk and one of them perished by way of it being very cold weather."

And if the Indians made it back to their villages, violence all too often erupted. During the winter of 1731 an Indian named Simon Hue, "being stirred up and instigated by the devil," kicked and beat one Jethro Quanset, then pummeled him with a "cordwood stick." Quanset lingered for close to two weeks, but eventually died. An Indian-English Superior Court jury found Hue guilty of manslaughter, determining that he "be branded in the brawn of the thumb in his left hand and with a hot iron with the letter T [for thief] and pay costs of prosecution," meaning, in effect, that he would work off his sentence in the whale fishery.

In 1739, two Indians by the names of John (also known as Happy) Comfort and John Elisha returned to their village after a drinking bout. Happy accused his companion of attempting to steal his corn and proceeded to beat him to death with what seems to have been a fairly common weapon among the Indians—a cordwood stick. Comfort was ultimately hanged at the gallows that stood beside the Newtown Gate, one of at least ten Indian executions performed on Nantucket during the eighteenth century, a particularly daunting statistic given that not a single murder occurred during the same period on the Vineyard. (Whether or not he served as the town's executioner, an Indian known as "Hangman" is listed in eighteenth-century town records.) For the Indians, the gallows must have provided a sobering reminder of the differences that existed on either side of the Newtown Gate.

Coinciding with the shift in settlement pattern was the rise of Quakerism among the English—a development that seems, if anything, to have increased the growing divide between white and native worlds. There is indirect evidence that Nantucket's Indians looked rather dimly on the rise of Quakerism among the English. Although his Puritan bias means that we must treat his testimony cautiously, Daniel Gookin recorded this account of a meeting between some Quaker missionaries and some Indians on Martha's Vineyard:

> [T]he Quakers...told the Indians, that they had a light within them, that was sufficient to guide them to happiness.... The Indians heard all this discourse patiently; and then one of the principal of them that could speak English, gravely answered the Quakers

after this manner, "You tell us of a light within us, that will guide us to salvation, but our experience tells us, that we are darkness and corruption, and all manner of evil within our hearts.... We cannot receive your counsel, contrary to our own experience of our ancient and good teachers...."

In 1704 the itinerant Quaker minister Thomas Story visited Nantucket, ultimately traveling to the property of John Swain who lived in the midst of the island's Indian territory out in Polpis. There he found "a great company of Indians and other people together, having been raising a timber house" for Swain. Story reported that "two priests were among" the Indians, one of whom had been "wrestling with a young Indian, and came into the house with his coat rent." While the non-Quaker minister joked that "we must all wrestle with flesh and blood," the disapproving Story shook his head and solemnly declared, "Thou must wrestle in another power than thy own, or else thy wrestling will be in vain." Just as on the Vineyard, the Quaker's words were not appreciated by the Indians; "in a few minutes time," Story noted, "they left the room, and the company departed, for they did not like our gravity, nor we their lightness."

Following the precedent of Story, Nantucket's emerging Quaker community chose to distance itself from the island's Indians. In a certain sense this was as it had always been on Nantucket. Ever since the Mayhews had begun traveling to Nantucket in the 1650s, off-islanders had been attending to the religious and educational needs of the Indians. In the seventeenth century the lack of on-island supervision enabled the Indians to maintain a healthy autonomy relative to the growing English settlement. In the eighteenth century, however, as the island's whaling economy became increasingly dependent on native workers, autonomy—at least this kind of autonomy—was not always appreciated by the English.

Something like a labor union, the organization that linked the Indians together was the Congregational church. In time, Indian churches would serve as centers of protest, providing the support system by which the island's native people would assert their traditional beliefs and practices in an increasingly hostile environment. All the more frustrating for English Nantucketers was the fact that those churches were supported financially by the New England Company—a missionary society that had the temerity to impose "Boston notions" upon Nantucket's insular world.

Given those circumstances, it is not surprising that white Nantucketers, no matter what their religious persuasion, had little enthusiasm for supporting the educational and religious life of the island's Indians. Nantucket's Congregational minister, Timothy White, who arrived in 1725 and preached to both the English and the Indians, was unable to persuade his own white congregation to support him financially. Instead, he was forced to rely on Boston Congregationalists for whatever salary he received over a twenty-five-year period.

The Quaker records, although full of references to collections made for worthy off-island causes, are devoid of any mention of the Indians. The Quakers might have declared their opposition to slavery in 1716, but that did not prevent their men's meeting clerk, Nathaniel Starbuck, Jr., from willing "all my Indian men with their debts" to his wife in 1753. On Nantucket, where whaling might be described as the Englishmen's true religion, commercial and legal obligations were what increasingly determined a white Nantucketer's relationship with the Indians.

It had been different in the early days of the English settlement when the whites had had no choice but to recognize the native Nantucketers' point of view. As we have seen, the Indians never accepted English notions of land ownership and winter grass rights. They might have signed documents that said otherwise, but that did not mean that the English held them to it. Compromises occurred regularly in the first decades of the settlement, culminating in the distribution of horse commons among the Indians in the 1680s.

By the end of the seventeenth century, however, with the Indian population down to around eight hundred, the English became less willing to negotiate. According to petitions filed by the Indians with the Massachusetts General Court, white Nantucketers began to confiscate cattle. They also began to remove Indian houses from land that the English declared was theirs. And with the rise of whaling, they kept accounts with inflexible precision. Because the Indians had signed the deeds and accepted the offers of credit, the English were doing nothing that was technically illegal.

From the Indians' perspective, however, everything had changed. Instead of simply working things out, the English were now insisting on the letter of a law that had never before mattered all that much. In 1702 the sachems Daniel Spotso, Peter Musaquat, and the curiously named Cain and Able (Wanackmamack's grandchildren) petitioned the General Court, claiming that if the English persisted they would "be forced in a short time to leave their habitations, and be utterly ruined." Prominent citizens such as John Gardner, who had once been on the Indians' side (when it served his political purposes), were now directing the constable to impound Indian cattle. Without effective legal recourse, the Indians could speak only to what they considered to be fair and just: "not versed in English law yet taught our wrong by the light of Nature," the Indians asked that the court take "pity to our distress."

Although white Nantucketers dismissed the Indians' charges out of hand (as have, by and large, Nantucket historians), there were some influential contemporary observers who sympathized with the Indians. In 1700, when he called the English winter feed rights a "circumvention and fraud," Massachusetts Governor Bellomont also informed Nantucket's James Coffin that he "would not give assent to any bill that should put a further hardship on those Indians." In 1722 Chief Justice Samuel Sewall addressed a letter to the Quaker Jethro Starbuck pleading the case of a "sober [and] industrious" Indian named Pekenney. According to Sewall, "I hear there is an unwillingness in the English that this Pekenney should pasture in common with his English neighbors; which they manifest by [im]pounding his cattle although he turns in to feed a very modest proportion."

Sewall and Bellomont's points were essentially the same: white Nantucketers should quit flaunting their deeds and account books and do what was right–especially since many of the native Nantucketers (whom Bellomont described as the "soberest best sort of Indians in America") were simply attempting to lead quiet, productive lives. As Sewall pointedly reminded Starbuck: "The English are many, and potent; but that should make them more careful to keep themselves far from being in the least injurious to those that desire to live peaceably with them."

By the second decade of the eighteenth century, English Nantucketers were in a position to devote their sole attention to whaling, ultimately transforming the town into a major port. Although native labor was critical to the fishery's success, the inexorable growth of the English population meant that by the 1720s the Indians no longer possessed the overwhelming demographic advantage they had traditionally held on Nantucket. What had once been an island frontier, requiring constant give-and-take between the Indians and English, was rapidly becoming an island city, with a predominantly Indian underclass scattered throughout Nantucket's outlying areas.

By the 1730s Indian-English relations on Nantucket appear to have reached their nadir. It was the one decade from the first half of the eighteenth century for which there are no surviving Indian petitions to the General Court. There is, however, plenty of other evidence suggesting that, more than sixty years after the outbreak of fighting on the mainland, Nantucket may have been on the verge of its own King Philip's War.

According to Obed Macy, it was during the 1730s that the Indians reached the point that "they became so bold as to threaten the English with total extermination, if they refused any longer to listen to their complaints." He adds, "Whether [the Indians] intended to carry their threats into execution, and whether they had a settled plan of action to this intent is uncertain."

The English, however, were not about to take the threats lightly. As far back as 1689 an Indian veteran of King Philip's War named Joseph had walked into a tavern in Rochester on Buzzards Bay and "in an insulting and ranting manner" claimed that the Indians of Nantucket were to be the leading force in an armed uprising also involving Indians from Martha's Vineyard and Chappaquiddick. Whether or not such reports were believed, English Nantucketers maintained a small fort on an island in the middle of Lily (originally Wesco) Pond (just to the northwest of town) in case of, according to Macy, "Indian attack." When a French privateer plundered the island in 1695, the Indians showed none of the loyalty they had displayed on previous occasions. Quoting from the French captain's report, the governor of Acadia wrote: "The more than two hundred savages there were very friendly to [our men] while they pillaged the English, and moreover [the English] have turned them into peasants by selling them no weapons and requiring them to fish and farm the land."

Not until the 1730s, by which time the white ascendancy on Nantucket was a virtual fait accompli, did the Native Americans openly begin to threaten the English with physical violence. Then, in September 1738, the white Nantucketers' worst fears were seemingly realized. An Indian came into town and "carefully, though very privately" reported that "the Indians had entered into a conspiracy to rise upon them, on a certain night, and to massacre men, women, and children."

An account recorded in 1895 by Eliza Mitchell, who as a young girl had spoken with an old Quaker woman who had been four or five years old at the time of the threatened uprising, describes the English response. Initially, the men kept the news to themselves. Then, once night had fallen, they announced to their families that there was "trouble brewing with the Indians." Some of the men remained in town to guard the women and children who "after many fears and some tears" were gathered together. Other "companies" were assigned the task of patrolling the foggy outskirts of town.

After a long and tense night, "not the least indication of any disturbance could be discovered." The next day, the English did their best to discover the "meaning of it all." According to Obed Macy, who also speaks of the uprising, "the high sheriff, with fifty well armed men, issued out of the town to reconnoiter the settlements of the natives, and ascertain whether they were making any hostile movements." Instead of angry war parties, the English found "all quiet; it was harvest time and the Indians were merrily husking their corn."

The native leaders immediately wanted to know who had told the English of the rumored uprising. As it turned out, the informer had spent the last three days in a drunken stupor, having used the money the English had paid him to purchase rum. According to Mitchell, the Indians were "so highly incensed [that] they came near tearing him apart." Eventually it was decided that he should receive no less than thirty lashes at the town's whipping post.

When it came time to inflict the punishment, a large crowd had gathered in front of the town hall, near where the Civil War monument now stands on Main Street. Passions had cooled somewhat, so it was agreed to reduce the number of lashes. Still, Mitchell's informant remembered, "it was all brutal enough," and afterwards the Indian was "proclaimed an outcast among his people." Whether or not a collective sense of shame had anything to do with it, the whipping post was "soon removed," making this, according to Mitchell, the last public whipping on Nantucket.

Testifying to the fact that white Nantucketers may have not been entirely convinced that their fears were groundless is a story that appeared in the *New England Weekly Journal* in October 10, 1738. After detailing the "horrid scheme...to set fire to the houses of the English inhabitants in the night, and then to fall upon them arm'd, and kill as many as they could," the story insisted that this was only part of an Indian conspiracy that reached beyond the island. Although there is no evidence that the insurrection existed, much less had spread to any Nantucket whaling vessels, the *Journal* could not resist fueling English paranoia by adding: "'tis said the above affair was concerted last spring, before the vessels sailed on the whaling voyages; and that the Indians who went out with the English on those voyages were in the confederacy, and were to do their part by destroying the English on the seas: As several of those vessels are not arrived tho' long expected; and as the great number in the crews were Indians, the consequences thereof is much to be feared."

No matter how unjustified the English fears may or may not have been, it would never be the same on Nantucket. After such an incident, white islanders were even less inclined to give the Indians the benefit of the doubt.

As far as English Nantucketers were concerned, the Indians had more land than they knew what to do with, and to a limited extent they had a point. Due to the Native Americans' declining population, the amount of land per Indian on Nantucket actually *increased* well into the eighteenth century, despite the sale of large tracts to the English. But as Kathleen Bragdon has written, "The significance of land to the Wampanoag went far beyond its products." When the Indians lost their lands, they lost an irreplaceable connection to their heritage–a loss that could not be measured in acreage.

In 1741, the Indians in Wanackmamack's territory made a bold but peaceful bid to reclaim their destiny. Gathered in the village of Occawa, which they now referred to as "Sakedan Indian Town," they drafted what might be described as a declaration of independence. In the petition the Indians complained that their sachem, Benjamin Abel (great-grandson of Wanackmamack), had been selling off their lands without his people's permission. And since a sachem's authority traditionally depended upon the consent of his village, they felt justified in taking measures to "put down" Abel who "had no other power but only what he had from us."

That this decision was not entered into lightly, and that the Indians' churches played a key role in civic affairs, is made clear by the petition: "The church people and town people were together that day and after this all our elders in our town tell us we may put down Benjamin Abel from being sachem in our place and we may choose another man to be sachem over us." Turning once again to "our fathers and our good old [men]" for advice, the Sakedan Indians chose John Quaab as their new sachem.

As Kathleen Bragdon has observed, petitions such as these– which are very similar to documents written by Indians from Mashpee, Natick, and elsewhere–"have the ring of formulaic protest which may have been aboriginal in origin." Just as Wanackmamack and Nickanoose pled their cases before Massasoit and King Philip, so did these Indian petitioners appeal to the General Court, displaying a diligence and expertise that came as an unpleasant surprise to English Nantucketers. Thus the island's Indians found yet another way to adapt their traditional practices to an ever-changing world.

A subsequent petition makes it clear that the Sakedan Indians felt that they needed a new sachem to defend them from both the English (who "take our land away from us and in all manner try to hurt us") and rival Indian villages. The petitioners maintained that certain "town Indians" from Squatesit to the west, led by Barnabas Spotso and James Papamoo, had been encouraged by the English to steal wood from Sakedan territory. By that point, the Indians had taken it for granted that any hope for redress lay in English, not Native American counsels. Boston had replaced Mount Hope.

It was not just a matter of land and land use. In other petitions the Sakedan Indians complained that the English refused to respect their desire to observe the Sabbath, which, as we have seen, was never a high priority among Nantucket's white community:

> When the Englishmen take us out whaling with them
> to sea they will let us no time to rest on the Sabbath
> days if they see whale or whales then we must row
> after them if it be on the Sabbath day all day long, we
> must be rowing after whale or killing whale or cutting
> up whale on Sabbath day when we should be at rest
> on that day and do no worldly labor only to do some
> holy duties to draw near to God and when on land
> then we have no time to go to the meeting and then
> we are call[ed] to go away again to sea whaling. How
> can we serve God or...worship him...when our
> masters lead us to darkness and not in light[?]

By the eighteenth century, the Christian Indians' churches had become the focal point of their cultural identity, providing the ceremonial center that held them together as a people–a center that

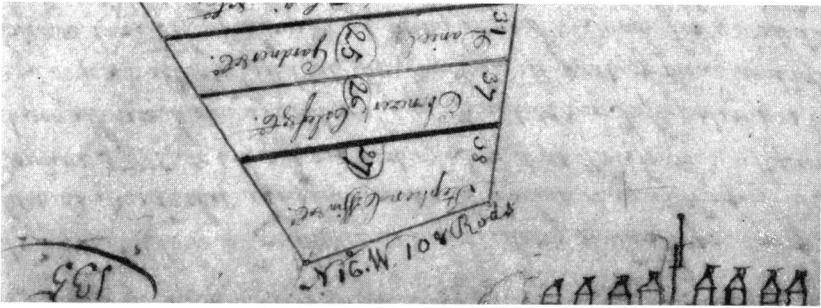

Fig. 44

The doodle at the lower right-hand corner of a plot-plan in the Nantucket town records, circa 1775, is our only surviving representation of what a Nantucket whale station looked like: two-room 'Sconset-like shacks (big enough to accommodate a six-person whaleboat crew) surrounding a two-piece lookout mast. *Photo by James McIntosh. Registry of Deeds, Town of Nantucket, Massachusetts.*

Fig. 45

It may have been engraved almost half a century after the heyday of alongshore whaling on Nantucket, but this representation of the codfishing village of Siasconset (made up, for the most part, of old whale houses) in 1797 helps to communicate a sense of what life was like at an island whale station. Not only was there the action out on the water, but the continual coming and going of inhabitants of all ages, who came to transport goods, see loved ones, or simply take in the scene. Engraving by David A. Leonard. *Courtesy of the Nantucket Historical Association.*

Fig. 46
The object of the hunt: the right whale. The men have begun to cut the blubber into strips. The man at the left clutches the whiskery tip of a piece of baleen, referred to as whalebone. Note the whale's huge, oil-filled tongue. We can only imagine the overpowering smell. *Courtesy of the Nantucket Historical Association.*

Fig. 47
A knife made of whale skeletal bone purchased at a flea market in New Bedford by Wampanoag Tribal Historian Russell Gardner. Although the knife appears to be an Eskimo snow knife from the nineteenth century (which could have come to southern New England from Hudson's Bay via a whaleship), the knife may have a connection to an earlier whaling era on Nantucket. In addition to several crude designs of anchors and whales, there are what Gardner interprets to be the names of several Indian driftwhalers from Nantucket (Wannawappog, Nathowa, and Job), along with the date 1671. The theory has been advanced that the inscriptions on the knife might represent a later copy of a seventeenth-century artifact from the island. *Photo by Russell Gardner.*

Fig. 48

An 1867 photograph of Stephen "Talkhouse" Pharoh, a Montauk Indian. In the early days of alongshore whaling on Nantucket, seventy-five percent of the whalemen were Native American. *Permission of the East Hampton Library, Long Island Collection.*

Figs. 49 and 50

The technology of alongshore whaling remained relatively static through the centuries. Note the similarities between the tryworks pictured in the English engraving, circa 1625, and that in the photograph of a whaling operation at Wainscott, Long Island, circa 1907. On Nantucket, alongshore whaling lasted from 1690 to 1760. *Old Dartmouth Historical Society-New Bedford Whaling Museum* (top) *and Collection of Barbara O. Meyer.*

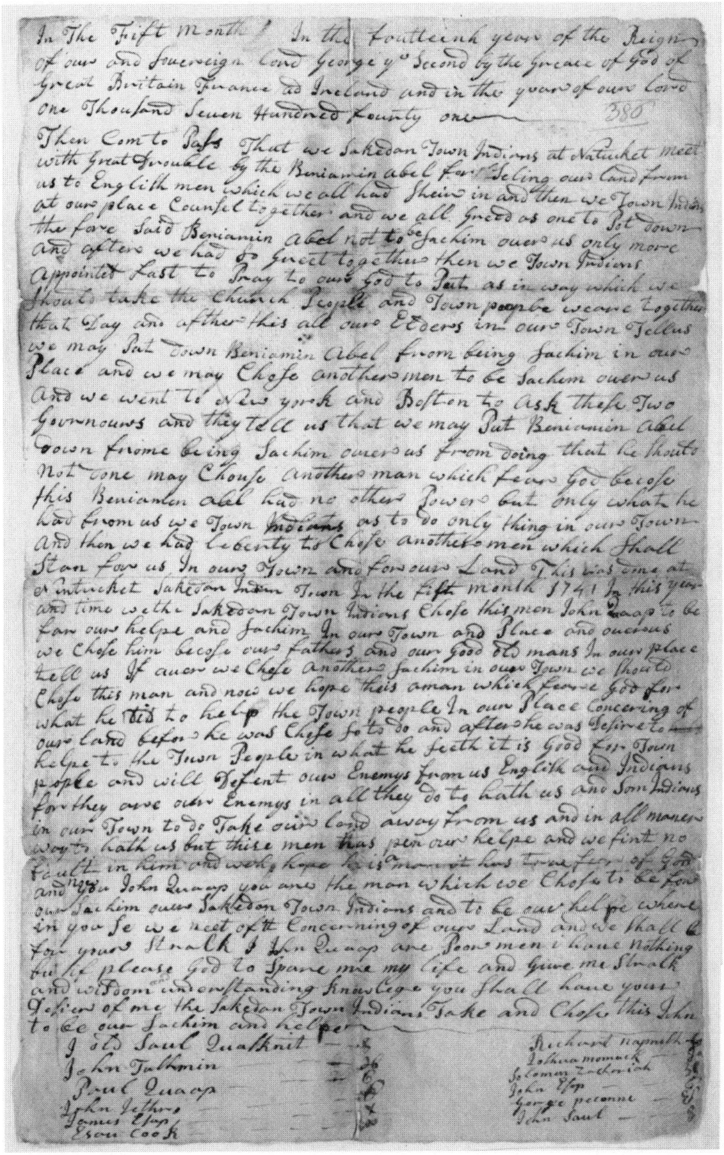
In The Fift month In the fourteenth year of the Reign
of our and Sovereign Lord George ye Second by the Greace of God of
Great Britain France and Ireland and in the year of our Lord
One Thousand Seven Hundred Fourty one
380
Then Com to Pass That we Sakedan Town Indians at Natucket meet
with Great Trouble by the Beniamin abel for Seling our Land from
us to English men which we all had Sheir in and then we Town Indians
at our place Counsel together and we all greed as one to Sit down
the fore Said Beniamin abel not to be Sachim over us only more
and after we had so Greet together then we Town Indians
appointed Fast to Pray to our God to Put as in way which we
Should take the Church People and Town people weare Together
that Day and after this all our Elders in our Town Tellus
we may Put down Beniamin Abel from being Sachim in our
Place and we may Chose another man to be Sachem over us
And we went to New york and Boston to ask these Two
Governours and they Tell us that we may Put Beniamin Abel
down frome being Sachim over us from doing that he Should
Not done may Chouse another man which fear God becose
this Beniamin Abel had no other Power but only what he
had from us we Town Indians as to do only thing in our Town
and then we had Leberty to Chose another men which Shall
Stan for us In our Town and for our Land This was done at
Natucket Sakedan Indian Town In the fift month 1741 In this year
and time we the Sakedan Town Indians Chose this man John Quaap to be
for our helpe and Sachim In our Town and Place and over us
we Chose him becose our fathers and our Good old mans In our place
tell us If ever we Chose another Sachim in our Town we Should
Chose this man and now we hope this aman which fear God for
what he did to help the Town people In our Place Concerning of
our Land befor he was Chose So to do and after he was Desire to
helpe to the Town People in what he seeth it is Good for Town
people and will Defent our Enemys from us English and Indians
for they are our Enemys in all they do to hath us and Som Indians
in our Town to do Take our Land away from us and in all maner
ways to hath us but this men has pen our helpe and we fint no
fault in him and we hope his man it has true fear of God
and you John Quaap you are the man which we Chose to be for
our Sachim over Sakedan Town Indians and to be our helpe where
in you se we neet of it Concerning of our Land and we shall be
for your Strangth I John Quaap are Poor men i have Nothing
but if please God to Spare me my life and Give me Strength
and wisdom understanding knowlege you shall have your
Desier of me the Sakedan Town Indians Take and Chose this John
to be our Sachim and helper

Old Saul Qualknit
John Talkmin
Paul Quaap
John Jethro
James Esop
Esau Cook

Richard Napmith
Joshua Momack
Solomon Zachariah
John Esop
George Petonne
John Saul

Fig. 51
A 1751 petition to the General Court in Boston from Nantucket Indians living in Sakedan Town at the east end of the island. In the petition the Sakedan Indians tell how they have "put down" their former sachem, Benjamin Abel, for selling their lands without the town's consent, replacing him with a new leader, John Quaab. *Courtesy of Massachusetts Archives.*

Fig. 52

1763: The Plague Year on Nantucket, the "Birth of the Whaling Industry" in New Bedford. This painting by William Wall, set in the very same year that a mysterious epidemic killed 222 of 358 Indians on Nantucket, shows the symbolic beginning of what would become the mainland's whaling capital. As a whaling sloop is being off-loaded in the background, whale blubber is being tried out in the foreground at right while an Indian (a jug of rum beside him) sells his baskets and moccasins to the English. The whale merchant Joseph Rotch, a Nantucket transplant, is shown speaking to an African-American at left. *New Bedford Whaling Museum-New Bedford Public Library.*

was becoming increasingly difficult to hold. According to the Indians, the decline in church attendance could be attributed not only to the demands of their English masters but to a breakdown in their own internal system of justice. In a 1746 petition, the Indians recalled how in the days of John Gardner, the English "let us have Indian justices in our towns so when Indians did anything...unlawful we punish[ed] them.... Now [the English] will not let us [have] Indian justices...and we cannot punish one another for our unlawful deeds."

As a result, increasing numbers of Indians were spurning the ways of their elders: "if [the] masters of those Indians have nothing for them to do on the Sabbath days then these Indians [would] rather go to see their friends...than come to meeting that day." Between the work demands of the English and the restrictions placed on their ability to discipline themselves, Nantucket's Indians were inevitably becoming more and more like their godless, whale-killing masters: "We...do what we can to serve God but these Englishmen...are no ways like Christians for if they was they would go by rules of the Gospel and should be in true fear of God."

The claims made in these petitions bear an intriguing similarity to an observation recorded in the 1680s by two Dutch travelers during a visit to the Indian-whaling heartland of Long Island: "The Indians hate the Quakers very much on account of their deceit and covetousness, and say they are not Englishmen, always distinguishing them from all other Englishmen, as is also done by almost all other persons. The Indians say 'they are not Christians, they are like ourselves.'" It may come to us in the context of religious prejudice and from a different island and time, but the suggestion that the Indians viewed the Quakers as demonic doppelgangers warrants further exploration in the context of English-Indian relations on Nantucket.

The island's Quakers would become famous for their emotional restraint, but that restraint, like that of Melville's Ahab, could sometimes turn ugly. According to one account, "the anger which [the Nantucket Quakers] are forbidden to express by outward actions, finding no vent, stagnates the heart, and, while they make professions of love and good will to their opponents, the rancor and intense malevolence of their feelings poison every generous spring of human kindness." The anthropologist William Simmons has described a similar behavior pattern among the Wampanoag during the seventeenth century. Like Nantucket's Quakers, the Indians were forbidden to express anger openly. As a consequence, a "covert form of interpersonal aggression" developed in the form of sorcery. Whether the conflict was personal or political, Indians used sorcery as a culturally sanctioned means of retaliation.

Indian and English Nantucketers each had their own form of sorcery during the eighteenth century. For the Indians it was, ironically perhaps, the written word. By barraging the General Court in Boston with petition after petition, Nantucket's Indians were able to cast a kind of spell over the English, requiring that they continually justify themselves to off-island authorities. When the Indian petitioners claimed that "we will tell no lies concerning these Nantucket whalemen for we [are in] no ways angry with these men," they were disingenuously carrying forward a covert attack campaign in keeping with the curses cast by powwows prior to English contact.

For the Quakers it was debt, a form of sorcery against which the Indians increasingly felt defenseless, particularly since white Nantucketers tended to inflict it on them at the worst of all possible times. According to one petition: "[The English] will not give Indians account of what they get at such times whaling or fishing, and let Indians live as long as he will.... [But] when he dies English will take all what may be found to his estate, and English will leave nothing for Indian's wife or children, and so they become poor." In the Indians' view, debt was the white Nantucketers' voodoo, capable of transforming a prosperous family into paupers as soon as the father's labor was no longer available to his English master.

The extent to which Indian debts provided Quaker masters with a vehicle to act out their harsh and uncompromising attitudes toward Native Americans is suggested by a petition authored by the Indian Paul Quaab: "[My master] never would make up our accounts...but when he was mad with me then we must make up our accounts between he and I and I know his heart was not with me then.... He reckoneth up for him things which I payeth for before." Quaab's master was Ebenezer Gardner, whose marriage in 1709 was the first Quaker wedding on Nantucket. One wonders how Gardner responded to being named in a court document written by his own servant.

Quaab was apparently something of a rabble-rouser. In the same petition he describes a confrontation he had with Barnabas Spotso when he caught the Squatesit sachem in the act of taking wood from Sakedan Town lands. Spotso complained to the English magistrate, who subsequently fined Quaab more than £2. The fine was quickly paid by Ebenezer Gardner, who, of course, now had an even firmer hold on his difficult servant.

If Quaab is to be believed, the English were not above resorting to physical force in order to silence the voice of Native American protest. In a petition from May 1747 he claimed that the English constable burst into his house in Sakedan as he was preparing for an impending court appearance. Even though Quaab showed the official "the writing I had from General Court at Boston," the constable claimed that he must serve on a whaling voyage to pay off a debt. When Quaab protested that he was "no ways obliged," the constable and two other men "laid hands" on him, ultimately carrying him for nearly a mile before lashing him to the neck of a horse and riding him into town. According to Quaab, "this they do to send me out whaling that I should not be at home when the Court sits."

The Indian town at Sakedan, along with Squam to the northeast (an eastern alliance that dated back to before the English), appears to have been the center of Indian protest on Nantucket in the middle of the century. According to an English account, Sakedan contained from twenty-eight to thirty families, with between 1,000 to 2,500 acres at their disposal. In addition to a church (whose timber frame dated back to the end of the previous century), there was a structure that Quaab describes as "made by our forefathers...for the town's use or for their sachem" around which the rest of the Sakedan Indians had "agreed to set their houses"–probably a mixture of wigwams and English-style structures.

Providing a potential glimpse into what this sachem's house was like is a legend from the Vineyard describing a "noble Indian residence" at Gay Head: "'Twas dug in the side of a hill, with a warm southern exposure, walled up with stones, well roofed with wreckage from the sea.... The floor was of beautifully pounded earth, kept in a fine state of firmness and black polish by constant sweeping." It was in such structures that Nantucket's Indians met to discuss the issues that concerned them, exerting a degree of control over their own culture and destiny that cannot be effectively measured by the patchwork of documents available to us today.

Rather than simply being passive servants to the English, Quaab and the people of Sakedan demonstrated that the Nantucket Indians were still a force to be reckoned with. Given their on-going disputes with the English, it is probable that the legends concerning the wars between the eastern and western Indians gained a new and inspiring immediacy with each retelling in the communal confines of the sachem's house. The legends of Maushop and their portrayal of an increasingly hostile taskmaster may have also taken on new relevance for the island's Indians.

In 1755, the English made what may have been their final attempt to silence Paul Quaab. First, Ebenezer Gardner once again successfully sued his servant for debt. Then Zephania Coffin–with corroborating testimony from the Indians Eben Corduda and John Poted–claimed that Paul Quaab had stolen "a fish boat" valued at more than £7. What makes this case more than a little suspicious is that the theft was reported to have occurred eight years earlier! Quaab was found guilty and sentenced to serve Coffin "four years for payment."

Not all Indians were locked in a covert war of petitions and accounts with the English. Many, if not most, Indians on Nantucket were too involved with the day-to-day challenges of making a living to be overly concerned with the injustices inflicted on them by the English. And besides, since whaling was one of the few non-war-related occupations open to Indians in New England, Nantucket was for many a place of genuine opportunity. In the late 1740s a significant number of off-island Indians relocated to Nantucket–a phenomenon that resulted in a temporary increase in total Indian population from approximately eight hundred to more than nine hundred.

And while whaling was the driving force behind the Nantucket economy, many, if not most, island Indians established niches that did not require them to ship out regularly on a whaler. According to the estimates of Kathleen Bragdon, two out of three male Indians on Nantucket worked in "ancillary industries on shore" rather than pull an oar on a whaleboat. This meant that the spectacular growth of whaling on Nantucket probably had less of an impact on the daily life of the island's Indians than it did on the English.

Probate records suggest that many of Nantucket's most financially successful Indians were not whalemen. From the cooper Peleg Duch to the weaver Jeremiah Netowa to the carpenters Madequecham Micah and Micah Phillips, Indians who reached the point that they could afford a house, some rudimentary furniture and a cart kept their feet firmly planted on dry land. According to Zaccheus Macy, those Indian weavers and carpenters conducted themselves "very well and precisely, and lived in very good fashion." But if the Indians were to maintain their cultural independence relative to the English, they needed what the Indians in Mashpee and Gay Head would retain well into the nineteenth century: their own lands.

In 1751, the Indian Ben Joab attempted to turn back the clock. While Nantucket's town records appear to have remained off limits to the island's Indians, the Vineyarder Enoch Coffin was perfectly willing to provide Joab with copies of the relevant Indian documents on record in Edgartown (a seat of government for both islands in the seventeenth century). Armed with a sheaf of six documents, many of them dating back to the time of Nickanoose and Wanackmamack, Joab petitioned the General Court in Boston, claiming that his people still rightfully owned at least half of Nantucket, even though the English considered almost all of it theirs. Of particular interest was an order dated June 20, 1672, from the General Court in Edgartown requiring that land on Nantucket be set aside for the island's Indians "perpetually."

By that point, it had become clear to many of the "East End Indians," as they called themselves in one petition, that the English were intent on transplanting them to the badlands in the vicinity of Miacomet, where "no corn will grow"–a move that would also make it easier for the English to round up Indians for service on whaling sloops. In this last desperate appeal to the paper trail left by their great forefather Nickanoose (whose heirs, in particular Daniel and Barnabas Spotso, had sold off almost all of the sachem's lands), the Indians attempted to save what was left of their future through an appeal to the past.

Perhaps influencing this strategy was the knowledge that more than twenty years before, in 1730, the English on Nantucket had been thrown into a panic by the appearance of an Indian from Cape Cod named Joshua Jethro. Joshua, it turned out, was the grandson of Jethro, the prodigal son of Nickanoose who had left the island to live in Harwich. Since court records revealed that Nickanoose had acknowledged his son's right to half his lands, the English quickly realized that they could lose everything they had purchased from Nickanoose's on-island heirs. As a consequence they "held a parley" with Jethro and agreed to buy, according to Zaccheus Macy, "all his right, title and property." Clearly, there was no better way to get the white Nantucketers' attention than to question the validity of their deeds.

Much to the irritation of the English (who claimed that several of Joab's documents were forgeries), the General Court in Boston took the Indian challenge in 1751 extremely seriously. But it would not be until seven years later, in 1758, that a formal hearing took place on Nantucket. Since it was, according to Obed Macy, "a subject of great magnitude," the proceedings attracted more spectators than could fit in the island's court house, requiring the use of the much larger Quaker meetinghouse, capable of seating up to 1,500 people. A benign counterpart to the rumored Indian uprising that began this era of thrust and parry, it would end the Indians' claims with a decided whimper. Says Macy:

> The parties, by their deputies, were heard, the records, and other evidence adduced, and the cause ably argued on both sides. The trial lasted three or four days, and when the parties had concluded, the judge addressed them in a long and ingenious speech, wherein he explained to the Indians, clearly and explicitly, that the English had clearly and legally purchased their lands; that they had produced good and lawful records to prove the same; that these records appeared without fraud, or intention to wrong them; that they were the best records of

purchases of land of natives he had ever met with; and that it was his judgment that they should be satisfied therewith, and quietly repair to their homes. On this conclusion the court rose, the Indians withdrew, and, though not satisfied with the decision, were never very troublesome about it afterwards.

Without recourse to the General Court, there was no longer a way for the Indians to make white Nantucketers listen, let alone respond, to their demands. As the Indians clearly recognized, the official's decision had robbed them of their last bit of magic.

10

AN EMPTY IVORY CASKET

Look now at the wondrous traditional story of how this island was settled by the red-men. Thus goes the legend. In olden times an eagle swooped down upon the New England coast and carried off an infant Indian in his talons. With loud lament the parents saw their child borne out of sight over the wide waters. They resolved to follow in the same direction. Setting out in their canoes, after a perilous passage they discovered the island, and there they found an empty ivory casket,— the poor little Indian's skeleton.

–Herman Melville, Moby-Dick

In August 1763 the eagle returned. More than one hundred and fifty years after the English explorer Harlow's predatory sweep across the region, a giant bird of death revisited the island. But it did not come from across Nantucket Sound; it came from across the Atlantic.

By this point the island's Indian population had come upon very hard times–falling from around 900 in 1749 to only 358 in 1763. Although the effects of disease (such as tuberculosis) and alcohol inevitably took their toll, there is indirect evidence that significant numbers of Indians chose to move away from the island, despite its employment opportunities. As Nantucket's native population plummeted, the number of Indians in Gay Head grew by more than a hundred during this period to total 276, while Mashpee's Indian population swelled to approximately 300. Nantucket–still the most densely populated native place in New England–had become an island where an Indian might find a job, but little else.

By 1763 the English had accomplished what the Indians had long since recognized was their original objective: to relocate the majority of the native population to the west–specifically to the village of

Miacomet. Miacomet contained very little good farmland, but there was plenty of water, with Miacomet Pond and, in the eighteenth century, a northerly draining swamp, or "slough," that stretched all the way from the pond's headwaters to the harbor in the vicinity of the Creeks. From an English perspective, the site had one overwhelming advantage: it was close (but not too close) to town, which greatly facilitated the supervision of Indian servants and whalemen.

And besides, so the English claimed, by this stage the Indians were so "addicted" to rum that allowing them to maintain substantial tracts of farmland served little purpose. In 1752, Nantucket's two court-appointed "guardians unto the Indians of Nantucket," the Quakers Richard Coffin and Abishai Folger, provided this account of the "miserable care" the Indians applied to their crops: "They have so little regard to their own welfare that as soon as their corn is ripe the greater part of them for the sake of rum begin to make sale of it so that they are out of corn before the winter is past and by the spring of year the English are obliged to supply them with corn on credit or they would go nigh to perish with hunger."

As memories faded of how it had once been on Nantucket—when the island's Indians had been a numerous and potentially dangerous people—the easier it became for the English to blame the Indians' decline on the Indians. Obed Macy voiced the opinion of most English Nantucketers when he wrote "some of them were devout and seemingly religious and lived regular lives, but generally they were a loose irreligious people—given to intemperance, but never very hostile or ferocious toward the English." While in Maine during the nineteenth century, Henry David Thoreau observed how extreme poverty can erase the kinds of cultural distinctions that had once counted for so much on Nantucket: "There is, in fact, a remarkable and unexpected resemblance between the degraded savage and the lowest classes in a great city.... In the progress of degradation the distinction of races is soon lost."

Whether or not that observation applied to Nantucket's Indians, once they were concentrated in the swamplands of Miacomet they had no choice but to rely on whaling and other non-agricultural pursuits to support themselves. Although several Indian families possessed English-style houses clustered around a meetinghouse built in 1732, most of Miacomet's Indians lived in wigwams and led lives characterized by extreme poverty. But unlike Nantucket's Quakers, who seem to have turned their backs on the needs of non-Quaker islanders, the Indians took it for granted that everyone in a community had a responsibility to take care of the less fortunate. Zaccheus Macy went so far as to insist that "[t]here were no poor persons among" the Indians: "For when any of them grew old and helpless, and went to a neighbor's house, they were made welcome to stay as long as they pleased." Thus, white Nantucketers could absolve themselves of responsibility for their native neighbors.

The tendency to assume that the Indians could manage just fine on their own (even if they lived on some of the island's poorest lands) reinforced the separation of Indian and English spheres on the island–especially as the English increasingly began to look off-island for labor. By 1763 the Nantucket whale fishery had reached new and spectacular heights. The island's fleet now included more than sixty vessels that annually brought in more than 9,000 barrels of oil. Nantucket whaling sloops had made it as far north as the Davis Strait, in 1746, and as far east as the coast of Africa, in 1763. Since the Indian population on Nantucket had been more than cut in half during this period of expansion, whaling merchants were forced to seek labor not only on the Vineyard and the Cape but throughout southern New England. By 1763 the island's whaling hierarchy was already committed to a future based on off-island, not native, labor.

To say that Nantucket's Indian population–now centered in Miacomet–had become expendable would be to overstate the case, especially since the whale fishery could use all the labor it could get.

However, from the perspective of a town that wanted to spend as little time and money as possible on the poor, the new form of whaleman–who stayed on the island only long enough to find a whaleship and then spent a good deal of his earnings on rum at the end of a voyage before returning home or finding another ship–had some distinct advantages. And since increasing numbers of Indians appear to have moved off the island during this period, they, too, seem to have begun to look to Nantucket not as a home but as a way station.

As it would turn out, the migration of Indians from the island to the Vineyard and the Cape–in effect reversing the trend that had once made Nantucket an "island full of Indians"–was extremely well advised. The constriction of Nantucket's Native Americans into a ghetto-like living situation and their increasingly debased economic status soon proved catastrophic. In August 1763, 358 Indians lived on Nantucket. Six months later, 222 of them would be dead.

The story, as told, goes like this:

One day a brig from Ireland appeared at the Nantucket Bar in the vicinity of the Cliff. After a long transatlantic passage, the brig's crew seemed reluctant to leave; then, a few days after the vessel's arrival, the bodies of two women were found in the surf, having been "thrown into the sea and so drove on shore." The brig was a plague ship.

Initially, the Nantucketers suspected smallpox. Several men who had already had the disease were designated by the town to go aboard the vessel and assess the situation. They returned with some disturbing news: Instead of smallpox, it was yellow fever, a disease that had devastated Philadelphia only the year before. The selectmen subsequently ordered the captain of the brig to "throw no more dead overboard, but to bury them on the shore, for which purpose, spades and shovels were sent to them." And so, in the same area where the Indians had once struggled to bury the body of Mudturtle, Nantucketers supervised the interment of several Irish plague victims.

The selectmen also ordered an informal quarantine, determining "that no intercourse should be had between the inhabitants of the island and the people in the ship." But it was too late. Several passengers had already come ashore and taken up lodgings at the house of Joseph and Molly Quin, an Irish couple who lived in the vicinity of what is now known as Five Corners. Along the extreme southern edge of town, the area was evolving into a multicultural community comprising not only Irish but African-Americans. In the years ahead Azoreans and Cape Verdeans would be added to the mix, and by the early part of the nineteenth century the emerging village would be called New Guinea. In 1763, however, it was still known as Newtown and seems to have been as Indian as it was Irish or black. The Quin's house was known as a place where "Indians frequently resorted," and soon both Molly Quin and her Indian washerwoman, Mary Norquarta, had come down with the disease.

Quin, it was said, "had the sickness very severe and was very yellow with it, but recovered." Norquarta was quickly moved to her home in Miacomet, where she lived with the "family of the priest," and died "nine, or at the farthest, eleven days after being at the boarding house." Soon after that, people began dying in Miacomet "to an alarming degree in a short time."

Although Nantucketers have accepted this story for more than two centuries, the disease may have had nothing to do with an Irish brig. The only two contemporary accounts of the outbreak make no reference to such a vessel. The first mention of a plague ship does not appear until more than three decades after the event, providing ample opportunity for English Nantucketers—just as native Nantucketers had been doing long before them—to mix and conflate differing historic events into a single mythic narrative. No documentation has been found, either in Ireland or the United States, verifying the existence of such a ship.

As it is, there are some troubling inconsistencies in the account that has been passed down to us. As Shubael Coffin realized back in 1798, by the time the brig supposedly appeared at the Nantucket Bar, eight Indians in Miacomet had already died. When Coffin took the trouble to ask Molly Quin about her role in the outbreak of the disease, she informed him that she had never been sick and knew nothing about it. Rather than explaining the disease, the Irish brig story may be far more indicative of the degree to which English Nantucketers–like most colonists–mistrusted the Roman Catholic Irish underclass, whose numbers were beginning to increase throughout America.

Instead of the Irish, it may have been the Nantucketers themselves who introduced an epidemic to their island. As it happened, 1763 was the first year that Nantucket whaleships ventured to the west coast of Africa, where yellow fever, the disease named by English Nantucketers, is endemic. Instead of being carried by fleas or lice (the kinds of carriers that would be associated with laundry), yellow fever is transported by mosquitoes, capable of surviving a transatlantic voyage in the damp bilge of a ship or in open water containers.

It is certainly possible that yellow fever made its way into the water barrels of the Miacomet Indians. Then why didn't any of the infected mosquitoes bite any white Nantucketers, who were just as susceptible to yellow fever as the Indians? Dr. Timothy Lepore, an island physician and researcher, has theorized that instead of yellow fever, the epidemic was caused by a disease with almost identical symptoms that is transmitted by lice, not mosquitoes. Known as louse-borne relapsing fever, the disease has also been referred to as the yellow plague and yellow famine fever. Andrew Spielman, an infectious-disease expert who has done extensive work with tick-borne diseases on modern-day Nantucket, agrees that the Indian Sickness was probably louse-vectored. However, given the high death rate, Spielman is inclined to think that it was typhus–generally a far more "fulminant" disease than relapsing fever.

Whether it was typhus or louse-borne relapsing fever, the Indians' custom of picking and eating lice would have only hastened transmission of the disease. For the English, on the other hand, a louse-vectored disease would have been relatively easy to avoid. As long as it originated in Miacomet and the English did not come in direct contact with the Indians and their clothing, they would have been able to remain disease-free.

Both typhus and louse-borne relapsing fever tend to hit groups of impoverished, overcrowded people who have been afflicted by colder than normal temperatures, just the conditions that the Indians of Miacomet experienced in the spring and summer before the outbreak. As we have already seen, it was fairly common for the Nantucket Indians to suffer shortages of corn throughout the eighteenth century. The winter of 1763, however, had been worse than usual. The hardship associated with the "great scarcity of corn among the Indians" was compounded by an unusually "moist and cold" spring and summer. Severely malnourished and crowded into the wet reaches of Miacomet, Nantucket's Indians were perfect candidates for the outbreak of typhus or louse-borne relapsing fever.

Although we may never know how it was introduced to the village of Miacomet, we do know that the transmission of a louse-vectored disease is greatest in the winter months, when people tend to wash less and bundle up more. Once again, this is how it would play out among the Miacomet Indians, who were hit the hardest as the temperatures declined in the fall and winter of 1763-64.

The statistics are appalling, suggesting that the disease struck with the savagery of a virgin-soil epidemic. Of the Indians who were infected with the disease, eighty-seven percent would die–a kill ratio matched only by the plagues of 1616-19. Of the dead, seventy-five percent were adults, indicating, once again, that the native population had no antibodies for this disease.

It began with a severe headache, soon followed by a yellowing of the skin and eyes, the yellow turning to a livid white just prior to death as the sufferer lapsed into a feverish delirium. Some died in only forty-eight hours, their faces and particularly their eyes swelling "in a shocking manner"; others lasted eight or nine days, then miraculously recovered. Some had "glandular swellings" that eventually burst, the "blood and juices appearing to be highly putrid." Some people's throats were so badly swollen that they suffocated; many bled from the nose. Although the red rash commonly associated with typhus was not mentioned, one account stated that about sixty percent of the sick had "a sore to break out under the ear."

One of the first white Nantucketers to become aware of what was happening in Miacomet was Richard Mitchell. The account that follows appeared in the Nantucket *Inquirer* in 1833, and, although it may take some liberties, seems to be based on Mitchell's description of discovering Nantucket's very own Valley of Death:

> The streets of the village were deserted–the silence of the grave pervaded every habitation. [Mitchell] reached the cabin [of an Indian named Peto]. He opened the wicket and entered. The first object he beheld were the corpses of Peto and his wife nearly naked on the floor, while two little papooses clung to the necks of their dead parents and wildly conjured them to awake and provide something to eat.
>
> Mr. Mitchell lifted the children from the floor and endeavored to soothe them, but they were faint and unable to stand without support. Their cheeks were

hollow, and their sunken eyes red with weeping.

"Why did you not go to your neighbors and procure some food?" he asked.

"We did, we did," was the reply, "but they were all asleep, and would not answer us."

Mr. Mitchell knew too well what manner of sleep it was that had rendered the neighbors deaf to the supplications of the poor creatures. He looked around upon the rude furniture of the little hut, and everything bore witness that Peto and his wife had long been unable to help themselves—while the low moan of a starved cow that thrust her head in at the window filled up his idea of complete desolation and famine. He took the children in his arms and silently strode along the village where he had been accustomed to receive the fond welcome of many voices— now a ghastly cemetery of the dead. When he returned to Sherburne with the two orphans, measures were immediately taken by the whites to relieve their unfortunate neighbors.

To say that "measures" were taken seems to overstate the case. According to another account, "the sick had no medical assistance, physicians refusing to go among them." The town's doctor, Thomas Tupper, "seemed unwilling to go among the Indians in this sickness." Tupper's take on the disease was that "it was infectious like the plague in Europe" and therefore best to leave well enough alone.

It was gradually discovered, however, that the disease appeared to have no effect on the English. According to Obed Macy, "The whites, apprehensive that the disorder would spread amongst themselves, were at first cautious in approaching the sick, but they at length found that the natives only were affected by it, for how much so ever they exposed themselves, not one was taken sick." For his part Mitchell claimed to have gone "several times among the sick Indians, into their houses to carry some necessaries and victuals."

Zaccheus Macy was another white Nantucketer who attempted to help the Indians. But he did so only after taking extreme precautions, suggesting that even though it was clear that the Indians were the ones at risk, English Nantucketers kept their contact with the infected to a minimum. According to Christopher Hussey, "When the Indians were being swept away by the dreadful plague, [Macy] daily, as long as it lasted, had one or two sheep killed and cooked as Indians did, in an oven of heated stones in the ground. These he would carry to a certain place and set a flag as a signal, while he kept to the windward and waited until he saw the food taken."

When the disease appeared among Indians living in an English-style house in Polpis, a neighboring white family responded much as Zaccheus Macy had. A woman who was only a young girl at the time of the outbreak remembered how she and her mother had carried a pail of food to the edge of a stream that flowed between her house and the Indians' residence. According to Christopher Hussey, who recorded her account many years later, "For fear of taking the sickness she would put her pail by the stream, shout to the Indians, and leave."

Meanwhile, Miacomet was a horror show. Two Indians, who may or may not have been employed by the town, had the grim task of burying the dead. Filling their mouths with tobacco and rum as a precaution against infection, they entered the houses and wigwams and dragged out the bodies. Since it was just the two of them and there were so many dead, they were forced to do as best they could: "[T]hey would sometimes dig a hole near the house or wigwam and so pull the dead ones out and cover them up without putting the corpse into any coffin. Then they would set fire to the wigwam to burn up all that was left in the house."

Several observers commented on the racial nature of the disease.

Although Mitchell called it an "Irish and Indian" disease (claiming that the first Indian to die, Mary Norquarta, was "a quarter Irish"), most described it as a disease that killed only Indians. In fact, of the thirty-four who recovered (some of whom were nursed back with "nothing but Bohea tea and cranberry porridge"), many were only part Indian, while of those who died, all were, according to at least one account, full-blooded Indians. As a consequence the plague of 1763-64 became known as the "Indian Sickness."

Whether or not it amounts to a cover-up, neither the town records nor the records of Nantucket's Quaker Meeting, to which most white islanders belonged, make any mention of the Indian Sickness. Documents do, however, exist. Zaccheus Macy, for one, kept a detailed list of statistics. While 222 of 358 Indians died, thirty-four were known to have contracted the disease and recovered, while only thirty-six of those living in Miacomet never became ill. The other Indians who survived were either at sea whaling (eighteen), servants with the English (forty), or living in Madaket (eight). In October 1764, Andrew Oliver, a high-ranking colonial official who had been involved in the hearings concerning the Nantucket Indians' petitions to the General Court in the 1750s, wrote a brief report to the Royal Society in London concerning the Indian Sickness.

But the most remarkable document concerning the sickness—a list of the 222 Indians who died—was lost until 1890, when it was discovered in an eighteenth-century bible. Although the historian Alexander Starbuck determined that "its accuracy is so uncertain that it does not seem worth while to publish it," the Nantucket Indian expert Elizabeth Little thought otherwise and published a brief study of the document in 1979. According to Little, the list records the order in which the Indians died. Instead of Mary Norquarta, the washerwoman whom Mitchell claimed was the plague's first victim (and who does not appear anywhere in the document), the list begins with Sarah Tashma, or Tashama, a member of one of Miacomet's foremost families. Before the sickness had run its course, three more Tashamas (John, Christian, and Abigail) would be dead.

Susanna Ease was the second person to die. (Five more Eases would die.) Abigail Titus was the third. (Seven Tituses would die.) A total of forty-six families are represented in the list, including the names of Quaab (four dead), Punkin (six), Sampson (five), Secunet (three), Saul (five), Netowa (six), Never (seven), Panchama (seven), Micah (six), Monkey (two), Paupamo (seven), Jethro (four), Pock (two), Aaron (six), Boney (four), Corduda (three), Dingel (two), Smugg (five), Spotso (nine), Taster (seven), Easake (two), Toddy (seven), and Woosoo (three). There are also forty-six individuals listed, including the grandmother Abram Quary would never know, recorded as "Jo Quadys wife."

Whatever the disease was, the fact that it did not spread beyond the Indian population is testimony to the impermeability of the boundary between English and Indian Nantucketers. Only because white Nantucketers had been so successful in insulating themselves, culturally as well as physically, from the island's Native American settlement did they not fall victim to the Indian Sickness of 1763-64.

Still, there were some extremely close calls. According to one account, some of the Indian servants who were "livers among the English" came down with the sickness (perhaps after visiting friends and family in Miacomet) while in the homes of their masters. Instead of being whisked back to Miacomet, they remained "in the houses they lived in and were not removed before they died." As long as the Indians did not transport any infected lice into their masters' houses, the English were safe from the disease, even as their servants sickened and died before their eyes.

At one point, an Indian appeared at the door of a house on Orange Street, not far from Stone Alley, to pay a debt he owed to a Mrs. Gardner. According to a tradition recorded by Christopher Hussey, "He said, 'I want to settle with you, Mrs. Gardner, for I shall not live long.' She tried in vain to dissuade him from this feeling. 'I see it,' he said, 'under my finger nails. I feel it all over. The Great Spirit has shown it to me.' The business was settled with much kindness and he started for his home at Squam Head, about nine miles away, at the east end of the island, but did not reach there, his prediction being fulfilled at a wigwam on the way."

Whatever the disease was, it created a chilling scenario: two peoples sharing an island, even sharing a home, and only one of those peoples being struck down by what the English assumed to be the hand of God. Recorded Christopher Starbuck: "upon the whole it was very wonderful and remarkable.... That it did not spread among the white people here may at least serve to show us that the works of the Almighty are beyond our comprehension and what human knowledge cannot foresee or prevent."

Given that a significant number of native Nantucketers appear to have moved off the island prior to and after the outbreak, it was only a matter of time before the disease followed them to Gay Head and Mashpee. In December 1763 it appeared on the Vineyard, where, according to Oliver's 1764 report, "[i]t went through every family, into which it came, not one escaping it: fifty-two Indians had it, thirty-nine of whom died; those, who recovered, were chiefly the younger sort." The sickness also appeared in Mashpee where, according to church records, Sam Pognit and "the squaw from Nantucket" introduced "yellow fever." For whatever reason, the touch of the disease was relatively light in Mashpee, killing only five Indians. Almost a hundred and fifty years after the plague of 1616-19, the island that had once served as a refuge had become the source of a disease that would ultimately kill close to thirty percent of the Native Americans on the Cape and islands.

On February sixteenth, the Indian Sickness on Nantucket "ceased as suddenly as it commenced." According to Obed Macy, "for on the evening preceding the date...there was no apparent abatement of the disease, but on the following morning all the sick were convalescent throughout their different places of abode." Without a human population of sufficient size and density, a disease such as typhus or relapsing fever (sometimes referred to as "crowd diseases") cannot sustain itself and disappears relatively quickly. With 222 of 358 Indians dead, Nantucket seems to have reached that point on February 16, 1764. In just over a century, Nantucket's Indian population had dropped from approximately 3,000 to 136.

Then, four months later, in June 1764, the bluefish that had been coming to the island's waters since time immemorial failed to appear. According to Benjamin Franklin Folger (as quoted by the novelist Joseph Hart), the Indians issued a prophecy. But it was also a curse, a curse that would one day search out the very Quakers who were still thanking the Lord as late as 1798 for their deliverance:

> The superstitious natives looked upon the unaccountable disappearance of the bluefish, which previously they had caught in immense numbers, as the sure forerunner of the total extinction of their Indian race.... "But," said they in bitterness, "when our fire is extinguished, and our wigwams have become razed, then the bluefish will return. Then let the shad-belly and the long-tail, (as they call the Quakers,) look out for HIS dwelling and his landmarks, and that the stranger wrest not his inheritance from him as he has wrested ours from us!"

It was the prophecy of Roqua all over again, but this time it included the whites. If the Indian Sickness had killed with what must have seemed a Divinely directed selectivity, God's wrath worked in even more mysterious ways when it came to English Nantucketers, a people who would never completely emerge from the shadow that had fallen across the island on August 16, 1763.

11

WHILE THE BLUEFISH WERE GONE

[As the Pequod *sinks beneath the waves, the Indian Tashtego–per Ahab's orders–hammers a red flag to the masthead.] A sky-hawk that tauntingly had followed the main-truck downwards from its natural home among the stars, pecking at the flag, and incommoding Tashtego there; this bird now chanced to intercept its broad fluttering wing between the hammer and the wood; and simultaneously feeling the ethereal thrill, the submerged savage beneath, in his death-grasp, kept his hammer frozen there; and so the bird of heaven, with archangelic shrieks, and his imperial beak thrust upwards, and his whole captive form folded in the flag of Ahab, went down with his ship....*

–Herman Melville, Moby-Dick

With the disappearance of the bluefish, the countdown began. As far as just about everyone on Nantucket was concerned, it was only a matter of time before the 136 survivors of the Indian Sickness had diminished to zero. A few years after the epidemic, Hector St. John de Crèvecoeur visited the island and recorded that a small group of Indians "still live together in decent houses along the shores of Miacomet pond." But Crèvecoeur saw the writing on the wall: "They are hastening towards a total annihilation, and this may be perhaps the last compliment that will ever be paid them by any traveler."

But it would not be the last. In 1775, Mary Holyoke wrote of a day trip "to a part of the island called Shimmer where a number of Indians live." Here she enjoyed what would be an ancient Nantucket tradition by the middle of the nineteenth century: "They treated us...with roasted Paqwaws (a sort of clam)."

In June of 1781, the itinerant Quaker George Churchman recorded that the Indians "had been observed greatly to decrease." In 1792 the elderly Zaccheus Macy reported to the Massachusetts Historical Society that there were only sixteen Indian women and four men remaining on the island. During his visit to the island in 1807, James Freeman noted that it had dropped to six women and two men.

By then, Obed Macy was keeping careful track of Nantucket's remaining Indian population, which had fallen to only five Indian women after the deaths of Isaac Tashama, Joshua Chogin, and Peter Micah in 1801. In 1817 both Mary Abel and Abigail Derrick passed away, followed the next year by Elizabeth Mingo. In 1821, Sarah Tashama died at the age of seventy-five and then, on January 20, 1822, Abigail Jethro, whom Macy described as "the last survivor of the Indian race belonging here," died.

By focusing on only full-blooded Indians, white Nantucketers placed a premature end point to a culture that continued to exist on the island well after the death of Abigail Jethro. As we have already seen, Abram Quary and Dorcas Honorable (daughter of Sarah Tashama) would carry forward Nantucket's Indian traditions for many years to come. However, it cannot be denied that the Indian Sickness of 1763-64 marked the end of something—something that English Nantucketers began to appreciate and record only after the bluefish were gone.

One of the Indians to survive the sickness was the minister and schoolteacher Benjamin Tashama. He may have escaped for a simple reason: his house was located not in Miacomet but to the east, on a rise of land (known as Tashama's Island) amid Gibbs Swamp—not far from Philip's Run, the stream that flows to the southeast to Tom Nevers Pond. Just to the north of the fifth mile marker on Milestone Road, he owned a small house, a dilapidated barn (described as a "hovel" in probate records), a cow, a horse, and a cart. He also owned a set of twelve chairs that were probably used for his young Indian pupils.

To the northeast of Tashama's home was a ghost town. Sakedan Indian Town (otherwise known as Occawa) had disbanded long ago, with only the empty church, the first timber-framed house of worship built on the island, left standing. Whether or not it was true on Nantucket, there were old Indian churches in both Gay Head and Rhode Island where at night passersby heard the ghostly sounds of singing. In 1770, the year of Tashama's death, Peleg Swain moved the church into town where it served as a "dwelling house" until 1838.

Tashama was widely credited with being the one who held his community together in the terrible aftermath of the Indian Sickness. In 1834, about the time that the bluefish would return, Joseph Hart, an off-islander with some strong Nantucket connections, published a historical novel entitled *Miriam Coffin, or the Whalefishermen,* which contains some detailed descriptions of Tashama. Although he adopted the mode of fiction, Hart (whose mother was a Coleman) based his story on extensive research conducted on Nantucket when he interviewed several people who had been alive prior to the Revolution, the period in which the novel is set. At one point Hart says, "There are a few aged people still living at Nantucket...who remember the old chief Tashama, and will attest that there is but little romance in the faint outline here given of his occupations." Hart may be guilty of taking certain novelistic liberties, but he has left us with one of the best descriptions of Indian life on Nantucket that we have.

Hart describes in detail the village in which Tashama lives, conflating several historical Indian sites (Miacomet, Squatesit, Occawa, Wannasquam, etc.) into the "hamlet" of Eat-Fire Spring, borrowing the romantic name from an actual location along the eastern edge of Polpis Harbor. Hart's village of twelve wigwams is clustered around

a spring and a large weeping willow; a "small garden patch" surrounds each wigwam. Inside, Tashama's wigwam is more English
than it is Indian. A wall divides the dwelling into two rooms that
include a pine dresser and a variety of "mugs, pans, and platters, of tin
and pewter" beside "wooden bowls...of red cedar, together with pails
and buckets of native manufacture," a description largely borne out
by probate records. In addition to a loom, the wigwam contains beds
"covered with sheets and counterpanes of incomparable whiteness."
The wigwam's earth floor is covered with a green carpet "woven of
the broad flag-leaf found in all swampy grounds." According to Hart,
"The only things which in any way betrayed the nationality of the
indwellers, were an ancient calumet, or council-pipe, crossing the
stem of a rude arrow, tipped with a sharp angular piece of semi-trans-
parent stone; and both were secured against the slight ceiling over
the mantel piece."

Not far from Tashama's wigwam is the "Indian schoolhouse,"
where the schoolmaster himself is surrounded by "some twenty
Indian boys and girls." According to Hart, "Each of the little urchins
was provided with a convenient board upon which a paper had been
pasted, containing numerous combinations of words in the Indian
tongue. These were illustrated by sensible signs or pictures." Hart
claims that Tashama "had nourished the vain hope of
preserving...the language of his people in its pristine purity" and that
his "numerous books and lessons were all in manuscript." If this is
true, if the collected writings of a Nantucket Indian did once exist, it
is an incalculable loss. Remarks Hart, "it is to be regretted that the
printer was never called in to aid in their preservation."

Benjamin Tashama may have provided a kind of final refuge for
a people blighted by, in Hart's words, "withering decay," but there
was another side to Nantucket's Indian legacy that was anything
but peaceful and retiring. And where Tashama may have attempted to preserve his people's language in its original "purity," he

knew full well that (despite what white Nantucketers such as Obed Macy might think) to be an Indian on Nantucket no longer involved racial purity.

For years, Nantucket Indians had been intermarrying with other groups. In the beginning and throughout the eighteenth century, it was with Indians from beyond their island. According to Crèvecoeur, Indians from the mainland "came over to the Vineyard [and Nantucket] to reunite themselves with such societies of their countrymen as would receive them." Even those Indians who only came to Nantucket "on business" inevitably interacted with the island's own native community. In 1770 eight Pequot Indians were sent by the labor agent Oliver Smith of Stonington for service on the whaleships of Nantucket's William Rotch, with one of them, Benjamin Charles, landing in court for "beating a squaw."

Increasingly, however, as the number of Indians not only on Nantucket but throughout southern New England continued to decline, Nantucket's Native Americans intermarried with other racial groups. By the Indian Sickness of 1763-64, there were Nantucket Indians with Dutch and Irish blood in their veins. In this regard, it is no accident that surnames such as Mooney, Egin, Hoite (Zachary Hoite had been Tashama's predecessor as minister at Miacomet), and Duch were common among the island's Indians.

Members of Nantucket's leading English families also contributed to the racial mix. In *Miriam Coffin*, a Quaker whaling merchant remembers having "many an innocent romp with the Indian maids" as a young man. According to a tradition also recorded in Hart's novel, Benjamin Tashama's daughter Sarah, as a consequence of one of these "innocent romps," had a child who would grow up to be Dorcas Honorable. Abram Quary, the son of Sarah Apie Quary, was also known to be half-white; whether or not it came from his father, he used the middle name of Pinkham. Whereas English-Indian intermarriages are known to have occurred on Cape Cod and the

Vineyard, none have been documented on Nantucket during the eighteenth century, a product, perhaps, of the Quakers' distinction between themselves and the "world's people."

The vast majority of Nantucket Indians intermarried with what the English termed "people of color": African Americans and, eventually, Cape Verdeans, who began to make their way to the island in growing numbers. For example, after his first wife Sarah died in the Indian Sickness, Benjamin Tashama married a black woman named Jenny. Although most referred to him as "Ben Negro," the Nantucket seaman Benjamin Walmsley (1773-1803) was a descendant of the Wampanoag sachem Massasoit. Absalom Boston, recognized as the leading member of the island's African-American community throughout the first half of the nineteenth century, was the product of a marriage between a Nantucket Indian woman named Thankful Micah and the manumitted slave Seneca.

Many Native Americans, fearful that their people's racial and cultural identities were in danger of becoming lost, viewed the mixed marriages with mounting trepidation. As late as the mid-nineteenth century, it was recorded that Indians in Gay Head were "jealous of the influence of [black] foreigners, having had much trouble with some of those who have intermarried with their women and settled amongst them."

Inevitably, the Indians' oral traditions began to reflect this anxiety. Several Gay Head legends recount the disturbing circumstances that introduced "kinky" or "snarly" hair into a formerly "straight-haired" people. In this regard, Nantucket's own monster of discord, Mudturtle (comprised of a seemingly random assortment of body parts "from the far corners of the world") was reputed to have hair that was "black, bristly [and] twisted into thongs, [giving] his head the appearance of a caulker's mop." Thus a legendary figure that may have been inspired by the arrival of Christianity on Nantucket may have acquired a new meaning (not to mention new hair) in the eighteenth century as increasing numbers of primarily black whalemen made their way to the island "from the far corners of the world."

Although the number of white off-islanders on Nantucket whale-ships would take a momentary jump in the years prior to the Revolution, the island's past and its future depended on labor provided by "seamen of color." And given that English Nantucketers had begun whaling with almost all Indian crews, providing them with the opportunity to develop their own island-based brand of labor control, Nantucket was better prepared than most New England towns for handling this diverse workforce.

White Nantucketers viewed the form of servitude that had evolved on the island as a kind of work-release program for a people who would otherwise be in jail or the poorhouse. In *Miriam Coffin*, a whaling merchant explains,

> To keep [the Indians] from becoming a charge to the town, when they refuse to work for the support of their squaws and papooses, the s'lackmen send them aboard the whale-ships, where they are compelled to earn a share of the cargo equal to that of any other mariner afore-the-mast. They possess a dogged disposition, and will endure much hard labor at sea without complaining. To be sure, they skulk a great deal; but, in pulling the oar in a whaleboat, when the eye of the mate or boat-steerer is upon them, they do their duty well enough.

But as we have seen, what worked as an effective system of labor control for white Nantucketers had a disastrous cumulative effect on the Indians, creating a legacy of degradation that would continue to impact the Indians of Mashpee and Martha's Vineyard for many years to come. In 1818 the court-appointed guardians of the Chappaquiddick Indians (whose Tomokommoth forefathers had also

traveled to Nantucket to whale, but under extremely different circumstances) provided this account:

> It is not uncommon for [the Indians] to go to
> Nantucket to engage on a whaling voyage around
> Cape Horn, sell half their voyage profit for half its
> probable value to furnish themselves with clothing,
> then a quarter for money to spend in liquor, and then
> an eighth to another [and] so on that when they
> return from the voyage they have not a cent to
> receive and are often in debt....

What had once been rationalized as a way to keep the island's own
Indian community in line had evolved into a region-wide network of
increasingly exploitative commercial relations, reaching out to the
very communities that had once looked to the island as a refuge.
While in Gay Head in 1809, Edward Kendall reported, "Ship-owners
come to [the Indians'] cottages, making them offers, and persuading
them to accept them.... [L]iquor, goods and fair words are plied, till
the Indian gets into debt, and gives his consent...hence, an Indian,
that goes to sea, is ruined, and his family is ruined with him." In 1795
Mashpee's white minister Gideon Hawley reported on how the
increasingly long voyages (two, sometimes three years) made it difficult for the whalemen to become integrated into the rhythms of daily
life: "When they come home there is little else but drinking, whoring,
fighting, etc., etc. I generally rejoice with almost all my neighbors
when they are gone again." Whaling's reach extended to the women
of Wampanoag communities throughout the region. An 1802 report
claimed that Indian women from Mashpee "go to the large sea-port
towns for months together, and serve in gentlemen's kitchens, to the
great injury of their morals."

Nantucket shipowners had long since adopted the policy of deliv-
ering Indian crewmembers as a group to a waiting whaleship. As

early as 1715 four Indians (plus an African American named Jockey) were, according to death records, "all drowned in the harbor...endeavoring to board a sloop out of a fish boat." In 1760 the whaleman Peter Folger recorded in his journal that he "went over the Bar in company with Stephen Paddack and come to anchor and waited for our Indians."

The nautical equivalent of a chain gang, this facilitated the control of what was considered to be the most difficult to control part of the workforce. According to James Freeman, "as they are more addicted to frolicking, it is difficult to get them aboard the ship, when it is about to sail, and to keep them aboard, after it has arrived." In *Miriam Coffin*, the only ones not granted a final shore leave on a whaleship are the six Indians: "The trouble of collecting these fellows again;–for it was believed they would not voluntarily return,–was the reason assigned for the denial to them of a few hours' liberty ashore. They formed a mess by themselves."

In October 1767, just such a mess of Indians–detained on board the schooner *Sally* after a whaling voyage–erupted into the kind of rum-induced violence that, as we have already seen, so often afflicted Indians on Nantucket. But instead of cordwood sticks, these Indians had harpoons and lances at their disposal. At one-thirty in the morning, the seaman Robert Ellis was awakened by a cry from the Indian Robin Narre that "the Indians are killing one another." Once on deck, Ellis found Peleg Titus dying from a stab wound in the back as the Indians Nathan Quibby and John Charles stood over him with whale lances in their hands. Quibby then jumped down into the forecastle and proceeded to stab to death the Indian Isaac Jeffrey. Ellis testified in court that Quibby threw the knife he'd used overboard before Ellis was able to "confine" him. According to another witness, Quibby later claimed that Charles was "as guilty as I am."

Once they were in jail, Quibby would also murder Charles before he was finally sentenced to hang on May 26, 1768. Although clearly an exceptional and sensational case (which Hart would use to good effect in *Miriam Coffin*), Quibby's was only one of four hangings during a two-year period on Nantucket, with the Indians Tom Ichabod, Polly Clicia, and Sampson Hind also succumbing to the hangman's noose in 1769. Despite the pacifist pretensions of the island's Quaker hierarchy (who seem to have had no qualms about the use of capital punishment when meted out by others), violence was a disturbing fact of life on colonial Nantucket, as it was in ports up and down the Atlantic coast.

Although it would ultimately become mythologized into America's first strike for freedom, what became known as the Boston Massacre began under circumstances that would have been familiar to any seaman of color associated with the Nantucket whale fishery. In fact, Crispus Attucks, a giant of a man originally from Framingham who was half African-American and half Indian, was reported to have been on shore leave from a Nantucket whaler when he became the leader of a mob that John Adams later described as "a motley rabble of saucy boys, Negroes, mulattos, Irish teagues and outlandish jack-tars."

The disturbance had been sparked by a fight between some Boston laborers and some off-duty British soldiers, but as several historians have argued, colonial seamen played a pivotal role in creating the climate of protest that would eventually culminate in the American Revolution. For decades, unreasonable British impressment policies had been making the lives of American sailors, which included a significant number of Indians, a kind of living hell. Several Indian legends from Gay Head specifically mention incidents associated with the depredations of British press gangs on the island. It was no accident that the Boston mob that confronted a well-armed group of British soldiers on March 5, 1770 comprised at least twenty "outlandish jack-tars," with a black Indian whaleman at the fore.

The six-foot-two-inch Attucks took up a weapon that had long been in use among Indians on Nantucket: a cordwood stick. Wielding the stick, Attucks "threw himself in, and made a blow at the officer," crying, "Kill the dogs, knock them over." The soldiers fired, and Attucks became the first martyr to the cause of American liberty.

Five years later, a similar "riot and affray" broke out on Nantucket only a few weeks after the start of the Revolution at Lexington and Concord. The only reference to the skirmish, which probably occurred in the neighborhood that would soon be called New Guinea, comes from a letter written by Abraham Williams of Sandwich who describes "some particulars I have heard about Nantucket" to Colonel Nathaniel Freeman in Watertown. According to Williams, "the Negroes and Portuguese [were] on the one side and the inhabitants on the other; in consequence whereof many of our Indians and mulattos are come off" the island to the mainland.

What were these African Americans, Cape Verdeans, Indians, and mulattos rioting against–and why did many of them decide to leave the island? As New Englanders to the north rallied around the cause of freedom, the island's seamen of color may have taken a stand against Nantucket's version of impressment: the shipowner's willingness to use debt, alcohol, and even force to recruit Indian and black whalemen. Thirty-seven years after the rumored Indian uprising and thirteen years after the court decision that had ended the Indians' attempts to retake their lands, the spirit of protest lived on among Nantucket's people of color.

In the late 1820s, an itinerant Pequot minister named William Apess spoke on Nantucket, probably at the African Meeting House at the center of what was now called New Guinea. Apess would eventually end up in Mashpee, where in 1833 he helped draft a petition protesting the discriminatory practices of the Indians' guardians and white Congregational minister. Soon after, Apess–much like Nantucket's foremost Indian petitioner, Paul Quaab–prevented some white men from cutting wood on Mashpee Indian lands. (Instead of being sentenced to servitude on a whaleship, Apess spent thirty days in jail.) Known as the "Woodland Revolt," the publicity generated by Apess's actions was instrumental in winning the establishment of the Indian District of Mashpee–an autonomous enclave–in 1834. One cannot help but wonder if a similar victory on Nantucket in the eighteenth century might have allowed for the preservation of the island's own Native American community and culture.

In the meantime, the spirit of protest remained alive and well on Nantucket. New Guinea's leading African-American citizen was the former whaling captain, Absalom Boston, whose mother was a Nantucket Indian named Thankful Micah. In the 1840s, Boston's daughter Phebe and another black girl, Eunice Ross, were denied access to Nantucket's all-white high school. The denial instigated a sometimes bitterly fought campaign to desegregate the island's schools, culminating in the boycott of the African School–perhaps the first instance of a black boycott in the United States. The result was that Nantucket, in 1847, became one of the first towns in America to open its public schools to children of all races. Given that Absalom Boston's daughter Phebe was at least a quarter Indian, this historic desegregation decision might also be viewed as the culmination of a tradition of Native American protest on Nantucket that dated back to the subversive legends of Maushop.

In Paul Revere's engraving of the Boston Massacre, it was thought prudent to give Crispus Attucks a white face. Meanwhile, back on Nantucket, something very similar had happened. As the Indians either died or, like Absalom Boston, disappeared into the African-

American community, white Nantucketers were free to claim what had been largely a native whaling legacy as wholly their own.

By the time the whale fishery had entered its most spectacular era in the Pacific Ocean, the Nantucket whaleman had become as much an explorer as he was a hunter of whales–discovering uncharted islands on an almost daily basis. This meant that just as the fishery was losing touch with the Indians who had literally brought it into being a century before, yet another group of native people was coming into its orbit. Two hundred years after Harlow first landed on Nantucket, a circle was being turned.

In many instances, a Nantucket whaleman was the first white man a South Sea Islander (whom the Nantucketer called a "Kanaka") ever saw. A typical encounter is reported by the Nantucket *Inquirer* in March 1828:

> Capt. Joshua Coffin, 2d of the ship *Ganges*, of this place, in his last cruise in the Pacific Ocean, discovered four islands not laid down on his charts.... They were inhabited, and the natives came along side with canoes loaded with coconuts, etc. One of the natives stole a hatchet from the Ganges, and after he got into his canoe, and having manifested an unwillingness to return it, Capt. C. discharged a pistol at some distance over the heads of the natives in their canoes, when they all fell as instantly as if they had received an electric shock; and after lying apparently lifeless for a short time, they all started up, seized their paddles, and rowed off with an astonishing velocity. The natives probably had no knowledge of firearms.

A first-hand account of Harlow's use of "English guns" during his brief appearance on Nantucket in 1611 might have made for similar reading.

And just as Harlow had returned with a handful of natives to England, so was it only a matter of time before Polynesians began to appear on Nantucket. Taking up where the New England Company had left off in its support of the missionary efforts of the Mayhews and others, the island's Congregational Church included seven "natives of the Sandwich Islands" in its Sunday school in April 1822. That same year it was reported in a Boston newspaper that Nantucket had "long been the resort of youth from pagan countries" who regularly transformed the streets into a kind of New England Oahu by erecting "ensigned idols" before which they "in frantic orgies paid their homage to the Host of Heaven." Thus, Nantucket's tradition of native worship–Christian as well as "heathen"–was reestablished just as the island's own native people lost their last fullblooded representative.

It was also a time of unsettling transition for the island's white population. As the Indians had predicted after the sickness of 1763-64, white Nantucketers were suffering sea changes of their own. By the 1820s, the effects of two wars and the increased scope of the whale fishery had introduced traumatic change to the island. According to Obed Macy, "The great success in whaling…had no tendency to lessen the immoralities which were unhappily introduced into society."

When the bluefish returned some time between the death of Abigail Jethro in 1822 and the publication of *Miriam Coffin* in 1834, it was an event that Benjamin Franklin Folger, who makes a cameo appearance in Hart's novel, saw as announcing the demise of not one but two peoples. If the Indians' culture was on the brink of extinction, so was the world of the island's first white settlers as a relentless series of schisms fractured Nantucket's once dominant Quaker identity into a confusion of feuding sects. Says Folger, "The lineal descendants of the original proprietors are scattered over the world, and are disappearing from among us before the face of the strangers who have

Fig. 53
Paul Revere's engraving of the Boston Massacre of March 5, 1770. The first to die in this pivotal event was Crispus Attucks, an Indian-African American who was, according to one account, on shore leave from a Nantucket whaleship. In the engraving Attucks is depicted as white. *Courtesy of the National Gallery of Art, Rosenwald Collection.*

Fig. 54
Thirty-five years after a rumored Indian uprising on Nantucket, in which it was feared that native whalemen would "do their part by destroying the English on the seas," colonial dissidents disguised themselves as Indians in what became known as the Boston Tea Party of 1773–an incident that involved two vessels from Nantucket. From *The American Magazine of Useful Knowledge, 1840.*

Fig. 55
Although listed in Nantucket census records as a black seaman, Samson Dyer–shown here in a China Trade painting by the artist Spoilum, circa 1805–may have also been part Native American, as were many members of the African-American community on Nantucket in the nineteenth century. *Photo by Jack Weinhold, courtesy of the Nantucket Historical Association. Private collection.*

Fig. 56
After preaching on Nantucket, William Apess, shown here in a painting by Mura Booker Johnson, moved to Mashpee where in 1833 he led what became known as the Woodland Revolt. *Photo by Alicja Mann. Courtesy of Mashpee Wampanoag Indian Museum.*

Fig. 57
Both a whaling captain and leader of a successful campaign to integrate Nantucket's public school system, Absalom Boston was as Native American as he was African American, with an Indian mother named Thankful Micah. *Courtesy of the Nantucket Historical Association.*

Fig. 58
Figurehead of Awashonks, squaw sachem of Sakonnet, from a whaleship of the same name built in 1830. Sakonnet was where the legendary giant Maushop was reputed to have thrown his wife Squant, where she turned into a stone. *Old Dartmouth Historical Society-New Bedford Whaling Museum.*

Fig. 66
Descendants of Nickanoose on the deck of New Bedford's last whaleship. Russell Gardner, Wampanoag Tribal Historian, can trace his ancestry to Nickanoose, a seventeenth-century Nantucket sachem, and he is shown here in 1930 with his parents and a family friend (center) on the deck of the *Charles W. Morgan* when it was berthed at the Green Estate in South Dartmouth, Massachusetts. Gardner is also descended from sachems on Cape Cod and the Vineyard. *Collection of Russell Gardner.*

Fig. 67
Russell Gardner, or Great Moose, poses beside the Indian Burial Ground marker at Miacomet, Nantucket, in 1995. *Collection of Russell Gardner.*

Fig. 68
The late John Peters, or Slow Turtle, Wampanoag Tribal Medicine Man and Executive Director of the Massachusetts Commission of Indian Affairs, with the author, Nathaniel Philbrick, on Nantucket in 1995. *Collection of Russell Gardner.*

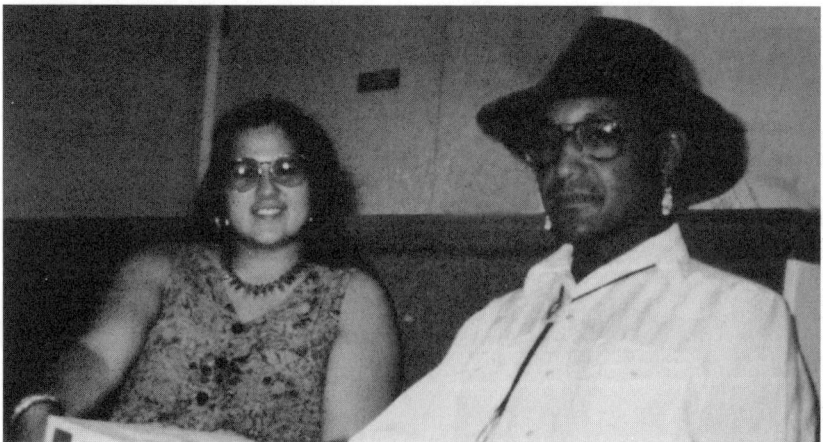

Fig. 69
The late Tony Pollard, or Nanepashamet, curator of Plimoth Plantation's Wampanoag Indian Program, and his wife Julie Marden, grand-niece of Lorenzo Jeffers, Supreme Sachem of the Wampanoag Tribe, 1960-74. They are shown here in 1995 (only a few months before Nanepashamet's death), when they, along with John Peters and Russell Gardner, attended a Native American symposium sponsored by the Nantucket Historical Association. *Collection of Russell Gardner.*

Fig. 70
One of the few acknowledgments of Nantucket's Native American past is the sign at the Overlook Hotel, where each room is named for an island Indian location. *Photo by Margaret S. Moore.*

Fig. 71
The man who killed Moby Dick: At the beginning of the twentieth century, Amos Smalley, a Gay Head Wampanoag (shown here beside Maushop's den near the Gay Head Cliffs), harpooned a white whale that was estimated to have been more than a hundred years old. *Courtesy of the Martha's Vineyard Historical Society.*

Fig. 72
This tribal logo memorializes the legendary Native American giant, Maushop, creator of Nantucket. *Courtesy of the Wampanoag Tribe of Gay Head (Aquinnah), Massachusetts.*

come into the isle.... [N]ot a single custom of our ancestors is adhered to in its ancient purity,–all–all is giving way before the spirit of innovation that now stalks abroad in the island."

It was at this moment in the island's history that Samuel Jenks, editor of the Nantucket *Inquirer*, published the legend of Mudturtle. Just as the Indians' oral traditions had evolved to accommodate changing historical circumstances, so was it inevitable that Jenks's account of Mudturtle should reflect the times in which the newspaper editor lived, times that had seen the virtual demise of Nantucket's native culture. Unlike today, there were still, in 1827, "very satisfactory indications" of the island's Indian past. According to Jenks, "The ruins of their encampments, and the remains of their cemeteries may still be traced in remote and deserted spots, where the curious wanderer may find vast masses of broken shells, and fragments of rude pottery, half buried in the shifting sands, or bleaching on the surface–with now and then an arrowhead of stone, or some dilapidated instrument of mischief." Instead of being hidden beneath the ground, remnants of the island's Indian culture were there for all to see.

In the legend recorded by Jenks, Mudturtle is buried a total of four times in front of his shoreside cave to the west of Brant Point. As the horror that will not go away, Mudturtle might be seen as a creature of survivor guilt, symbolizing a Native American legacy that was far more messy and catastrophic and lingering than most people on this increasingly image-conscious island would have liked. It was in an attempt to close the door on this legacy that Nantucketers transformed Abram Quary into their very own "last Indian."

According to Joseph Hart, whose best-selling novel made Abram a national celebrity: "He is THE LAST of the Indian race.... Without known relative upon the face of the earth, he wanders about the island an object of curiosity." The next step for white Nantucket was to incorporate the myth of the island's "last Indian" into its own rosy, self-serving version of the island's past. Some time after Quary's death in the town's poorhouse on November 25, 1854, an anonymous Nantucketer recorded what would become the party line when it came to the island's Indians:

> The relations that existed between the settlers of Nantucket and the Indians were amicable and the land which the whites bought in nearly every case was honestly paid for. They entered into one another's councils and the whites tried to educate and civilize them. So far as Christianizing them to the faith of the Gospel was concerned, the persevering Quakers succeeded better here than anywhere else. But all efforts were in vain, the race was doomed to perish. One by one they departed to the happy hunting grounds, there nevermore to be disturbed. In 1822 the last full-blooded Indian wrapped his blanket around him and slept with his fathers, which was less than two centuries and a quarter from the discovery of the island. In 1854 Abram Quary at the age of eighty-two passed peacefully away. In this man's veins ran the last drop of Indian blood, a once happy and prosperous people.

This simple, tidy myth of extinction enabled white Nantucketers to wish away the complexities of the island's Native American legacy. Sanitized of conflict, the myth casts the Indians as passive zombies. But as we have seen, Nantucket's Indians were anything but passive. From the diplomatic machinations of Nickanoose to the eloquent protests of Paul Quaab, native Nantucketers insisted on being heard. And as we have also seen, Nantucket's Quakers were hardly good Samaritans; they were, in Herman Melville's words, "Quakers with a vengeance" whose motivation, at least when it came to the Indians, was almost wholly materialistic. It is no accident that so many Nantucket Indians in the second half of the eighteenth century chose to relocate to the Vineyard and the Cape, beyond the ferocious undertow of the whale fishery.

It is also important to recognize that a remarkable partnership had been established in the early years of the fishery, a partnership that would have a lasting impact on the region. For it was the Indian-English Nantucket whale fishery that ultimately brought together the racial mixture–Native American, Dutch, English, African American, Irish, Cape Verdean, Polynesian, etc.–that flows through the veins of Indians throughout southeastern New England to this day.

No matter what white Nantucketers in the second half of the nineteenth century might have said, there was never a last Nantucket Indian. As late as 1944 John Barreau wrote to the Nantucket *Inquirer and Mirror* wondering why Abram Quary "is credited by many as being the last man with Indian blood in him." Barreau reported that he had "met several [on the island] who claim to trace Indian lineage." There are Native Americans today in Mashpee, Gay Head, and elsewhere who are descended from Nantucket Indians. For example, Wampanoag Tribal Historian Russell Gardner, or Great Moose, from the area of Middleborough, Massachusetts, can trace his ancestry to the great eastern sachem Nickanoose.

At some point, however, Nantucket lost a living, on-island connection to its Native American past. When John Peters, the Wampanoag Tribal Medicine Man who died in October 1997, came to Nantucket, it was, in more cases than not, to inspect the dead. As executive director of the Massachusetts Commission of Indian Affairs, Peters (who also went by the name of Slow Turtle) was called to the island whenever Native American skeletal remains were discovered. Sometimes it was more than just a skeleton.

In a curious and ironic twist of fate, when the time came for Nantucket to address the issue of affordable housing amid the real estate boom of the 1980s, the land chosen was the sandy, poorly drained area of Miacomet. It was here on December 21, 1987, that a plumber digging a trench uncovered evidence of the long-lost Indian Burial Ground dating to before the Indian Sickness of 1763-64.

In 1992, another Indian burial ground was discovered in Shawkemo, not far from Abram's Point. Elizabeth Little has speculated that this may have been the sacred place that Abram Quary defended more than a century and a half ago.

Nantucket, once home to the largest Native American community in the region, has returned to what it was when Maushop first followed a giant eagle in its direction: an island where only the bones remain.

EPILOGUE

PORT OF THE *Pequod*

In waters where no charts avail,
Where only fin and spout ye see,
The lonely spout of hermit-whale,
God set that isle which haunteth me.

—Herman Melville, Clarel

For Herman Melville it began on a Nantucket whaleship in 1841: the strange interpenetration of myth and experience with which this book began. Instead of an Indian wigwam, he was in the cramped confines of the forecastle. Instead of imprinting the stories of the elders in his memory, he was given a book, the narrative of the *Essex* disaster. And instead of Maushop, the once-benevolent giant who would destroy his own family before disappearing, the book told of a large sperm whale, "proverbial for its insensibility and inoffensiveness," suddenly possessed by "resentment and fury" as it repeatedly rammed and sank a Nantucket whaleship. Many years later Melville would remember: "The reading of this wondrous story upon the landless sea, and close to the very latitude of the [*Essex*] shipwreck had a surprising effect on me."

Later, of course, Melville would write *Moby-Dick*, a novel in which a ship named for a defeated Indian tribe, the *Pequod*, sets out in pursuit of a white whale. And as happened to the *Essex*, Moby Dick sinks the *Pequod*, among whose crew is the Gay Head Wampanoag, Tashtego.

In 1901, half a century after the publication of *Moby-Dick*, a twenty-five-year-old Gay Head Indian named Amos Smalley shipped out of New Bedford on the bark *Platina*. While cruising off the Azores, the crew encountered a large albino sperm whale, which Smalley subsequently harpooned and killed with a bomb lance. More than ninety feet long, the whale was estimated to be between a hundred and two hundred years old by the bark's captain, Thomas McKenzie.

Not until thirty-five years later, when a history professor named Marcus Jernegan made the trip out to Smalley's house in Gay Head and asked him about his experiences, did the Indian learn about Melville's mythical whale: "From him I heard the story that whalers used to tell some fifty years before my time of a white sperm whale that raged around the Pacific and was more ferocious than anything ever met on land or sea." Word quickly spread that "Uncle Amos" (as he was affectionately known on the Vineyard) had killed Moby Dick.

In 1956 Smalley was invited to the premier of John Houston's film version of Melville's novel, where he shook hands with Hollywood's Ahab, Gregory Peck. In 1957 an article (credited to "Amos Smalley as told to Max Eastman") appeared in *Reader's Digest* entitled "I Killed 'Moby Dick.'" In November of that year, Smalley appeared on the television show "I've Got a Secret." All of America had been given a lesson in the reality of mythic thinking.

In 1981–three years after the Mashpee Wampanoag were denied federal recognition as a tribe (a status later conferred on the Gay Head Wampanoag)–the anthropologist William Simmons sat down with a Mashpee woman named Nosapocket who told him a story about Maushop. According to Nosapocket, the Creator changed Maushop into a white whale named Moby Dick after the giant unduly pampered the people of Gay Head "by doing many of their labors [so] that they themselves became lazy." After describing Maushop's emotional farewell to the Gay Head Indians, Nosapocket related how "I met a fellow named Amos Smalley when I was younger, and he told me that he was the one that killed the Moby Dick. He was a very old gentleman when I met him...he was an

Aquinnah Wampanoag, Gay Head.... And it could have only been a Wampanoag, in my mind, that could have killed a Moby Dick, sought after by so many whalers."

As Nosapocket (who today has a web page on the Internet) makes clear in other stories, Smalley did not so much kill Maushop as become the vehicle for a change in the giant's "state of being." (Maushop has appeared to Nosapocket in the form of a small green bird; for a Maushop legend told by Russell Gardner, or Great Moose, which accounts for events that occurred as recently as 1992, see the Notes.) More than 360 years after he was supposed to have left them, Maushop lives on in the legends of his people, legends whose symbolic meanings remain firmly rooted to the real, ever-changing world.

Today on Martha's Vineyard, the Gay Head Wampanoag are thriving. Now that they have gained federal recognition, more and more people are returning to the tribe, whose numbers have increased to almost eight hundred, with more than three-hundred living on the Vineyard. A brand-new, state-of-the-art tribal office, along with an affordable housing complex with units that resemble traditional long houses yet boast all the modern amenities, sprawl across a rolling hillside overlooking the Atlantic. Each year, a pageant based on the story of Maushop is reenacted on an outdoor stage beside the tribal office. The new tribal logo shows the giant proudly holding up a whale by its flukes beside the Gay Head cliffs–a far cry from the Massachusetts Bay Seal of 1629 in which an Indian (possibly based on Nantucket's very own Sakaweston) says, "Come over and help us." In the spring of 1997, the town of Gay Head voted to change its name back to the original Aquinnah.

On July 6, 1852, less than a year after the publication of his whaling masterpiece, Herman Melville visited Nantucket for the first time.

During his stay on the island, Melville traveled to the fishing village of Siasconset, to the new lighthouse at Sankaty Head, and had dinner with the astronomer Maria Mitchell and her parents. At some point he also met George Pollard, captain of the ill-fated *Essex*, whose home was just across the street from Melville's hotel at the present-day Jared Coffin House. Although we have no proof that Melville visited the town's Atheneum, it is difficult to believe that he did not make a point of exploring its collection. In addition to a library and the newly hung portrait of Abram Quary, the Greek revival building housed a growing assortment of artifacts from the South Seas.

And besides, Melville had already read about Nantucket's last Indian in *Miriam Coffin*, an important source for *Moby-Dick*. It is also possible that his father-in-law and traveling companion, Justice Lemuel Shaw, told him about the time when Abram was hauled into court for threatening to shoot the trinket gatherers. Maybe, just maybe, Melville even made his way out to Abram's house in Shimmo. But instead of a frail recluse, whose white flag might be interpreted as a signal of surrender, the thirty-two-year-old novelist found something else.

More than twenty years later Melville would publish a long meditative poem called *Clarel* about a pilgrimage to the Holy Land that resonates with references to Nantucket, the Holy Land of *Moby-Dick*. In the pivotal, final section of the poem, there is the character of Ungar, an Indian. Like Abram, Ungar is of mixed parentage, with an "Anglo brain, but Indian heart." Whether or not Melville had read Captain John Smith's account of Harlow's voyage to Nohono, Ungar is, like the Nantucket captive, Sakaweston, a mercenary. More to the point, Ungar looks very much like the Anglo-Indian in the Atheneum painting:

> His shoulders lithe
> Were long-sloped and yet ample, too,
> In keeping with each limb and thew:

Waist flexile as a willow withe;
Withal, a slouched reserve of strength,
As in the pard's luxurious length;
The cheek, high-boned, of copperish show
Enhanced by sun on land and seas;
Long hair, much like a Cherokee's,
Curving behind the ear in flow [and]...
Brown eyes, what reveries they keep–
Sad woods they be, where wild things sleep.

Here Melville grants the Quary portrait the power of speech. And, as one might expect given Quary's known willingness to take up arms against white trinket gatherers–not to mention the grim irony of having your portrait placed beside an exhibit of native "trinkets" collected by Nantucketers in the South Pacific–Melville's last Indian is not happy with the way things have turned out.

In the midst of a wide-ranging discussion concerning the current state of the world, Ungar lashes out against the "Anglo-Saxons" and their depredations in the "New World." In words that Abram Quary could have related to, Ungar labels white men "grave looters" who in the "name of Christ and Trade...[d]eflower the world's last sylvan glade." When last seen, Ungar's face has acquired "that strange look / Of one enlisted for sad fight / Upon some desperate dark shore."

Anger, fear, resignation, and, in the end, unshakable resolve: that is what Melville saw in Abram's eyes.

NOTES

Abbreviations:

HN	*Historic Nantucket* and *Proceedings of the Nantucket Historical Association*
MHS	*Massachusetts Historical Society Collections*
MA	Massachusetts Archives
NA	Nantucket Atheneum Library
NAS	*Nantucket Algonquian Studies*
NCCR	Nantucket County Court Records, 1721–85, Office of Superior Court, Nantucket
NCD	Nantucket County Deeds, Registry of Deeds, Nantucket
NCP	Nantucket County Probate Records, Probate Court, Nantucket
NHA	Nantucket Historical Association
NI	*Nantucket Inquirer* and *Inquirer and Mirror*
SCJ	Superior Court of Judicature, Court of Assize, Suffolk County
SNET	*Spirit of the New England Tribes, Indian History, and Folklore, 1620–1984*

Prologue—Abram's Eyes

The best place to start for the documentary evidence on Abram Quary is Elizabeth Little's "Abram Quary of Abram's Point, Nantucket Island," to which I am indebted. In the novel *Miriam Coffin, or the Whale-Fishermen* (1834), Joseph Hart anticipated Quary's becoming, almost twenty years later, the subject of a painting by the artist Herminia Borchard Dassel (still on display at the NA): "The lineaments of his face are those that a painter or sculptor might choose to copy after, with the certainty of transmitting to posterity an accurate and strongly marked specimen of the aboriginal countenance." In *Miriam Coffin*, Hart also states that Nantucketers refer to quahogs as "pooquaws," while J.O. Lewis in *Abraham Quary, A Sketch* (1836) describes Quary as a kind of "last Indian" exhibit: "many of his visitors come for the sole purpose of indulging in the very natural curiosity of looking upon the last of the Nantucket Indians." For a discussion of the "last Indian" phenomenon, see Robert Berkhofer, Jr.'s *The White Man's Indian: Images of the American Indian from Columbus to the Present*. According to Berkhofer, "The tragedy of the dying Indian, especially as represented by the last living member of the tribe, became a staple of American literature and art."

Phebe Coffin Hanaford (1829-1921), a noted Universalist minister, educator, and abolitionist born on Nantucket, remembered a conversation with Quary in which he "expressed sorrowful yet Christian submission to the Divine will" [Grace Brown Gardner's "Abraham Quary and his Portrait"]. The "Friends of Art" are all listed by name in the NA's Donation Book; the Quary painting was donated to the Atheneum on the condition that the trustees purchase a frame. The reference to Quary's "girl-friend" from Sandwich is in the updated introduction to J. O. Lewis's *Abraham Quary, A Sketch*. Mrs. Sturgis's account of Abram appears in Frank G. Speck, "Territorial Subdivisions and Boundaries of the Wampanoag, Massachusetts and Nauset Indians." According to Earl Mills, Sr., Chief Flying Eagle of Mashpee, Mrs. Sturgis lived to be ninety-seven and was one of ten children of Ezra and Sarah Jones Attaquin [*Son of Mashpee*]. Jean O'Brien, in *Community Dynamics in the Indian-English Town of Natick, Massachusetts, 1650-1790*, describes the "dynamics of migration" of which Quary was a part: "A network of locations with different sized Indian populations was in place in the region, and Indians frequently traveled among them. These pockets of Indian population constituted a kind of community in itself that was much larger than any one Indian town"; see also Kathleen Bragdon's *Another Tongue Brought In: An Ethnohistorical Study of Native Writings in Massachusett* for an in-depth account of the interchange among Indian communities in the region.

The anecdote concerning Abram's brush with the law is in "Miss Macy Carved Portrait of Abram Quary," New Bedford *Standard Times* (September 1, 1957). Benjamin Franklin Folger's "Story of 'Abraham Quary,' the Last Indian of Nantucket" appeared shortly after Quary's death in 1854 and is in Grace Brown Gardner scrapbook #20 at the NHA. When Henry David Thoreau was on Nantucket, he noted in his journal on December 28, 1854: "The last Indian, not of pure blood, died this very month, and I saw his picture with a basket of huckleberries in his hand" [*The Journal of Henry D. Thoreau*]. Thoreau also left an interesting account of Benjamin Franklin Folger: "a singular old hermit and genealogist, over seventy years old, who, for thirty years *at least*, has lived alone and devoted his thoughts to genealogy. He knows the genealogy of the whole island, and a relative supports him by making genealogical charts from his dictation for those who will pay for them. He...lives in a very filthy manner, and G. helped clean his house when he was absent about two years ago. They took up three barrels of dirt in his room." (One can only wonder if this "dirt" contained some precious historical documents.)

Eliza Mitchell's account of visiting Benjamin Franklin Folger was written in 1895 in a book of reminiscences at the NHA. In 1992, more than a century and a half after Eliza Mitchell made almost the exact same request of Benjamin Franklin Folger, the writer Douglas Preston asked a young Navajo if he could write down their conversation. He received a most Folger-like explanation of why he should simply listen: "When someone says something important to you, if you have to write it down...in order to remember it, then it means you didn't understand it. The only really *good* things are those things you can never possibly forget" [Preston's *Talking to the Ground*].

Arthur Gardner's account of the Indian legend appears in *Wrecks Around Nantucket*. Eva Folger made the disparaging comment concerning the Maushop legends in *Nantucket: The Glacier's Gift*. That the legend of Maushop's moccasins had been told on Nantucket long before Folger recorded it in 1911 is indicated by "An Old Story," a poem written by Maria Mitchell in 1844 (in *Seaweeds from the Shores of Nantucket*, Boston, 1853) that summarizes the legend, then ends,

> Ill-judging sachem! Would that you
> Had never shaken here that shoe;
> Or, having done so, would again,
> And join Nantucket to the main!

Meredith Marshall Brenizer's *The Nantucket Indians: Legends and Accounts before 1659* remains an enjoyable and important book, with useful sections by Paul Morris, Jr., and Elizabeth A. Little.

Elizabeth Little's articles concerning Nantucket Indians, many of them (but by no means all) included in her series *Nantucket Algonquian Studies* (subsequently referred to as *NAS*), must provide the starting point for any exploration of Nantucket Indian history and archeology. Her "Indian Politics on Nantucket" makes groundbreaking connections between Nantucket Indian legends and the island's history. William S. Simmons first spoke in detail about Maushop in "Return of the Timid Giant: Algonquian Legends of Southern New England." For a Maushop sourcebook, see Chapter 9, "Maushop and Squant," in Simmons's *Spirit of the New England Tribes* (subsequently referred to as *SNET*).

One of the oldest and most detailed of the Maushop legends (a portion of which is quoted at the beginning of Chapter 4–"The Killers Come") is Benjamin Basset's "Fabulous Traditions and Customs of the Indians" purportedly "communicated...by Thomas Cooper, a half-blooded Indian, of Gay Head, aged about sixty years; and which, he says, he obtained of his grandmother, who, to use his own expression, was a stout girl, when the English came to the island." The reference to the mixing of history and myth is in Jonathan Hill and Robin Wright's "Time, Narrative, and Ritual

Historical Interpretations from an Amazonian Society." George Hamell's statement concerning the time it took for contact experiences to be reflected in the Indians' legends is in "Strawberries, Floating Islands, and Rabbit Captains: Mythical Realities and European Contact in the Northeast During the Sixteenth and Seventeenth Centuries."

For a compilation of Indian legends from a noted folklorist, see Stith Thompson's *Tales of the North American Indians,* while Christopher Vecsey's *Imagine Ourselves Richly, Mythic Narratives of North American Indians* provides a useful overview of the latest trends in interpreting Indian myths and legends. When it comes to the distortions introduced by white society to Indian oral traditions, even Abram's own last name comes to us in an Anglicized form. Since the Massachusett language has no sound for the letter *r,* he pronounced his name Quady instead of Quary (just as it was originally Podpis, instead of Polpis, Harbor). For a guide to the Massachusett language, see Ives Goddard and Kathleen Bragdon, *Native Writings in Massachusett.* The essays (including Robin Ridington's "Fox and Chickadee") contained in *The American Indian and the Problem of History,* edited by Calvin Martin, offer probing insights into the problem of mixing history with Native American legends. The reference to the mistaken assumption that Indian myths are "flawed history" is from Ridington.

Chapter 1—An Island in Time

John Winthrop called Nantucket "an island full of Indians" in *The History of New England from 1630 to 1649.* For accounts of Nantucket's geologic origins, see Barbara Blau Chamberlain's *These Fragile Outposts: A Geological Look at Cape Cod, Martha's Vineyard, and Nantucket* and Robert Oldale's *Cape Cod and the Islands: The Geological Story.* Overviews of how climatic and ecological changes related to the developing human cultures in New England are provided by Dena Dincauze in "A Capsule Prehistory of Southern New England" and Esther Braun and David Braun's *The First Peoples of the Northeast.* See Howard Russell's *Indian New England Before the Mayflower* for an overview of Native American culture in the Northeast. Peter Dunwiddie's "Postglacial Vegetation History of Coastal Islands in Southeastern New England" and Elizabeth Little's "Essay on Nantucket Timber" provide useful information concerning Nantucket's botanical history.

In the collections of the NHA is a paperweight-sized mastodon tooth dredged from the harbor in the 1890s. In the 1950s, a soapstone bowl from the Late Archaic period was uncovered and inadvertently crushed by a bulldozer while grading a driveway at the Nantucket High School; see Edward Roy's "A Steatite Vessel from Nantucket." For a summary of the latest thinking on where Native Americans in coastal New England chose their village sites, see Little's "Where are the Woodland Villages on Cape Cod and the Islands?" The French explorer Samuel Champlain (in *Forerunners and Competitors of the Pilgrims and Puritans*, edited by Charles Levermore) described the wigwams he saw on Cape Cod in 1607: "they are large, of a circular shape, and covered with a thatch made of grasses or the husks of Indian corn. They are furnished only with a bed or two, raised a foot from the ground, made of a number of little pieces of wood pressed against each other, on which they arrange a reed mat." In *New England's Prospect*, William Wood told of the differing seasonal configurations of an Indian wigwam: "Their houses are smaller in the summer when their families be dispersed by reason of heat and occasions. In winter they make some fifty or three score foot long, forty or fifty men being inmates under one roof." He also remarked: "They be warmer than our English houses. At the top is a square hole for the smoke's evacuation.... These be such smoky dwellings that when there is good fires they are not able to stand upright, but lie all along under the smoke."

The Indians planted their crops on southern-facing hills, a technique apparently adopted by white Nantucketers; as late as 1854, Henry David Thoreau recorded in his journal, "Half-way to Siasconset I saw the old corn-hills where they had formerly cultivated, the authorities [the town proprietary] laying out a new tract for this purpose each year." Such cornhills were visible in parts of New England well into the twentieth century; see Russell's *Indian New England*. Roger Williams's comments concerning the Indians being "full of business" is in *A Key into the Language of America* (subsequently referred to as *Key*). Williams's remark concerning how an Indian can envision "the face of the country" also appears in this invaluable source. Henry Barnard Worth in *Nantucket Lands and Landowners* speaks of groundnuts (which were referred to simply as "roots" on Nantucket) in the swamps near Siasconset. Edward Winslow's reference to memory holes is from *Good News From New England* (1624). Indians in Rhode Island, Martha's Vineyard, and Mashpee were also known to leave stones and pieces of wood at specific sites, often near a large rock; see *SNET*.

The account of Indians from the Northwest using songs to help guide them on their voyages appears in Anne Cameron's *Daughters of the Copper Woman* and is cited in Bruce Chatwin's *What Am I Doing Here*. In *The Songlines*, Chatwin describes the narratives by which an aboriginal people connected themselves to their lands and to each other: "they were the means by which man marked out his territory, and so organized his social life." Until the beginning of the eighteenth century, it was the practice of Nantucket Indians to "strengthen and refresh" themselves before a voyage by retiring to a sweathouse: a cave-like dwelling dug out of the sand dunes and brought to temperature with a "parcel of heated stones." Paul Dudley offers a detailed account of the sweathouses in a clipping dated 1724 in the "Indian" folder at the NA.

Hector St. John de Crèvecoeur in *Letters from an American Farmer* described Nantucket as "the uneven summit of a sandy submarine mountain...; other submarine ones lie to the southward of this, at different depths and different distances. This dangerous region is well known to the mariners by the name of Nantucket shoals: these are the bulwarks which so powerfully defend this island from the impulse of the mighty ocean and repel the force of its waves, which, but for the accumulated barriers, would ere now have dissolved its foundations and torn it in pieces." In a personal communication (August 1996), erosion expert Wesley Tiffney, Jr., predicts that Nantucket may wash into the sea in as little as 600 years.

The present state of archaeological investigation on the island is best summarized in two articles by the NHA archaeologist Elizabeth Little: "Locus Q-6, Site M52/65, Quidnet, Nantucket, Massachusetts" and, with John Pretola, "Nantucket: An Archaeological Record from the Far Island." For those wanting to know how the excavated artifacts were actually used by the Native Americans, an excellent sourcebook is C. Keith Wilbur's *The New England Indians*. For information on stones and projectile points specific to Nantucket, see Little and Leona Champeny's "Nantucket Stone Type Collection: Artifacts and Beach Pebbles," an exhibition description from 1979 on file at the NHA, as well as Little and Dena Dincauze's "Nantucket Indian Stone Artifact Styles," another NHA exhibition description from 1978. For an account of Nantucket's modern-day group of arrowhead hunters, see Mary Lancaster's "Arrow Heads," *Nantucket Beacon* (November 20, 1996). The two accounts of native burials with dogs come from Harry Turner's "Vanished Treasures" and Ripley Bullen and Edward Brooks's "Three Burials at the Hughes Site, Nantucket, Massachusetts."

A summary of Michael Gibbons's preliminary findings concerning his study of the skeletal remains in the holdings of the NHA appeared in "A Report on the NHA Symposium: Nantucket and the Native American Legacy of New England" *HN* (Fall, 1995). According to the published synopsis of Gibbons's presentation: "Although the incidence of periodontal diseases among the Nantucket Indians was unusually large, and osteoarthritis was fairly prevalent as well, [the Indians] were taller, more powerful and robust, longer lived, and, for the most part, healthier than their mainland counterparts." James Athearn Jones's 1830 legend of Maushop claims that "his teeth, which were only two in number, were green as the ooze raked up by the winds from the bottom of the sea" (in *SNET*).

Drawing upon accounts from the voyages of Bartholomew Gosnold, Martin Pring, and George Waymouth, David Quinn and Alison Quinn speak of apparent height variations among Indians on the New England coast in *The English New England Voyages, 1602-1608.* That Maushop should be considered an example of the "reality of mythic thinking" is supported by the work of Vine Deloria in *Red Earth, White Lies, Native Americans and the Myth of Scientific Fact.* According to Deloria, who has tracked references to giants in native traditions from across the country, the legends are describing real "people of more than average height" who display "cultural behavior comparable to the Indians in many respects, physical size being one important distinction which made these people memorable." (Instead of nutrition, Deloria attributes height changes to variations in the levels of carbon dioxide in the air.)

David Quammen speaks of islands and evolution in *The Song of the Dodo, Island Biogeography in an Age of Extinctions.* An excellent study of the cultural and historical implications of island living is Greg Dening's *Islands and Beaches, Discourse on a Silent Land: Marquesas, 1774-1880.* Little speaks about the growing scarcity of deer on Nantucket in "Locus Q-6." As S. F. Cook in *The Indian Population of New England in the Seventeenth Century* points out, in "purely coastal habitat the subsistence regime of natives was so altered in adapting to marine resources that [population] density is referable to length of shore line rather than to extent of exposed land areas." Crèvecoeur claimed that Nantucket's once large native population could be attributed to "the great plenty of clams, oysters, and other fish on which they lived, and which they easily catched, [and which] had prodigiously increased their numbers." Little's "Observations on Methods of Collection, Use, and Seasonality of Shellfish on the Coasts of Massachusetts" describes the principal shellfish habitat on Nantucket; her analysis of shellfish seasonality indicates that significant quantities of quahogs, scallops, surf clams, and mussels wash ashore during fall and winter storms.

The first recorded Maushop legend tells how crabs came to Nantucket; written by John Winthrop in 1702 after a visit to the Elizabeth Islands, it tells how the giant was building a stone bridge (in most accounts from Gay Head to Cuttyhunk) when a crab caught him by the fingers. Maushop then "snatch[ed] up his hand and flung it towards Nantucket, and the crabs breed there ever since" (*SNET*). See Little's "Drift Whales at Nantucket: The Kindness of Moshup" for a discussion of the relatively large number of driftwhales that came ashore on Nantucket. As Kathleen Bragdon has pointed out in *Native People of Southern New England,* the caloric content of a single pilot whale (prone to mass strandings on the Cape and islands) is the equivalent of thirty-six deer! Emil Guba in *Nantucket Odyssey* charts the temperature differences between Nantucket and the mainland. James Freeman in "Notes on Nantucket, August 1st, 1807" recorded that "two kinds of clay, one of which is of a yellow, and the other of a blue color, are found on the island" and claimed that they were still used "for the making of cisterns to hold whale oil." Barbara Luedtke in "Regional Variation in Massachusetts Ceramics" writes that relative to pottery sherds found on mainland New England, "Nantucket pots were apparently rather thick walled and a large proportion had coarse temper," indicating that Nantucketers may have made bigger, cruder vessels. However, recent investigations associated with the construction of the Polpis Bike Path seem to suggest that vessels made on Nantucket were not significantly different from elsewhere in the region [personal communication, Mary Lynne Rainey, November 1997].

Crèvecoeur speaks of the Nantucket Indians using strings of sun-dried clams as a kind of currency, while Freeman reported that they did not use wampum. Champlain observed that the Indians on Cape Cod had relatively few skins, while Freeman recorded the claims that Nantucket Indians dressed in grass mats and roasted, instead of boiled, their food. A detailed description of a "subterranean oven"–the native cooking method that would eventually evolve into the New England clambake–is in Samuel Jenks's "The Legend of Mudturtle" (1827): "[Nantucket Indians] excavated the ground to the depth of about three or four feet, making a pointed hollow that might contain some three or four bushels, and lining the sides with smooth stones weighing from six to ten pounds each. Within this subterranean oven they kindled a fire, and heaped on fuel until the stones became duly [hot]; then removing the coals, they threw in promiscuously their respective contributions, gathered from the sea, the [beach], the ponds, and the [soil]; overlaid the whole with a thick lid of seaweed. When this medley was thus sufficiently seethed, the covering was withdrawn, and the feast ensued." Although she makes no reference to Jenks's description (which is one of the earliest accounts of this cooking method to appear), see Kathy Neustadt's *Clambake, A History and Celebration of an American Tradition*. My thanks to Peter Gow for pointing out the fuel efficiency of this roasting/steaming method and that Tandoori cooking in India (where firewood is extremely scarce) relies on a similar method. According to James Athearn Jones's legend of how Maushop created Nantucket (published in 1830): "First he dug a great hole in the earth, into which he threw many heated stones" along with the "live embers [from his pipe]...." (in *SNET*).

Chapter 2—An Eagle in the Year of *The Tempest*

The description of the Indians in Newport Harbor appears in *The Voyages of Giovanni da Verrazano*, edited by Lawrence Wroth. My thanks to C. S. Lovelace for pointing out how Verrazano memorialized his annoyance with the waters of Nantucket Sound. For a collection of the primary sources associated with European explorers in New England (including Harlow, Gosnold, Champlain, Smith, and others), see *Forerunners*, edited by Charles Levermore. According to Kathleen Bragdon in *Native People of Southern New England*, the name "Wampanoag...now used to designate the modern descendants of the Pokanokets, was probably derived from the name Wapanoos, first applied by Dutch explorers and map-makers to those Natives near Narragansett Bay, with whom they had no personal experience, based on information from the peoples of the lower Hudson. The term means 'easterner' in Delaware, and was probably not an original self-designation."

Information on Bartholomew Gosnold's voyage comes from three sources: a letter to his father and accounts from two crew members, John Brereton and Gabriel Archer. In *The English New England Voyages*, David Quinn and Alison Quinn provide definitive discussions of Gosnold's much debated route to Cuttyhunk and Waymouth's 1605 voyage to the region that debunk long-standing claims by island historians that these two explorers both saw Nantucket; the Quinns also speculate that Gosnold's men may have traded with the father of Massasoit. The Velasco map is at the General Archives of Simancas, Spain, and is referred to by the Quinns.

Our knowledge of Edward Harlow's voyage is based almost exclusively on a teasingly brief account by Captain John Smith. Neal Salisbury's *Manitou and Providence: Indians, Europeans, and the Making of New England, 1500-1643* provides an insightful overview of early European-Indian contact, but mistakenly places Edward Harlow's first three abductions in Maine. At one time, the early chronicler of British exploratory efforts in America, Samuel Purchas, possessed a copy of Harlow's report of his voyage, but it has been lost. The Quinns reprint "A document, apparently by Edward Harlow, being the 'Description' and other sources as a guide for Nicholas Hobson's voyage of 1614." Although this brief document (which is at the British Library) first appeared in print in David Bushnell, Jr.'s "New England Names," it has, according to the Quinns, "not been used by historians of New England." Smith's account claims that Harlow and Hobson sailed together in 1611, but the 1614 document suggests that Hobson was not part of the earlier voyage. William Hubbard's *A General History of New England* contains this account of Harlow's voyage: "At one of the islands at Cape Cod, (by Captain Smith called Nohone,) they took in that voyage an Indian called Sakaweston, who, after he had lived divers years in England, went a soldier into the wars of Bohemia, as saith Capt. Smith."

Before it succumbed to rising sea levels, the Isle of Nauset also had the more colorful name of Slut's Bush, possibly a reference to the Siren-like perils associated with this scrubby, shoal-surrounded island. That the name "Nohono" had, at best, a loose connection to the native name for the island is demonstrated by Harlow's memory of the island as "Natcea" in the 1614 document, which the Quinns claim "would appear to be Nantucket (the Nohono seen by Harlow in 1611)." (Other seventeenth-century names for Nantucket include "Natocko" and "Nautican.") In his instructions Harlow also mentions "Capawick" (Martha's Vineyard) and "Akeucanack" and "Ioucanoke," which may refer, according to the Quinns, to Chappaquiddick and Tuckernuck/Muskeget, which may have been joined at that time.

Henry Barnard Worth in *Nantucket Lands and Land Owners* provides translations of many Indian place names on Nantucket, including that of Coatue. Jenks's "Legend of Mudturtle" claims that the Indian on the Massachusetts seal was based on an eastern sachem who "was a warrior of great prowess, though peaceably disposed." William Wood relates that the Indians thought the first European ships were islands. The legend from Dighton, Massachusetts, referring to a bird taking Indian captives is in *SNET*. The Nantucket-based legend about the bird is from Freeman and is also included in *SNET*. George Hamell in "Strawberries, Floating Islands, and Rabbit Captains: Mythical Realities and European Contact" refers to a Shawnee tradition recorded in 1803 in which a European ship is at first taken to be "a great bird, but [they] soon saw it was a monstrous canoe." In "History, Narrative, and Temporality, Examples from the Northwest Coast," Michael Harkin refers to a Tlingit account of an encounter with a French ship in 1786 in which the ship was taken to be "a great supernatural bird, Yehleh (Raven), with a flock of small dark crows."

Harkin states that "[i]t would be difficult to imagine a more epitomizing class of event than that of contact with an alien culture," while claiming that "the manifest content of myths…is most commonly historical, in that it relates a series of events that lead up to the present state of the world." See also Christopher Miller and George Hamell's "A New Perspective on Indian-White Contact: Cultural Symbols and Colonial Trade." Some later versions of the eagle myth (some of which place it on the Vineyard instead of Nantucket) claim that Maushop found and killed the giant bird; see *SNET*.

Paralleling Maushop's experiences with the giant eagle are the legends from Indians in Maine describing the giant Gluskap. According to one legend, before the arrival of the Europeans in America, Gluskap crossed the Atlantic in a stone canoe, eventually paddling up the Thames to London. The English wanted to trade a large wooden vessel for his stone canoe, but spurning the offer, Gluskap paddled to

France. After receiving gifts from the French king, Gluskap returned to Maine [Horace Beck's *Gluskap the Liar and Other Indian Legends*]. Just as the Maushop legend of the giant eagle possibly evolved around the appearance of European ships in the vicinity of the Cape and islands, so may have this particular Gluskap legend emerged as the Native Americans' version of a discovery myth in the wake of Indian captives returning from Europe.

Simmons in *SNET* refers to John Josselyn's 1675 account of poke, "known variously as white hellebore, Indian poke and *tabac du diable*," and speaks of its hallucinogenic properties. John Strong in *The Algonquian Peoples of Long Island from Earliest Times to 1700* lists pokeweed as *Phytolacca Americana* and claims that it was used not only as a medicine but also as "salad greens." In 1792 Zaccheus Macy wrote that the Nantucket Indians "had a sort of weed or herb they called *poke*, which they used instead of tobacco" [Obed Macy's *History*]. In the legend of Mudturtle, Samuel Jenks mentions a shaman's use of "poke-weed" and claims that Nantucket Indians traded with Indians from Naushon, one of the Elizabeth Islands, for tobacco. According to Kathleen Bragdon in *Native People of Southern New England, 1500-1650*, "Birds are…linked to the experience of drug-induced 'flight,' a linkage marked by the common association in Native North America between birds…and smoking pipes." Bragdon also speaks of the Indians' use of "vision quests, the seeking out of sacred places, dreams, and induced trance."

Chapter 3—Escape from Golgotha

The reference to Nantucket being a "naval power" appears in Hart's *Miriam Coffin*. George Churchman recorded the comment concerning the Indians' lack of canoes during a visit to Nantucket in June 1781 [Henry Cadbury's "An Off-Islander's Impressions"]. The unavailability of large trees on the island may have been a contributing factor to the absence of canoes among year-round Nantucketers. Samuel Champlain observed a canoe being made in the Merrimack River region: "After cutting down, at a cost of much labor and time, the largest and tallest tree they can find…, they remove the bark, and round the tree except on one side, where they apply fire gradually along its entire length.… It being hollowed out as much as they wish, they scrape it all over with stones…" [*Forerunners*]. In "Seasonality of Fish Remains from Locus Q-6 of the Quidnet Site, Nantucket Island, Massachusetts," Catherine Carlson speculates that Nantucket may have been "an inviting summer retreat from the mainland during prehistoric times, just as it is today."

Bernard Stockley made the comments concerning archaeological evidence for two different groups on Nantucket in "Preliminary Report, Ram Pasture I, A

Stratified Site on Nantucket Island, Massachusetts." In the "Legend of Mudturtle," Samuel Jenks freely admits to inventing the names Khaud and Taumkhod for the island's eastern and western Indians. Frank Speck speaks about Nantucket being the possible focal point of a two-pronged Indian "invasion" in the seventeenth century in "Territorial Subdivisions and Boundaries of the Wampanoag, Massachusett and Nauset Indians." Elizabeth Little discusses the east-west divide on Nantucket in "Indian Politics on Nantucket."

Neal Salisbury in *Manitou and Providence* provides the best account of the restless interplay between the Indians and the English; he was the first scholar to see the Pilgrims' raid on Wessagusset from the Indians' perspective. In his *History of New England* (in *Forerunners*), John Smith provides his surprisingly even-handed take on European-Indian interaction in the region; Smith speaks of the Indians' treatment of the French captive and his prophecy. For accounts of the plague of 1616-19, see Arthur Spiess and Bruce Spiess's "New England Pandemic of 1616-1622: Cause and Archaeological Implication" and Dean Snow and Kim Lanphear's "European Contact and Indian Depopulation in the Northeast: The Timing of the First Epidemics." Williams's reference to the Narragansett response to infectious disease is in *Key*. In *The Sin and Danger of Self Love* (1622), Robert Cushman speaks of "civil dissensions and bloody wars" erupting in the midst of the plague. Thomas Morton refers to a "new found Golgotha" in *New English Canaan* (1637). Dermer's account is in *Forerunners*.

Warner Foote Gookin discusses Dermer's activities on Nantucket in *Capawack alias Martha's Vineyard* and speculates that Dermer was referring to Harlow's "former report" of Nantucket. Dermer reported saving two of the French sailors taken prisoner by the Indians; he also stated that the Wampanoag "bear an inveterate malice to the English" because a group of Indians had been recently murdered in cold blood on the deck of an English vessel. Dermer visited Epenow on the Vineyard twice. During his second visit, fighting broke out; although Dermer escaped, he was severely injured and later died in Virginia. Another good summary of Dermer's activities in the region is in Jerome Dunn's "Squanto Before He Met the Pilgrims." For an account of the Pilgrims' early years in New England, see *Mourt's Relation* (1622); Edward Winslow's *Good News From New England* (1624) in *Chronicles of the Pilgrim Fathers*; and William Bradford's *Of Plymouth Plantation, 1620-1647*.

Warner Gookin in *Capawack alias Martha's Vineyard* translates Capawack as "the refuge place." Matthew Mayhew's remarks concerning Indian "strangers" appears in "A Brief Narrative of the Success Which the Gospel Had Among the Indians of

Martha's Vineyard." The reference to Maushop disappearing when the Indian population increased comes from Basset's 1792 version of the legend. A version of the Poot
Pond legend is in Brenizer and is reprinted in full in *SNET*; the legend originally
appeared in *NI* (February 28, 1829), with "Homtas" listed as the author. Homtas
claimed to have learned the legend from his great-grandfather who had heard it from
the Indian "Eaaooptooicoo," described as "Great Medicine of the Western Tribe." In
an unpublished manuscript from the 1840s, Obed Macy recorded another version of
the Poot Pond legend, reprinted in Alexander Starbuck's *The History of Nantucket*: "an
Indian alleged that he saw a whale rise from the water in the Chord of the Bay [which
extends from Great Point to the harbor entrance] and immediately sound again, and
come up again in the southern pond. Going down for the third time, he reappeared
off the south shore of the Island, and then disappeared for good."

Chapter 4—The Killers Come
Simmons discusses the Narragansett use of the word "Mausup" to designate their
supreme sachem in *SNET*. Peter Nabokov in "Present Memories, Past History" (in
The American Indian and the Problem of History) speaks of the "in-jokes" that were an
inevitable part of the Indians' traditions. While Nabokov's comments are directed
toward how the Indians made light of the Europeans, Peter A. Thomas's analysis of
the fur trade in Connecticut convincingly demonstrates that it wasn't always a question of Indian-European conflict. Just as the English didn't always see eye to eye with
their officials, so were there instances in which the Indians felt victimized by their
own leaders–particularly a wheeler-dealer such as Massasoit. As Thomas states,
"Individual motives on both sides molded the process of change.... Native
Americans on the southern New England frontier were not passive witnesses to their
own demise. Rather, for better or worse, and with varying degrees of success, many
were active participants in shaping their own destiny" (in "Cultural Change on the
Southern New England Frontier, 1630-1665").

Other Maushop legends portray additional violence and brutality inflicted on the
giant's wife, whose name was Squant. According to a legend recorded by Mary
Cleggett Vanderhoop on Martha's Vineyard in 1904, "Squant was broad, but finely
proportioned, with coal-black hair, which she wore over her face, so as to cover it as
with a veil. The reason for this–as given by the few who had beheld her face while
the veil was lifted, and as told by our forefathers in tones of awe–was that Squant's
eyes were square. They had been cut and thus shaped by an enemy who one day
found her asleep on the marsh. Thus, her beautiful hair was used to cover her
hideous deformity" (in *SNET*).

Jones's Maushop legends are in *SNET*; Peter Thomas speaks of "Big Men" in the Connecticut Valley fur trade in "Cultural Change on the Southern New England Frontier." That Maushop's cruelly flippant treatment of his children was in keeping with the behavior of Massasoit, a sachem/Big Man with a reputation for manipulating others, seems to be borne out by an anecdote recorded by Massachusetts Governor John Winthrop in 1634. One day Edward Winslow, the Pilgrim who had saved the sachem's life in 1622, visited his "old ally" Massasoit. The Wampanoag sachem offered to accompany Winslow back to Plymouth but, unknown to his English friend, "sent some of his men to Plymouth to tell that Mr. Winslow was dead." Massasoit's messengers even showed "how and where he was killed, whereupon there was much fear and sorrow at Plymouth." The next day, when the sachem arrived with Winslow by his side, he was asked "why he sent such word." His reply: "It was their manner to do so, that they might be more welcome when they came home." Whether or not his behavior was culturally justified, this was a sachem who was willing to go to great lengths to mislead and even lie to his apparent friends– English and Indians alike [Winthrop's *History*].

Williams speaks of whales in *Key*; see also Elizabeth Little and J. Clinton Andrews's "Drift Whales at Nantucket." In 1605, Waymouth (who saw "many whales" in the vicinity of Cape Cod and the islands) witnessed the division of a dead whale in Maine: "They call all their chief lords together, and sing a song of joy: and those chief lords, whom they call Sagamos [or sagamores, the northern equivalent of a sachem], divide the spoil, and give to every man a share, which pieces so distributed they hang up about their houses for provision: and when they boil them, they blow off the fat, and put to their peas, maize, and other pulse, which they eat." Although the chronicler of Waymouth's voyage described how the Maine Indians pursued the whale in their canoes, stabbed it with a harpoon made out of bone, then killed it with their bows and arrows, that seems to have been an exceedingly rare occurrence in southern New England [Little and Andrews].

Another good source concerning early New England whaling is Glover Allen's *The Whalebone Whales of New England*. According to Elizabeth Little, Abram Quary's last name is short for Scuhtquade, which is also the title of a minor official in Dutch ["Abram Quary of Abram's Point"]. Little mentions the presence of Massasoit Bridge in "Indian Politics on Nantucket"; as Little states in that article, the Nantucket historian R. A. Douglas-Lithgow in *Nantucket, A History* (1914) claimed that Massasoit had visited the island.

A question remains concerning Indian driftwhaling: How did they try out and store the oil? European iron pots or kettles, in which the blubber would have been boiled into oil, were readily available to the Indians even before the beginning of the seventeenth century. On their way down the New England coast in 1602, Gosnold and his men ran across a group of Indians in a Basque-style shallop with an iron kettle. On Cape Cod in 1620 the Pilgrims discovered "a great kettle which had been some ship's kettle and brought out of Europe" beside a wigwam. According to Timothy Dilliplane in "European Trade Kettles," the Dutch used iron and brass kettles as trade items in the seventeenth century. When it comes to the storage of the oil, there is an intriguing reference by Freeman in 1807 to the use of Nantucket clay to manufacture "cisterns to hold whale oil." Might this have been a holdover from the Indian driftwhaling days when the Indians stored the oil and even the unprocessed blubber in cisterns while waiting for the arrival of European traders? For a reference to the construction and use of a clay-lined blubber storage pit in the Northern Isles of Britain that was used to collect the oil that oozed from decomposing blubber before it was tried out, see Ole Lindquist's "The Auskerry Whale, 1777: Processing and Economy." (My thanks to Klaus Barthelmess for bringing the reference to my attention.)

Freeman refers to King Philip's having "power" over some Indians "not belonging to the island." Little and Andrews cite the 1677 court document describing Massasoit's (referred to by this time as Ussemequin) order concerning driftwhaling on Nantucket; as they point out, Nantucket was the only place in the region where Indians maintained their driftwhaling rights throughout the seventeenth century, a possible indication that diftwhaling was already big business on the island prior to the arrival of the English. Little theorizes that Attapeat was a Vineyard driftwhaler who, as Zaccheus Macy described, "got his lands by his bow." Macy's "Account of the names of the old Sachems" is reprinted in Obed Macy's *History*. Jones's account tells how the Vineyard sachem Hiwassee refused to let his daughter marry a young Indian of humble birth until Maushop provided the young man with his own island [*SNET*].

Instead of cuddly creatures from Sea World, killer whales were notorious in coastal New England for ganging up on a young right whale: "Some will lay hold of his tail to keep him from threshing, while others lay hold of his head, and bite and thresh him, till the poor creature, being thus heated, lolls out his tongue, and then some of the killers catch hold of his lips [and] feed upon the tongue and head" [Paul Dudley, "An Essay upon the Natural History of Whales, with a Particular Account of the Ambergris Found in the *Sperma Ceti* Whale"].

Prior to the arrival of the English, Tuckernuck was the territory of the Vineyard sachem Pattochohonet, whose heirs maintained driftwhaling rights on the island well into the eighteenth century. Obed Macy's account of the massacre at Madaket is reprinted in Starbuck; Brenizer also includes a version of this tale. Roger Williams describes Indian warfare in *Key*. According to Michael Gibbons, one of the skeletons in the NHA holdings sustained a "blow to the head" approximately 800 years ago ["Inventory of Native American Human Remains Currently in the Possession of the Nantucket Historical Association," Report Prepared by Michael A. Jehle, 1995]. In Mary Lancaster's "Arrow Heads," Danny Haynes recounts discovering the body of a young Indian woman "without hands or feet, and a portion of her skull was smashed."

The legend of Roqua–billed as "Another Legend as Told by 'F' at 'Sconset in 1830"–first appeared in *NI*, a copy of which is in the "Indian" blue file at the NHA; a version also appears in Brenizer. Unfortunately, the legend seems to have been rewritten by a second party who did his or her best to make it sound like Longfellow; at one point, the author states: "I will relate [the tale] as near as I can in the nervous style of the original. It is clothed in all the wild dress of fanciful exaggeration, to which untaught nations are so prone." Experience Mayhew speaks of wars among the Island Indians in *Indian Converts*. Crèvecoeur describes in detail the Indians' "partition line" in *Letters from an American Farmer*.

Elizabeth Little provides a transcription of the 1678 Indian deed in "The Writings of Nantucket Indians." Concerning the Indians' unwillingness to speak the name of a dead sachem, Roger Williams states, "if any of their sachems or neighbors die, they lay down those names as dead." The portrait of Wanackmamack and the extended process of decision-making that emerges from the 1678 petition is in keeping with the description of an Indian sachem given by Isaack de Rasieres, who visited the Cape and Plymouth in 1627: "When any stranger comes, they bring him to the sachem. On first meeting they do not speak–they smoke a pipe of tobacco; that being done, the sachem asks: 'Whence do you come?' The stranger then states that, and further what he has to say, before all who are present or choose to come. That being done the sachem announces his opinion to the people, and if they agree thereto, they give all together a sigh…and [if] they do not approve, they keep silence, and all come close to the sachem, and each sets forth his opinion till they agree: that being done, they come all together again to the stranger, to whom the sachem then announces what they have determined, with the reasons moving them thereto" [*Narrative of New England, 1609-1664*, edited by J. Franklin Jameson].

Although we don't know what they were hunting, the mention of a "hunting meeting" at Manna in the Indian deed from 1678 (referring to events from a "long time ago") may indicate that deer were still present on the island as late as the mid-seventeenth century. The description of the area known as Manna comes from Elizabeth Little's "Indian Place Names at Nantucket." The text included in Reverend F. C. Ewer's 1869 map of Nantucket refers to 1630 being the end date of the Indian wars on the island. William F. Macy in *The Story of Old Nantucket* gives the same date for the end of hostilities. Bradford refers to the outbreak of smallpox among the Indians in his *Of Plymouth Plantation, 1620-1647*. Winthrop's account of Oldham's stop at Nantucket appears in his *History*. Brenizer refers to Wood's account of the Indian soccer-like game.

Chapter 5—The Black Book

Although Williams, whose account of his religious experience on an island appears in *Key* (as do the other references to Williams in this chapter), is known to have traveled to Martha's Vineyard, the possibility exists that this particular island was Nantucket. According to Zaccheus Macy, writing in 1792, the dialect variations among the region's Wampanoag villages meant that Nantucket Indians had trouble understanding Indians who lived as close as Dartmouth and Mashpee but had no trouble understanding the Vineyard Indians [Little and Sussek's "Zaccheus Macy's Account of the Indians of Nantucket: Three Versions"].

My account of Thomas Mayhew's early missionary efforts is based largely on his own letters collected in "The Light appearing more and more" (1651) and "Tears of Repentance" (1653). Mayhew's descendants also provide important information concerning the beginnings of the Vineyard mission: Matthew Mayhew in "A Brief Narrative of the Success Which the Gospel Had Among the Indians of Martha's Vineyard" and Experience Mayhew in *Indian Converts*. I have also depended on Charles Banks's *History of Martha's Vineyard* and Lloyd Hare's *Thomas Mayhew: Patriarch to the Indians 1593-1682*. William Simmons speaks in detail about the Mayhew mission in "Conversion from Indian to Puritan."

James Ronda in "Generations of Faith: The Christian Indians of Martha's Vineyard" argues persuasively that it was the flexibility of Mayhew's approach that made it so successful relative to the efforts of John Eliot: "It was in this more permissive environment, as Indian congregations and praying towns rose and flourished, that political power and cultural leadership remained in Wampanoag hands.... Christianity Indianized as well as Indians Christianized." Richard Cogley claims that Mayhew's success could be attributed to his focus on the powwows instead of the sachems in "Two Approaches to Indian Conversion in Puritan New England: The Missions of Thomas Mayhew, Jr., and John Eliot."

At the very beginning of the English settlement on the Vineyard, Thomas Senior announced his presence on the island not as a European claiming the Indians' island for his king but as a fellow, albeit superior, sachem. Matthew Mayhew relates how an Indian leader came to Mayhew's house and "being admitted, sat down": "Mr. Mayhew entered the room, but being acquainted with their customs, took no notice of the Prince's being there (it being with them in point of honor incumbent on the inferior to salute the superior). [A] considerable time being past, the Prince broke the silence and said, 'Sachem...Mr. Mayhew, are you well?'"

Concerning the Pilgrim's Wampanoag ally Hobbamock being named for a native god, Kathleen Bragdon in *Native People of Southern New England* notes that "mutuality of appellation" was an indication of "strong links between people...and their tutelary spirits." Father Biard's account of Indians having their fun with European missionaries appears in his *Relation of New France* (1610) in *Forerunners*. The Chappaquiddick sachem Pakeponesso–who was blasted by lightning in 1644–was one of the Indians whose lands at the west end of Nantucket were sold to the English almost twenty years later (see Little's "Indian Politics on Nantucket"); thirty-three years later in 1677 Pakeponesso witnessed a deed of the Nantucket sachem Nickanoose [Little's "The Writings of Nantucket Indians"]. Russell Gardner speculates that Towanquatick was the son of Epenow in "A Rare Aboriginal Artifact from Martha's Vineyard Island, With a Living Family History."

William Simmons speaks of the "massive erosion and change" suffered by the Indians in *SNET*; his reference to Mayhew's efforts resulting in the "most profound social conversion" in New England is in "Conversion from Indian to Puritan." Charles Cohen discusses how the Puritans' concept of sin was surprisingly compatible with the Indians' spiritual world in "Conversion Among the Amerindians: A Theological and Cultural Perspective." Robert Naeher in "Dialogue in the Wilderness: John Eliot and the Indian Exploration of Puritanism as a Source of Meaning, Comfort, and Ethnic Survival" talks about the "almost sensual joy of intimate communion with a living God."

William Kellaway's *The New England Company, 1649-1776: Missionary Society to the American Indians* is a comprehensive look at the company's activities and contains much information concerning the Vineyard and Nantucket. Mayhew's account of Massasoit's exchange with some Vineyard Indians illustrates the sachem's skepticism concerning Christianity: "He inquired what earthly things came with [the ways of God], and demanding of [the Vineyard Indians] what they had gotten by all they had done this way? One of them replied, 'We serve not God for clothing, not for any outward thing." William Hubbard speaks of the Vineyard Indians in *A General History of New England*.

Jenks's legend of Mudturtle first appeared in 1827; an abbreviated version of the legend appears in *SNET*; Simmons speculates that Mudturtle "could be a distorted memory of Maushop."

Chapter 6—Federated Along One Keel

In his somewhat garbled, but extremely important, "Account of the names of the old Sachems and some of the most respectable Indians" (reprinted in Obed Macy's *History*), Zaccheus Macy translates Nickanoose as "to suck the foreteat." Macy mistakenly claims that Nickanoose was the son of Wauwinet when the opposite was the case. Macy also speaks of Nickanoose having a brother "named Wawpordonggo, which in English is white face, for his face was one side white, and the other side brown or Indian color." Edward Byers's *The Nation of Nantucket: Society and Politics in an Early American Commercial Center, 1660-1820* provides the best review of the English settlers' motivations in coming to Nantucket. In reply to an Indian petition to the General Court in the early eighteenth century, the Nantucket Proprietary described Wanackmamack as "a man in years" when the first white settlers arrived; if he was sixty years old in 1659, Wanackmamack would have been a young boy at the time of Harlow's arrival on the island.

Zaccheus Macy's description of Nickanoose's territory betrays a Native American tendency to, in Roger Williams's words, "picture the face of the country on his mind": "his bounds begin adjoining to the northward of...Wanackmamack's land and run still along to the northward and take in all Squam, and run on to our long sandy point, called Coatue or Nauma, which in the English is Long Point, where our Massachusetts lighthouse now stands, and then to the westward to New Town, then to the southward to a place called Weweeder Ponds, which in the English signifies a pair of horns, by reason there are two ponds that run to a point next to the sea, and spread apart so as to leave a neck of land, called Long Joseph's Point; which two ponds spread apart so as to resemble a pair of horns."

Macy on Wanackmamack's territory: "Their lands or bounds began at a place on the south side of the island, called Touphchue Pond, and ran across to the northward to a brown rock marked on the west side, that lies to the northward of our washing pond, called Gibbs Pond, on the west side of Saul's Hills and so over towards Polpis swamp, and then to the eastward to a place, Sesachacha Pond by the east sea. At the Southeast part of said tract is a high bluff of land, called Tom Nevers Head; and about two miles to the northward stands our famous fishing stage houses, where our

sick people go for their health, called Siasconset; and about a mile still to the northward is a very high cliff of land called Sankaty Head, then about a mile still to the
northward stands another fishing stage called Sesachacha."

Attapeat's territory: "His bounds were at the said Weweeder Ponds, and from
thence to the northward to a place called Quonsue meadow at Monomoy, where we
now call New Town, and from thence westward along to the southward of the hills
called Popsquatchet Hills, where our three mills now stand, and so to the west sea,
called Tawtemeo, which we call the Hummock Pond.... [T]heir habitation was
Miacomet, which signifies a meeting-place, and their meetinghouse they called
Miacomor." Although it does not seem to be substantiated by the record, Macy
claimed that the sachem Pattacohonet, whose territories included the island of
Tuckernuck ("which signifies, in English, a loaf of bread") also possessed the northwest corner of Nantucket: "His bounds extended from Madaket down eastward to
Wesco, which in English is the white stone, and so on the north side of Attapeat's
land, all bought of him at the coming of the English, saving some particular tracts
that belonged to the Japhets and the Hoites [who lived in the vicinity of modern-day
Capaum Pond] and some others." A fourth sachem, Seiknout (who, like
Pattacohonet, was a Vineyarder), controlled the island of Muskeget.

For extremely useful genealogical charts of the sachems, see Little's "The Writings
of Nantucket Indians." See Henry Barnard Worth's *Nantucket Lands and Land Owners*
for a valuable glossary of Indian names, which as Worth readily admits, are in many
cases best guesses. In "Indian Politics," Little speculates that Askammapoo and
Spotso are the real-life subjects of "The Legend of Wauwinet," which, according to
a foreword to the poem, "was written by Miss Charlotte P. Baxter and read by her
at an excursion to the little hamlet of Wauwinet, at the head of Nantucket Harbor,
made by the Nantucket Shakespeare Club on the 20th of June, 1876. The legend was
written to the meter of Longfellow's '*Hiawatha*,' and it breathes of one of the old
Indian traditions of the island—a pretty love tale enacted in the days of the Red Man."
The poem was reprinted in *NI*, January 21, 1911.

James Freeman in his "Notes on Nantucket, 1807" recorded an alternative version
of the legend: "Tradition has preserved a pleasing instance of the force of love. The
western tribe having determined to surprise and attack the eastern tribe, a young man
of the former, whose mistress belonged to the latter, being anxious for her safety, as
soon as he was concealed by the shades of night, ran to the beach, flew along the
shore below the limit of high water, saw his mistress a moment, gave her alarm, and
returned by the same route before day-break; the rising tide washed away the traces

of his feet. The next morning he accompanied the other warriors of the tribe to the attack: the enemy was found to be prepared; and no impression could be made on them. He remained undetected, till several years after peace being restored between the two tribes, and the young man having married the girl, the truth came to light."

The term "Tomokommoth" appears in *Miscellaneous Records, 1659-1823*, NCD. Howard Russell's *Indian New England Before the Mayflower* provides an excellent summary of the wide range of plants used as medicines by the Indians. The information concerning the use of pokeweed to treat poison ivy, rheumatism, and hemorrhoids (which the Rappahannocks administered by squatting over a simmering pot) comes from the American Indian Heritage Garden at the National Zoo in Washington, D.C. My thanks to Susan Beegel for bringing this reference to my attention.

For the most part, the Nantucket deeds referred to in this and other chapters are reprinted in Starbuck. The area that Mayhew reserved for himself was on the west side of Polpis Harbor and was called Masquetuck, which means "the reed land" according to Zaccheus Macy. According to Henry Worth, "Land was to [the Indian] as free as the water or air. Nobody could have exclusive right to it. So when the white men came and obtained deeds from the sachems it was merely the admission of the new settlers on equal terms with themselves. It was not that the Indian had ceased to have the right to enjoy the land but that another had become his co-occupant. Hence the idea that an Indian could be guilty of trespass was a strange innovation." In "Daniel Spotso: A Sachem at Nantucket," Elizabeth Little details how Nickanoose's grandson took up–to a certain extent–where his ancestor had left off, describing the "synthesis of native American and introduced English ideas" that took place on Nantucket, incorporating "Indian customs of tribute (periodic payment of something of value) and usufruct (rights to the use of a sachem's land, generally in return for tribute) with the English customs of rent (temporary use of land for a fee) and commons (rights to use of undivided land held in common by the proprietors, who pay periodic taxes)."

A document dated August 24, 1654, in MA 1:ii speaks of Captain Humphrey Allerton keeping sheep on Nantucket. For an account of Macy and Starbuck's first winter on Nantucket see my *Away Off Shore, Nantucket Island and Its People, 1602-1890*. Joseph Sansom in "A Description of Nantucket" recounts the tradition concerning Edward Starbuck's interruption of an Indian powwow. An anecdote recorded by "An Old Settler" (*NI*, May 28, 1831) suggests that Nantucket's Indians may not have been as "peaceably disposed" as other traditions claim. According to the account, prior to their arrival on the island Thomas Macy and the other first settlers, "believing the Indians were ever fearful of people appearing in deranged state," decided that Edward Starbuck would pretend to be "a man that was insane, should any appearance be made by the Indians to be hostile." The article continues, "Finally, they landed; and for appearances the Indians were for battle; [Starbuck] appeared with a pole, and made chase…with all the antic motions that could be expected from a deranged person: the Indians discovering him in that attitude; dispersed upon a quick march, believing it real; and from that, whenever appearances bespoke mischief from the Indians, [Starbuck] exerted himself as an insane person." This account seems to be a variant of the anecdote concerning Edward Starbuck and the powwow referred to in the text.

Providing an indication of just how "messy" the sale of the west end of the island to the English was is Elizabeth Little's summary in "Indian Politics" of the Indians "displaced…from their lands: Pakepanessa [the Chappaquiddick sachem struck by lightning], Conpokanet (George Nanahuma), Harry the son of Wapscowet, Jonas, Kimmo, Tequamomemy, Mekowakin, John Hoyt (Wannaquin), Obadiah (Obadiah Japhet), Peteson (Matakekin), Jacob Pattacohonnet's son, Mr. Harry, and Ahkieman." In the first decades of the settlement, the English had no choice but to be extremely careful about compensating Indians for the losses they incurred from cattle feeding on their corn; almost every year throughout the 1660s and '70s committees were organized to "go among the Indians and see what stray there is done in their corn by the English cattle and to agree with them in point of satisfaction" [June, 1671, *Miscellaneous Records*, NCD].

William Simmons speaks of the Indians' attitude toward the color white in *SNET*. James Freeman recounts the tradition concerning the Indians' "delight" with English plows and guns in "Notes on Nantucket, 1807." For an analysis of Indian deeds in general and Nickanoose in particular, see Little's "The Writings of Nantucket Indians," "Daniel Spotso: A Sachem at Nantucket Island," and especially "Sachem Nickanoose of Nantucket and the Grass Contest."

Daniel Gookin speaks of Joel and the wreck on Coatue in *Historical Collections of the Indians in New England*. For information concerning Harvard's role in educating the Indians, see Samuel Eliot Morison, *Harvard College in the Seventeenth Century*. A letter from Colonel George Cartwright to Colonel Nicolls dated January 1665 [Vol. 3 of *Minutes of the Executive Council of the Province of New York*, edited by Victor Hugo Paltsits] speaks of the shipwreck and murders at Coatue: "This day we have certain news that the Indians upon Nantucket Isle, murdered and pillaged the sailors belonging to a bark which was by storm driven upon it; but fearing it may be stale news before this may come to your hands going with so great uncertainties I will trouble you no further." Reference to the murders appears under the date of February 7, 1665, in Vol. 4 of *Records of the Colony of New Plymouth in New England*, edited by Nathaniel Shurtleff.

Killing wreck survivors was an ancient, if not honorable, tradition on both sides of the Atlantic–particularly in the west of England where many of Nantucket's first settlers had been born. As late as 1707, a British admiral who had washed ashore alive along the southwest coast of England was killed by an old woman for his emerald ring (see Dava Sobel's *Longitude* [New York, 1995]). John Winthrop describes the discovery of Oldham's body in his *History*. The deed from Nickanoose to Quaquachwinnit dates from 1668 and is in Little's "Writings of Nantucket Indians." In a letter dated May 9, 1676, to New York Governor Andros (reprinted in Starbuck), Thomas Macy speaks of "a considerable company of Indians [who] have formerly owned themselves Philip's men." Roger Williams in *Key* describes how Indians looking for a favor typically approached a sachem: "I have seen the party do obeisance, by stroking the [sachem] upon both his shoulders, and using the word, Cowawnkamish, I pray you favor."

The reference to Philip on Nantucket in 1665 is in *Miscellaneous Records*, NCD. Although it has been generally assumed that Philip made only one visit to Nantucket, during which he not only appeared at a town meeting but also had a standoff with the English, it is more likely that the sachem made two visits to Nantucket. Zaccheus Macy provides support for this by saying that Philip came to the island to kill John Gibbs "about the year 1669"–four years after he appears in the town records. Betty Schroeder in "The True Lineage of King Philip (Sachem Metacom)" cites a treaty from 1662 in which, just as the Tomokommoths would do on Nantucket in 1665, Philip declared himself a "subject to the King of England." While Schroeder claims that Philip was the grandson, not the son, of Massasoit, George Horner argues persuasively in "Massasoit and his Two Sons: Wamsutta and Metacom" that Philip was, in fact, the son of Massasoit.

Chapter 7—The Shark Pool

See Elizabeth Little's "Indian Horse Commons at Nantucket Island, 1660-1760" for a definitive discussion of Nantucket's Indian population in 1659. Zaccheus Macy was the first to come up with the figure of 3,000, while S. F. Cook in *The Indian Population of New England in Seventeenth Century* estimated the number at 1,500. According to Little it was probably closer to 3,000 and was "a temporarily large Nantucket Indian population which declined irregularly after English settlement as a result of immigration, emigration, and epidemics." Daniel Vickers in "The First Whalemen of Nantucket" compares Nantucket's population density to that of western Europe, while Edward Byers in *Nation of Nantucket* comments that the island's population was at least ten times what it had been anywhere else in the region prior to the plagues. Concerning the possible shortage of wood on Nantucket, Roger Williams in *Key* writes, "For [the Indians] having burnt up the wood in one place, wanting draughts to bring wood to them, are fain to follow the wood and so to remove to a fresh new place for the wood's sake."

Crèvecoeur in *Letters from an American Farmer* claims that smallpox initially swept through the Indians. Although no information exists on how Nantucket's Indians dealt with the outbreak, Thomas Cooper (in *SNET*) recounted how Indians on the Vineyard initially attempted to stave off disease with a complex ceremony that ended with the construction and burning of a wigwam, out of which would burst a young man who was, to all appearances, dead. Eventually, however, the man would come back to life and tell of being carried "in a large thing high up in the air, where he came to a great company of white people" who agreed to "have the distemper laid." Although from a different island, the ceremony bears some eerie similarities to legends told on Nantucket. Just as Roqua burned the western Indians' wigwams, then foretold the coming of the English, so does this account speak of fire, truth-telling, and "white people"; and just as a huge eagle carried papooses from Cape Cod up into the sky to Nantucket, so is flight a part of the ceremony.

The reference to a committee speaking to the Indians about whales, as are the other references to town records in this chapter, is from *Miscellaneous Records*, NCD. In "Drift Whales at Nantucket," Little and Andrews speculate that the English avoided a tax on whale oil by claiming it was an Indian endeavor: "Whale oil from Indian drift whales may have been exported tax-free from eastern Long Island, and Nantucket, which belonged to New York until 1692. This consideration may have played a role in the agreement with the Indians about whales on Nantucket, and, if drift whales were adequate to sustain an industry, could account for the relatively late beginning of English along-shore whaling on Nantucket." Elizabeth Little in "Historic Indian Houses on Nantucket" traces Jacob Washamon's deed trail from No-Bottom Pond to Squam.

Thomas Macy's concern about the Indians "taking offense" is in the previously cited letter of 1676 to Governor Andros. An entry dated June 13, 1660, in Vol. 3 of *Plymouth Records* reads: "At the earnest request of Wamsutta, desiring that in regard to his father is lately deceased, and he being desirous, according to the custom of the natives, to change his name, that the court would confer an English name upon him, which accordingly they did, and therefore ordered, that for the future he shall be called by the name of Alexander Pokanokett, and desiring the same in the behalf of his brother, they have named him Philip."

For a more detailed and, to a limited extent, alternative account of King Philip's pursuit of John Gibbs (as well as a theory as to how Altar Rock and Saul's Hills got their names), see my *Away Off Shore*. While Nantucket has an Altar Rock, Martha's Vineyard has a Pulpit Rock where Indian church services were conducted for more than two hundred years; see Russell Gardner's "My Sancheckantuckett." Obed Macy's account of Philip's appearance is in his *History*; Zaccheus Macy's account appears in *MHS* (1st Series, Vol. 3). Although this published version claims that Philip came after Gibbs in 1665, Macy's original manuscript version (NHA Ms. Collection 96, Folder 44) gives the date as "about the year 1669." Macy adds, "The above story we have handed down to us from our fathers so that we do not doubt the truth of it." Preston Morris in "Interesting Landmarks on Nantucket" speaks of Altar Rock being holy to the Indians. On Philip's relationship with Sassamon, see Douglas Edward Leach's *Flintlock and Tomahawk: New England in King Philip's War* and Russell Bourne's *The Red King's Rebellion: Racial Politics in New England, 1675-1678*. Peter Nabokov speaks of "folklore as sedition" in "Present Memories, Past History." If the Maushop legends did evolve to reflect the circumstances surrounding King Philip's War, Maushop's angry hurling of his wife Squant to Sakonnet, Rhode Island, may speak to King Philip's unsuccessful attempt to intimidate Awashonks, the squaw sachem of Sakonnet, into joining his rebellion against the English.

For accounts of the flowering of Christianity among the Nantucket Indians, see Gookin's "Historical Collections," Lloyd Hare's *Thomas Mayhew, Patriarch to the Indians*, and S. D. Hosmer's "The Indian Churches on Nantucket." *Some Correspondence Between the Governors and Treasurers of the New England Company*, edited by John W. Ford, contains letters from Mayhew and Eliot that speak of Nantucket. Russell Gardner touches on the Vineyard sachem Wampamog's role as a Nantucket missionary in "A Rare Artifact from Martha's Vineyard." Wampamog was the grandson of Towanquatick; a cane Wampamog presented as a gift to the Vineyarder Nicholas Norton was at one time in the possession of the Edgartown D.A.R. The location of the cane is currently unknown. Mayhew's 1678 report on Nantucket appears, curiously enough, in Vol. 2 of the *Plymouth Records* and is dated June 24, 1678. John Gardner's 1694 remark concerning the decline in Indian pow-wows on Nantucket originally appeared in Cotton Mather's *Magnalia Christi Americana* (1702) and is reprinted in Starbuck. Zaccheus Macy's account of an Indian church service is reprinted in Macy's *History*. Samuel Eliot Morison in *Harvard College in the Seventeenth Century* describes the process by which Eliot published his translation of the Bible. Danforth's remarks are in "A Letter from the Rev. Samuel Danforth" (dated August 8, 1720). A rantum scoot is defined in William F. Macy's *The Nantucket Scrap Basket* as "a day's 'cruise' or picnic about the island, usually a drive, but it might be on foot. The distinctive feature of such an excursion is that the party has no definite destination, but rather a roving commission...."

Evidence that Nantucket Indians were regularly traveling "off-island" is found in Vol. 4 of the *Plymouth Records* under the date of June 10, 1662: "A certain Nantucket Indian named Tetannett, alias Ned, was, for pilfering and stealing sundry things from John Mayo, of Eastham, sentenced by the court to be publicly whipped, and also warned, according to former order, being a stranger in our government, to depart to his own place at Nantucket; and in case he...be found [in Plymouth County] any other than as a passenger on a journey or the like, that then he shall be taken and publicly whipped, and sent home again." The Indians' increasing participation in the English economy can be tracked in Mary Starbuck's Account Book with the Indians at the NHA; see Elizabeth Little and Marie Sussek's "Index to Mary Starbuck's Account Book with the Indians."

A 1696 petition filed by Matthew Mayhew and James Coffin (MA 30:380) talks about "cider and strong drink" coming to the islands from Rhode Island, while a 1711 petition filed by James Coffin (MA 31:85) claims that "Indians from [Nantucket] run over thither [to Tuckernuck] in the winter to avoid the payment of their just debts and other Indians from Rhode Island and the mainland carry over liquors and strong drink to them...[and] they get drunk, fight and commit gross disorders...." Thomas Mayhew provides an interesting account of the Indians' response to their own use of liquor: "It is strange to see how readily [the Indians] strip themselves to receive punishment for this sin [of drunkenness] of which our nation is much guilty" [*Plymouth Records*, Vol. 2]. Peter Mancall in *Deadly Medicine: Indians and Alcohol in Early America* tells the complex story of Native American alcohol use. Obed Macy's account of Stephen Hussey's wedding party is reprinted in Starbuck as is the tradition concerning Mary Gardner Coffin at the "Oldest House."

Christopher Coffin Hussey in *Talks About Old Nantucket* recounts a story told to him by the daughter of Hannah Meader, who once ran a "house of entertainment" in Polpis, that is similar to the Mary Gardner Coffin anecdote: "This aged woman told also of an intoxicated Indian who came to her mother's in the evening in the absence of her father, and clamored at the back door for admittance. She was a small girl, and a little child lay asleep in the cradle. The mother took from the 'mantle tree shelf,' as it was then called, a tortoise shell snuff box, and told her she would give it to her if she would sit still, make no noise, and rock the cradle till she returned. Thinking the Indian would not venture around to the front door, she went out that way and ran to the nearest neighbor, not less than a half mile, where she obtained two men who returned with her, and found the intruder still at his post. 'Let me open the door,' she said, which she did, and before the Indian was secured he made a wound on that brave woman's neck, the scar of which remained to her death." Thomas Macy's reference to Indian liquor use and John Gardner's role in it are in his letters to Governor Andros. Obed Macy speaks of Indians causing trouble only when they were drunk in his *History*. Zaccheus Macy (reprinted in Obed's *History*) claimed that Nantucket's Indians brewed a "good strong beer."

For an excellent overview of the ecological impact of the Europeans in New England, see William Cronon's *Changes in the Land: Indians, Colonists, and the Ecology of New England*. Virginia DeJohn Anderson's "King Philip's Herds: Indians, Colonists, and the Problem of Livestock in Early New England" offers insights into Indian-English interaction over the subject of land use, while Elizabeth Little places it in the context of Nantucket in "Sachem Nickanoose and the Grass Contest" and "Indian Horse Commons at Nantucket Island, 1660-1760"–two articles upon which much in this chapter is based. In *Key* Roger Williams speaks of the Indians' attraction to horses: "they covet them above their cattle, rather preferring ease in riding, than their profit by milk and butter from cows and goats." Governor Bellomont's description of the English winter grass rights as a "circumvention and fraud" is reprinted in Starbuck. Concerning the importance of dogs to the Indians, see Eva Butler and Wendell Hadlock's "Dogs of the Northeastern Woodland Indians" and John Strong's "Late Woodland Dog Ceremonialism on Long Island in Comparative and Temporal Perspective."

The John Gardner letter to Governor Andros is reprinted in Starbuck. For accounts of the Half-Share Revolt, see Byers's *Nation of Nantucket* and Starbuck. Thomas Macy tells of Gardner providing the Indians with rum in his letter to the governor. Peter Folger's long and entertaining letter to the governor is also reprinted in Starbuck; for a detailed account of Peter Folger, see Florence Bennett Anderson's *A Grandfather for Benjamin Franklin*.

Chapter 8—The Whale

The tradition concerning a whale appearing in the harbor is in Obed Macy's *History*. Macy's account does not make it clear which harbor the whale appeared in: the

Great Harbor to the east or the much smaller Cappamet Harbor. Adding to the confusion is that Macy seems to have been under the impression that the original settlement was at Madaket, not Cappamet, claiming that "when the island became more peopled, the present situation of the town was preferred to Madaket, and the latter was accordingly abandoned." Although Macy may have assumed the tradition referred to a whale in the Great Harbor, it may have in reality concerned Cappamet, hence my placing it in that location (for an alternative possibility see my *Away Off Shore*). Of interest is an 1876 reference to a "forty-barrel right whale...aground on the bar near Capaum Pond" (*NI*, November 11, 1876, cited in Allen). Apparently, old habits died hard; according to the account: "Preparations were made to kill the whale: a boat was manned, harpoons procured, and the party set forth to effect the capture, but by this time [the whale] had succeeded in freeing itself and though pursued for eighteen miles[!], eventually escaped."

William Wood describes the typical Indian canoe as "not above a foot and a half or two feet wide and twenty foot long"–similar to the dimensions of an early Nantucket whaleboat. Concerning the Indians' boat-handling skills, Wood comments, "In these cockling fly-boats, wherein an Englishman can scarce sit without a fearful tottering, they will venture to sea when an English shallop dare not bear a knot of sail, scudding over the overgrown waves as fast as a wind-driven ship, being driven by their paddles.... If a cross wave (as is seldom) turn her keel upside down, they by swimming free her and scramble into her again."

One of the best sources concerning alongshore whaling techniques is Everett Edwards and Jeanette Edwards Rattray's *"Whale Off!" The Story of American Shore Whaling*. Peter Matthiessen's *Men's Lives: The Surfmen and Baymen of the South Fork* also provides useful background on whaling; for information specific to Nantucket, see Elizabeth Little's "The Indian Contribution to Along-Shore Whaling at Nantucket." Zaccheus Macy claims that Ichabod Paddack arrived on Nantucket in 1690. Little in "Indian Horse Commons" speaks of wigwam poles and firewood being imported to the island by 1712. See her "Nantucket Whaling in the Early 18th Century" concerning the use of "bookkeeping barter" on Nantucket. Obed Macy's description of how Nantucketers kept accounts is in his *History*. James Freeman recounts the tradition concerning the Indians being "religiously punctual." In *The Middle Ground* Richard White defines the concept for which he named his study of Indians in the Great Lakes Region: "On the middle ground diverse peoples adjust their differences through what amounts to a process of creative, and often expedient, misunderstandings. People try to persuade others who are different from themselves by appealing to what they perceive to be the values and practices of those others. They often misinterpret and distort both the values and the practices of those they deal with, but from these misunderstandings arise new meanings and through them new practices–the shared meanings and practices of the middle ground." Elizabeth Little claims that "Indians sometimes donated labor or goods to Starbuck's store to be entered in a sachem's account" ["Probate Records"]. I describe Mary and Nathaniel Starbuck's business as the "Starbuck Company Store" in *Away Off Shore*.

An unpublished manuscript by Charles Banks at the Martha's Vineyard Historical Society entitled "Indian Bondage" refers to the 1672 law concerning debt. In 1674 the nearby Plymouth Courts determined that "such Indians as live idly and will not take care to pay their just debts after conviction, shall be made to serve either those to whom they are indebted or some other man until the debt be satisfied...." Matthew Mayhew speaks of "not privileged" Indians in *A Brief Narrative*. The seventeenth-century court references are at NCD; the eighteenth-century court references are at NCCR. The reference to Folger and Musaquat's "controversy" over a driftwhale is in Miscellaneous Records at NCCD; Little refers to this episode in "Whales, Grass and Shellfish." Little provides a summary of the record concerning driftwhaling in "Indian Whalemen of Nantucket: The Documentary Evidence." Little first offered the English-Indian driftwhaling tax dodge theory in "Drift Whales at Nantucket." Obed Macy recounts the "green pasture" legend in his *History*.

See Little's "The Indian Contribution to Along-Shore Whaling" for an analysis of the development of the four whale stations. Ichabod Paddack, a Quaker who would return to his native Yarmouth by the early part of the eighteenth century, taught the Nantucketers a form of whaling that dated back to the Middle Ages when Basques began pursuing whales off the European coast. It would be the Basques who would introduce alongshore whaling to America when as early as the fifteenth century they began whaling in Newfoundland and Labrador. That Native Americans were inevitably exposed to the European technology was made clear when in 1602 Bartholomew Gosnold encountered a sail-equipped "Basque-shallop" manned by six Indians off the coast of present-day New Hampshire. Paul Dudley provides a detailed description of colonial whaleboats in his "Essay Upon the Natural History of Whales." Once the whaleboat builders' needs outstripped local supplies of white and red cedar, Nantucketers looked to Webb's Island in the vicinity of Cape Cod's Monomoy Point, which they would entirely denude of red cedars before it was eventually washed away in the eighteenth century (in Freeman). See my *Away Off Shore* for an account of the capsized canoe in 1669.

When it comes to the economic nuts and bolts of alongshore whaling, see Daniel Vickers's "The First Whalemen of Nantucket." Obed Macy speaks of the Indians' "readiness to join" the English in whaling in an unpublished manuscript at the NHA (subsequently referred to as "Notes"). William Root Bliss records the tradition that "Tom Never was an Indian…appointed by the English settlers to be master of the section [now known as Tom Nevers Head], to watch for and oversee the 'cutting-up' of stranded whales." Crèvecoeur tells of the Indian phrase "Awaite Pawana." Although "Thar She Blows!" would ultimately become the cry used when sighting a whale, another native term, "townor," which eventually evolved into "Townho," remained the cry (according to the Oxford English Dictionary) when hunting tortoises in the Galapagos; see also "The Town-Ho's Story" in Melville's *Moby-Dick.* (My thanks to Robert diCurcio for pointing this out to me.) I have relied on Dudley, Crèvecoeur, Obed Macy, Allen, Edwards, and Little in my recreation of a whalehunt; see Little's "Indian Contribution" for a discussion of the use of drogues. In the margins of a first edition of Crèvecoeur's *Letters from an American Farmer* at the NA is a nineteenth-century reader's reference to the remains of a brick tryworks beside Hummock Pond.

For information on Indian whalemen listed in surviving account books, see Little's "Indian Whalemen of Nantucket: The Documentary Evidence," "Indian Horse Commons," and "Whaling Off Nova Scotia, Newfoundland and Greenland in the Early Eighteenth Century." My own analysis of NCP records reveals that between 1718 and 1741 seventeen white Nantucketers (of a total of fifty-eight, almost thirty per cent) possessed Indian debts. In an almost unheard-of move in 1749, the Indian Cain Haggai "pleaded abatement" against John Upham's claim that the Indian owed him money. The court declared, "No action ought to be brought against an Indian without being first allowed as law directs"–a process that does not seem to have been rigorously followed on Nantucket. Kathleen Bragdon speaks of Eben Smugg and his patron-client relationship with Nathaniel Starbuck, Jr., in "Native Economy on Eighteenth-Century Martha's Vineyard and Nantucket." Obed Macy's comments concerning the English providing the Indians with liquor is in "Notes." See my *Away Off Shore* for a more detailed account of Abraham Monkey's string of appearances in Nantucket courts. The Indians accused of stealing Pinkham's pocket-book are in NCCR; the references to Indian servants is in NCP.

Although Nantucketers (with their Quaker abolitionist reputation to protect) have been reluctant to call Indian debt servitude slavery, the Vineyard historian Charles Banks had no such qualms–at least when it came to his private notes. In a manuscript chapter entitled "Indian Bondage" at the Martha's Vineyard Historical

Society that was never included in his monumental history of the Vineyard, Banks cited several incidents of what he called "this form of human slavery," then concluded, "Further citations are unnecessary to show that it was not an infrequent spectacle on the Vineyard to see scions of the 'Noble Red Man' standing on the block…to serve a term as bond servant for trifling misdemeanors." Charles Carpenter and Mary Grace Carpenter in *The Decorative Arts and Crafts of Nantucket* discuss evidence of Indian slavery in Nantucket probate records. According to the Carpenters, "some Indians were slaves, although the word *slave* does not often appear in eighteenth-century Nantucket records. The probate court records usually refer to them as 'servants' or by such terms as 'the Indian boy.' Nonetheless, they were slaves and not indentured servants."

Vickers refers to the Punker petition, which along with almost all the Indian petitions referred to in this chapter, appears in slightly modified form in Starbuck. Richard Macy's account book is at the NHA; Little cites the agreement between Macy and Ephraim in her "Indian Contribution to Along-Shore Whaling." Edward Augustus Kendall (who is cited by Vickers) describes the Indians' not-inconsiderable bargaining power in their negotiations with the English, a bargaining power that Nantucket's present-day business owners on this frequently labor-starved island can readily appreciate.

James Axtell speaks of the "drawing power of Indian culture" in "The White Indians in Colonial America" in *The European and the Indian*. Walter Folger's account of Nantucket boys learning Indian phrases is in "A Topographical Description of Nantucket." Henry David Thoreau's description of an Indian moosehunter appears in *The Maine Woods*. *Moby-Dick* is filled with references to how the Nantucket whaleman is a product of his exposure to native cultures. For example, Ishmael discovers the *Pequod*'s Quaker owners in a temporary "wigwam" made of the "long, huge slabs of limber black bone taken from the middle and highest part of the jaws of the rightwhale." The *Pequod* itself is described as a "cannibal of a craft" while in another instance the statement is made: "your true whalehunter is as much a savage as an Iroquois." Richard Slotkin in *Regeneration Through Violence* writes convincingly of the ways in which Melville's Nantucketers embody "a cannibal Eucharist unifying the spirit of the white man with that of the Indian wilderness."

Elizabeth Little argues that Nantucket whalehouses should be considered Indian houses in "Historic Indian Houses of Nantucket." Henry Forman, on the other hand, in *Early Nantucket and Its Whale Houses* sees the structures as essentially English-medieval. In his *History*, Macy states, "It is remarkable, that, notwithstanding the people had to learn the business of whaling, and to carry it on under many hazardous circumstances, yet not a single white person was killed or drowned in the pursuit, in the course of seventy years preceding 1760." See Allen concerning deaths in the Cape's alongshore whale fishery. Zaccheus Macy's anecdote about a whaleboat being caught out in a storm is reprinted in Obed's *History*. Russell Gardner and Kathleen Bragdon have indicated in separate instances to me that Macy's version of Massachusett (in its use of sounds, such as r, not usually part of the dialect spoken on Nantucket) was a pidgin of English and Massachusett. Concerning Macy's tale, Vickers comments, "In Macy's conviction of the esteem in which Indian whalemen held the English, so that only the threat of a lost white man could rally them, even in the face of death, the story is almost touching. Men so apparently devoted to their masters were fond memories indeed." Little was the first to interpret the story as a wry Indian joke in "The Indian Contribution to Along Shore Whaling."

Chapter 9—The Light

The tradition concerning Richard Macy and the first sperm whale to wash up on Nantucket appears in Obed Macy's "Notes" under the title "A Short Memorial of Richard Macy, Grandfather of Obed Macy." Starbuck also recounts the incident. Henry Worth claims the name Wesco (which Zaccheus Macy said meant "the white stone") is "derived from 'Wohsumocqussuk,' and means 'a bright stone.'" See Byers's *Nation of Nantucket* concerning the shift from Cappamet to Wesco; also my *Away Off Shore*. For the changes in Nantucket's Indian population throughout the seventeenth and eighteenth centuries, see Little's "Indian Horse Commons," which contains a useful graph.

The town order concerning "Indians, Negroes, and other suspected persons" is from 1726 and is in *Miscellaneous Records*, NCD. Obed Macy speaks of intoxicated Indians dying from the cold in his "Notes." The court case from 1744 describing similar events is in MA 31:470. The 1732 court case involving Simon Hue is in SCJ Records at MA; as is the 1739 case involving Happy Comfort. Little's "Indian Horsecommons" lists the selling of a horsecommon from Daniel Spotso to "Sam Humphrey, Indian" in 1720; in 1752 Samuel Humphrey is identified as "hangman" when he sold the horsecommon to his son-in-law, John Tashama. For a detailed analysis of the trial associated with the killing of a Nantucket Indian women by her husband Sabo in 1704, see Little's "The Mattequecham Wigwam Murder." Yasuhide Kawashima's *Puritan Justice and the Indian* places Nantucket in a regional context; according to Kawashima, criminals were branded with A for adultery, B for burglary, T for thievery, F for forgery, and I for incest.

In his "Notes," Obed Macy includes "A list of Indians who have been hanged on Nantucket since the island was settled by the whites." Macy lists seven, beneath which are added another four by Walter Folger; not listed by either Macy or Folger are the Indians hanged in connection with the murders of 1665, making for a minimum of thirteen Indians hanged on Nantucket. Lloyd Hare in *Thomas Mayhew, Patriarch to the Indians* points out Nantucket's high murder rate relative to the Vineyard and states that native Nantucketers appear to have been "more ferocious" than their Vineyard counterparts.

See Gookin for his account of Quakers on Martha's Vineyard; also see Robert Leach's "Quaker Intruders on Martha's Vineyard." Charles Cohen in "Conversion Among Puritans and Amerindians" provides theological evidence that supports Gookin's account of the Indians' inability to relate to the concept of the Inner Light; Cohen states that their traditional spiritual framework meant that the Indians "had difficulties conceiving a god of love." Thomas Story's account of his visit to Nantucket in 1704 is reprinted in Starbuck. See Byers's *Nation of Nantucket* on the role of Indian churches on Nantucket.

For more information on Timothy White and his relationship with the island's Indians, see my *Away Off Shore*. In White's papers (at the NHA) are his records of the thirteen years (beginning in 1728) that he "preached lectures to the Indians." Although the vast majority of lectures/sermons were delivered at Miacomet, averaging about a dozen per year with between twenty and sixty Indians in attendance, he also preached at "Agawam" (Occawa?) in 1739 and on July 2, 1740, preached in the morning "to the Baptists about 30" and in the afternoon "to the Presbyterians at Squam–20 or 30," indicating that not all Indians on Nantucket were Congregationalists. White's papers also include a 1739 list of the names of more than twenty Indians, most of whom appear to have been widowed women. On May 31, 1740, White made an account book entry lisiting "The Negro Doctor," who may have served as the island's Indian physician. White also kept a school where, according to his own account, he had "three or four Indians," a number that White felt would have been much larger "were it not for the charge of victualizing abroad."

Nathaniel Starbuck's will is in NCP. The Indian petitions referred to in this chapter are at MA and reprinted in Starbuck. Daniel Mandell's *Behind the Frontier: Indians in Eighteenth-Century Eastern Massachusetts* amply demonstrates that native Nantucketers were not the only Indians in the region petitioning the General Court. Bellomont's and Sewall's comments concerning Nantucket Indians also appear in Starbuck. Macy speaks of the Indians threatening the whites "with total extinction" in his *History*. The testimony concerning a "ranting Indian" in Rochester appears in MA 35:129a; the Indian claimed "there was 500 at Martha's Vineyard, 700 at Nantucket, and 400 at Chappaquiddick, all very well armed and in better manner than him." Obed Macy's "Notes" speaks of a fort on Gull Island in Lily Pond. The French governor's report concerning the 1695 landing of a French privateer on Nantucket is in the Archives Nationales of Paris (Colonies C11d2). Eliza Mitchell's account of the Indian uprising is contained in her reminiscences at the NHA. Yasuhide Kawashima in *Puritan Justice and the Indian* refers to the *New England Weekly Journal* account of the uprising; Starbuck also refers to newspaper accounts of the uprising. Indicating that the rumored Indian insurrection on Nantucket was big news throughout the colonies is a story (which mistakenly places it on Martha's Vineyard) in Benjamin Franklin's *Pennsylvania Gazette* (cited by Peter Mancall in *Deadly Medicine*).

Daniel Vickers in "The First Whalemen of Nantucket" speaks of the amount of land per Indian actually increasing well into the eighteenth century. Kathleen Bragdon's remarks concerning Indian petitions and the importance of land to the Wampanoag appear in "Native Economy on Eighteenth-Century Martha's Vineyard and Nantucket." Besides the Sakedan Indians' troubles with the Indians from Spotso's Country in Squatesit, there is evidence of additional "internal" problems among Nantucket's Indian communities. When in the early 1740s sachem Isaac Musaquat's widow Hannah in Miacomet insisted on collecting rents from Indians–specifically Benjamin Tashama and Corduda–who had never before had to pay for the use of their lands, Tashama and Corduda petitioned the General Court in Boston. They were subsequently advised by the court to settle the case among themselves. The court's reasoning was that since the losing party would, in all probability, not be able to pay court costs, the litigation would result in the Indians being "put under servitude."

The statement made by Dutch travelers in Long Island is cited by Roy Harvey Pearce in *Savagism and Civilization*. William Comstock's comments concerning the "depravity" of Nantucket Quakers appears in *The Life of Samuel Comstock*. In *SNET*, William Simmons cites the work of Irving Hallowell in his description of the psychological characteristics of Indians in the seventeenth century. The Indians' petitions got the English Nantucketers in trouble with more than just colonial officials. High-ranking Quakers in Philadelphia and elsewhere took Nantucket's Quaker Meeting repeatedly to task throughout the middle of the eighteenth century for the islanders' treatment of the Indians; see Robert Leach and Peter Gow's *Quaker Nantucket, The Religious Community Behind the Whaling Empire.*

Even someone as substantial as Ben Abel, the sachem whom the Sakedan Town Indians "put down," was not immune to the economic black magic of Indian debt. He may have possessed several coats and blankets, an "old hat," a horse, a wheel-less calash (a simple cart), a saddle, some dishes, an iron pot, a pewter pot, some tools, a table, three old chairs, some feathers and some "old fencing stuff," amounting to a grand total of almost £90, but he owed close to £100 on his death in 1744. Of the nine Indians whose estates were inventoried in the Nantucket Probate Records (which, almost by definition, means that they were relatively well off) prior to 1763, three owed more than they were worth. This would suggest that many, if not most, Indian families were bankrupted by the demise of their providers. Robert Leach (in a personal communication) provided the information concerning Paul Quaab's master Ebenezer Gardner. Mary Vanderhoop included the description of the "noble Indian residence" in a legend recorded in 1904 (in *SNET*). Paul Quaab's legal troubles in 1755 are documented in NCCR.

Byers in *Nation of Nantucket* cites a 1746 account that claims there were 900 Indians on the island, many of them Vineyarders who had come to Nantucket "being a place of better employment." Bragdon speaks of Nantucket Indians in "ancillary industries" in "Native Economy on Eighteenth-Century Martha's Vineyard and Nantucket." See Little's "Probate Records of Nantucket Indians" for inventories of the estates of Duch, Netowa, Micah, and Phillips. Zaccheus Macy's comments concerning well-off Nantucket Indians and the "parley" between Joshua Jethro and the Nantucket proprietors are reprinted in Macy's *History.* Jethro was the son of Captain Joshua Jethro (and Nickanoose's grandson) who had died in 1722 and had served in Gorham's Rangers under Major Benjamin Church (in *Early Encounters*, edited by Delores Carpenter). Although Obed Macy in his *History* claims the final hearing concerning Indian lands was in 1753, Henry Worth and Alexander Starbuck argue convincingly that it occurred in 1758.

Chapter 10—An Empty Ivory Casket

In *A Brief History of Gay Head, or "Aquinuih,"* Helen Attaquin records that the town's Indian population grew from 165 in 1749 to 276 in 1764. While not as dramatic, the statistics provided by Francis Hutchins in *Mashpee: The Story of Cape Cod's Indian Town* indicate that Mashpee's Indian population certainly did not decrease during this period, hovering in the neighborhood of 300. Given that Nantucket's Indian population dropped dramatically during the 1750s, it seems likely that significant numbers of Indians moved off the island to the Vineyard and Mashpee. The eventual spreading of the Indian Sickness to both Gay Head and Mashpee is another indication that Indians were moving from Nantucket to other native communities.

For information on the Miacomet region, see Little's "History of the Town of Miacomet." The testimony of the Nantucket Indians' guardians is reprinted in Starbuck. Obed Macy's description of the Indians as a "loose irreligious people" appears in his "Notes." Thoreau's comments concerning the degradation of a native people is in *The Maine Woods*. A summary of those Indians who owned English-style houses in Miacomet (from Little's "History of the Town of Miacomet"): In 1736 the whaleboat captain Eben Corduda purchased an English-style house in Miacomet from none other than Ebenezer Gardner (Paul Quaab's master) who acquired the dwelling from the Indian George Monkey–undoubtedly as part of a debt settlement. In 1747 Corduda purchased a second house in Miacomet from the Indians Peleg and Bethiah Duch, a house that would be subsequently sold to Peter Micah, an Indian whaleman who had the benefit of an English education courtesy of Timothy White, the island's Congregational minister. John Diamond, another whaleman, would inherit the village's sachemship from his father-in-law, Peter Musaquat. In 1762, Diamond had an English-style house near the Miacomet Meetinghouse, for which Josiah Spotso had purchased 1,500 feet of boards in 1732. Also living near the meetinghouse in a framed dwelling was the family of Joseph Secunnet, who may have been a descendant of Seiknout, sachem of Muskeget. Other Indians with the financial wherewithal to live in English-style houses included Jonathan Caleb, who married the sachem Peter Musaquat's widow Hannah, and the whaleman John Mooney, whose driftwhaling ancestors had gone by the name of Pattacohonet and had controlled the sachemship of Tuckernuck.

Zaccheus Macy's remarks concerning the cooperative nature of Indian society is reprinted in Obed's *History*, which also details the rise in whaling on Nantucket at the time. See Daniel Vickers's "Nantucket Whalemen in the Deep-Sea Fishery: The Changing Anatomy of an Early American Labor Force" for an account of the off-island recruitment network that brought labor from throughout the region to Nantucket.

My account of the Indian Sickness of 1763-64 is based largely on Little's "The Nantucket Indian Sickness," Obed Macy's *History*, and Edouard Stackpole's "The Fatal Indian Sickness of Nantucket That Decimated the Island Aborigines," in which are reprinted Andrew Oliver's 1764 report to the Royal Society, and letters written in 1797 and '98 to Moses Brown in Providence, Rhode Island, by Christopher

Starbuck. Another important letter concerning the sickness was written by Shubael Coffin (also to Moses Brown, who was compiling, in Little's words, "a study of yellow fever which would show that it was not necessary to quarantine ships from the West Indies") in 1798 and (along with the Starbuck letters) is in NHA Ms. Collection 126, Folder 2. Yet another useful account was recorded by Dr. Joseph Parrish in 1805 and published in 1853 as "Remarkable account of the Yellow Fever as it prevailed among the Indians on the Island of Nantucket" ["Indian" blue files at the NHA]. Parrish wrote the account "after a visit to the island, and the facts were given by a gentleman who was one of the selectmen at the time of the epidemic." My thanks to Dr. Timothy Lepore for bringing this source to my attention.

Testifying to the anti-Irish feelings prevalent on Nantucket in the eighteenth century is a passage from the log of Peleg Folger written in 1752 while whaling along the coast of Newfoundland: "There the Irishmen cursed us at a high rate for they hate the whalemen... Here we lay till June 27th, and in that space of time bore many an oath of the Paddies and bogtrotters, they swearing we should not cut up our whale in the harbor." A copy of the account describing Richard Mitchell's discovery of the sickness at Miacomet is in the "Indian" blue files at the NHA and contains the note: "The following article was taken originally from a paper called *The Bunker Hill Auriea*, and printed in the *Nantucket Inquirer* in 1833." Christopher Hussey's anecdotes concerning the Indian Sickness are in his *Talks About Old Nantucket*.

See *NI* (June 21, 1890) for an article describing the discovery of the list of Indians who died. Apparently, traditions concerning the island's Indians were still alive and well in 1890, even if the memories reflected an underlying prejudice: "The few elderly people to whom this paper has been shown have recalled anecdotes about some of these Indians. Among these is one about the whipping of one of the women at the public whipping-post upon her body naked to the waist. Very likely there is more sentiment lavished upon the Indian of today, out upon the Western Plains, than the great grandparents of the present Islander bestowed upon his dirty, thriftless and thieving Indian neighbor. Another anecdote is told about Ben Cheegin's unsavory remark to one of the Island kings of his day." Little and Marie Sussek's "Nantucket Indians who died of the Sickness, 1763-64" provides an analysis of the 222 names of the dead. Backing up Christopher Hussey's claim that some of the last to die lived near the house of entertainment in Polpis is that the 222nd Indian listed is David Quaab, from a family with strong connections to, if not Polpis, the nearby Indian town of Sakedan.

Possibly betraying a certain anxiety concerning the plague that was raging among the Indians at their doorstep was an ongoing discussion among the selectmen throughout the fall of 1763 concerning the possibility of inoculating the townspeople for smallpox. Throughout his long life, Zaccheus Macy established a reputation as a Quaker medicine man, using traditional poultices and herbal medicines while setting bones on the island free of charge. In 1792 he estimated that he had set more than 1,700 bones–"some strangers, some blacks, and all sorts, rich and poor, old and young, good and bad."

In a presentation at the NHA symposium, "Nantucket and the Native American Legacy of New England," Dr. Timothy Lepore made a convincing case for the likelihood that the Indian Sickness of 1763-64 was louse-borne relapsing fever; see *HN* (Winter 1996). The information concerning louse-borne relapsing fever comes from *Theory and Practice in American Medicine*, edited by Gert Brieger; my thanks, once again, to Dr. Lepore for providing me with this source. The missionary John Eliot speaks of the Indians' habit of eating lice in his "Rules for the Praying Indians at Concord, Massachusetts" [Alden Vaughan's *New England Frontier*]. In a personal communication (August 1997) Andrew Spielman, Professor of Tropical Health at the Harvard School of Public Health, theorized that the Indian Sickness on Nantucket was typhus. Daniel Mandell in *Behind the Frontier* cites the reference to the disease spreading to Mashpee. Jared Diamond in *Guns, Germs, and Steel* discusses how "crowd diseases…need a human population that is sufficiently numerous and sufficiently densely packed." The bluefish prophecy appears in *Miriam Coffin*.

Chapter 11—While the Bluefish Were Gone

Death records list considerably more Indians (a total of thirty-four between the years 1784 and 1855) than accounted for by Obed Macy, but Macy may have considered many of them to be off-islanders or "half-breeds." Elizabeth Little has compiled a list from the town records in Table 4 of "The Indian Sickness at Nantucket." Mary Holyoke's diary account of her 1775 trip out to Shimmo to eat quahogs roasted by Nantucket Indians is cited by Kathy Neustadt in *Clambake: A History and Celebration of an American Tradition*; Churchman's reference is in Henry Cadbury's "An Off-Islander's Impressions." Obed Macy's list of last Indians, in which he refers to Abram Quary as "half-white," is in his "Notes." Little's "Probate Records of Nantucket Indians" includes Benjamin Tashama's inventory from NCP. Legends concerning haunted Indian churches are in *SNET*. Macy in his "Notes" speaks of Peleg Swain moving the Indian church in Sakedan to town. Hart's account of an Indian wigwam with many English touches is corroborated by descriptions of wigwams on the Vineyard and Mashpee. Edward Kendall, who visited Mashpee about the same time he came to the Vineyard and Nantucket, described a wigwam in Mashpee "with some mixture of European architecture....[T]he inside of the wigwam is perfectly neat. The furniture in the houses, here, is generally of the same description with that of the poorer whites."

On Dorcas Honorable's background, see Eliza Mitchell. The "eight Pequot Indians" are listed in Volume 1 of the *Financial Records of William Rotch, Sr.*–a huge ledgerbook in the collection of the Old Dartmouth Historical Society in New Bedford. (My thanks to Daniel Vickers for bringing this resource to my attention.) Concerning English-Indian intermarriages, see Daniel Mandell's *Behind the Frontier* in which is cited a state investigator's claim "that almost every marriage in the Yarmouth Indian community since 1700 had been between whites and Indians." On Martha's Vineyard Joseph Dagget, the first white settler of what is now Oak Bluffs, married the Indian Alice Sissetom (granddaughter of sachem Wampamog, missionary to Nantucket), beginning a family line known as the "bow and arrow Daggets"; see Russell Gardner's "My Sanchekantackett." Mandell cites the report to the state senate about the Gay Head Indians' resentment concerning the rising number of black men in their community. Whether or not it reflected his patrimony, there was a Nantucket Indian during the first half of the eighteenth century (who appeared frequently in court) with the name of John Swain but who was also referred to as "England." According to a family tradition, a Nantucketer with the last name of Marden married an Indian woman at the end of the nineteenth century and moved to Martha's Vineyard (told to the author by David Wood, June 1997).

Benjamin Tashama's second wife Jenny is listed in Nantucket Vital Records. Absalom Boston's Indian-black background, and his ultimate identification with the black side of his heritage, closely follows that of Paul Cuffe from the New Bedford area; see Lamont Thomas's *Rise to Be a People*. The Walmsley family (descended from Massasoit) would move from Nantucket to Rhode Island some time after Benjamin's death in the West Indies in 1803 as I learned in a personal communication (August 1997) from Russell Gardner. Two Gay Head legends concerning how "snarly" or "kinky" hair was introduced into the Indian population are in *SNET*. The report of the Chappaquiddick guardians and Mashpee's Reverend Hawley are cited by Daniel Mandell in *Behind the Frontier*. The mention of Indian women being drawn to major seaports is in "A Description of Mashpee, in the County of Barnstable, September 16th, 1802" [MHS (Vol. 3, 2nd Series, 1815)]. The drowning of four Indians and an African American on their way to a whaleship is recorded in *Vital Records*. Peter Folger's log is at NA. See Emil Guba's "The Trial and Execution of Nathan Quibby"

284   *Notes to Pages 215-218*

for court testimony concerning the murders on board the *Sally*. Although the list of
Indians hanged on Nantucket compiled by Obed Macy names four Indians between
1768 and 1769, a study of Supreme Judicial Court Records during this period (conducted by Elizabeth C. Bouvier, Head of Archives, and her staff) "found no murder
cases involving Indians residing in Nantucket County" (with the exception of Nathan
Quibby). Is Macy's list simply wrong, or were Nantucketers capable of hanging
Indians without benefit of a proper trial? After mentioning these executions in his
History, Macy (a Quaker) states: "The putting to death of these persons was, of
course, in accordance with the requirements of the law of the land, and cannot be
considered as expressing the opinion of the inhabitants on that mode of punishment.
We believe the sentiments of this community are, and always have been, strongly
against capital punishments."

On Crispus Attucks, see Sidney Kaplan's *The Black Presence in the Era of the
American Revolution*. On how seamen contributed to the rising tide of protest prior
to the Revolution, see Jesse Lemisch's "Jack Tar in the Streets: Merchant Seamen
in the Politics of Revolutionary America." Peter Linebaugh and Marcus Rediker's
"The Many-Headed Hydra: Sailors, Slaves, and the Atlantic Working Class in the
Eighteenth Century" talks of the multicultural aspect of this rebellious group. John
Adams's remarks concerning the Boston Massacre as well as court transcripts
describing what happened are in Vol. 3 of *Legal Papers of John Adams*, edited by L.
Kinvin Wroth and Hiller Zobel. The Gay Head legend that talks about British
press gangs is in *SNET*. Abraham William's letter concerning the "riot and affray"
on Nantucket is in NHA Collection 197. William Apess tells of preaching on
Nantucket in *On Our Own Ground: The Complete Writings of William Apess*, edited
by Barry O'Connell.

Mandell in *Behind the Frontier* summarizes the circumstances that allowed for
the survival of Indian communities after the Revolution: "Mashpee and other large
coastal Indian communities, such as Christiantown, Chappaquiddick, Gay Head,
and Herring Pond, barred white settlers from their reserves and continued to hold
their lands in common. Their lands were protected by the state law that barred its
sale to outsiders. Their relative isolation, often-abundant resources, sizable populations, and location along the coast gave these enclaves considerable advantages in
the struggle to survive." Of course, Nantucket's Indians were not allowed this
opportunity. Concerning Absalom Boston and his fight to desegregate the schools,
see Barbara Linebaugh's *The African School and the Integration of Nantucket Public
Schools, 1825-1847*.

Captain Joshua Coffin's encounter with natives from a previously undiscovered island is in *NI* (March 22, 1828). The South Sea Islanders attending Sunday school are described in *NI* (April 25, 1822); *NI* (May 9, 1822) contains the story describing their religious ceremonies in the streets of Nantucket. Town death records list three South Sea Islanders: a twenty-one-year-old "Sandwich Island Canackar" who died in New Guinea on October 24, 1836; a thirty-five-year-old "Sandwich Island Indian [who] came here in one of our whaling ships from Round Cape Horn" and was found dead on February 27, 1837; and a twenty-five-year-old "Canaca [from] S. Sea Islands" who died of "lung fever" on June 12, 1844.

Macy speaks of the disturbing "immoralities" overtaking Nantucket in his *History*. Although Christopher Hussey in *Talks about Old Nantucket* claimed that the bluefish returned with the death of Abram Quary, the evidence points to their return prior to 1834; see Catherine Carlson's "Seasonality of Fish Remains." In the legend of Mudturtle, Samuel Jenks pokes fun at the tendency to romanticize the phenomenon of the last Indian: "The contemplative mind would fain muse on various and solemn topics—ruminating on the rise and declension of nations—pondering on the vicissitudes of fortune—moralizing on the strange destiny of mortals—and making multitudes of other sad and sober reflections: all which, the kind reader is humbly desired to do at his leisure."

Some more details about Abram Quary: He was born in a wigwam in Miacomet on January 30, 1772, the son of Sarah Apie Quary, whom Benjamin Franklin Folger praised for her "strength of character and endurance," as well as her basketmaking. As late as the 1830s, Abram could still point out "the desolated hearth of his birthplace indicated by a confused heap of broken stones." As a young boy Abram—like so many Indian children before him—was placed in the home of a white family, the Stephen Chases. By the age of twenty-one he was a whaleman, and on July 30, 1793, he left his mark on a document in which he requests that Captain Zenas Coffin pay Randall Rice "all there is due to me for services in the ship *Lydia*." In 1806, the town's vital records report the death of one Abigail Quary, which an earlier census reveals to have been Abram's wife. Four years later, on November 7, 1806, the Nantucket Marriage Records indicate that Abram, who in an interesting throwback to the usage of his grandfather and great-grandfather, is recorded as "Abraham Skoote (int. Sootequary)," married a woman named Fanny Hall. By 1834, when the novel *Miriam Coffin* described Quary as Nantucket's "last Indian," Fanny Hall Quary was apparently dead, as was their child.

Benjamin Franklin Folger related an interesting anecdote concerning Quary's career as a Shimmo "caterer": A woman was once so appalled by the fact that Quary set his table with a bedsheet that she replaced it with a tablecloth of her own. She and her guests also took it upon themselves to move Abram's table into the middle of the room so that it could seat more people. Just as they sat down, Abram appeared at the door, a frown on his face. When asked what the problem was, Quary replied, "The table don't go so." Not until the room had been returned to its original condition would Abram let them proceed with their meal.

The "party line" concerning English-Indian relations on Nantucket is in NHA Ms. Collection 126, Folder 7. The letter from John R. Barreau about Nantucketers with Indian blood is in *NI* (November 4, 1944). Further proof that there was never a last Nantucket Indian: It turns out that Dorcas Honorable, who outlived Abram Quary by two months, had a daughter named Emmeline. Emmeline Honorable eventually became Emmeline Castro and had a daughter named Isabel. By 1895 Isabel Castro had married a man named Hiram Reed. The Reed children could claim the Indian school teacher and minister Benjamin Tashama as their great-great-great grandfather. In 1917, the massive 1,800-pound doorstone that had once fronted Tashama's home was moved to the entrance of the Nantucket Historical Association's building on Fair Street, a fire-proof structure that had been attached to the island's only remaining Quaker Meetinghouse (see *NI* [July 28, 1917]). (By then, the woman who was generally regarded as Nantucket's "last Quaker," Eunice Paddack, had been dead for seventeen years.)

In 1904, the Improved Order of Red Men—a nationwide fraternal organization whose roots reached back to before the Revolution—convened for the first time on Nantucket. Calling themselves the Wauwinet Tribe No. 158, the island's original seventy-five members elected Horace L. Gibbs as their "sachem." For many years to come, more than a few Nantucketers would mistakenly assume that the Red Men, who annually marched through the streets of town in western-style Indian headdresses, were the descendants of the island's native people; see Tim Desrocher's "The Red Men." Russell Gardner traces his Nantucket ancestry in "The Cape Cod-Nantucket-Martha's Vineyard Connection: A Traditional Lineage from Sachems of the Cape and Islands."

Russell Gardner, or Great Moose, is living proof of the strength of the Wampanoag's oral traditions, publishing articles in regional journals that draw not only on his extensive research but the knowledge handed down to him from ancestors. Gardner grew up knowing his grand aunt, Susan Look Ryder, who knew her great-grandfather, Joseph Look, who in turn knew his grandfather, Samuel Look, a

Wampanoag born on Martha's Vineyard in 1702 and whose wooden pendant is in Gardner's possession today. Writes Gardner, "This leapfrogging over generations has a telescoping effect…, shortening the distance in time and allowing for more accurate transmission of oral tradition, too often scorned as hearsay" [in "A Rare Aboriginal Artifact from Martha's Vineyard Island, With a Living Family History"].

For a brief account of the rediscovery of the Miacomet Indian Burial Ground, see Little's "History of Miacomet." Throughout the nineteenth century, the burial ground at Miacomet had been pilfered repeatedly by trinket hunters and amateur phrenologists. In *NI* (May 26, 1840) is this account of the burial ground: "It is without a fence, or headstone of any description, to protect or distinguish this humble, but thickly peopled cemetery…. We count some twenty excavations within the space of as many yards, which must have been made within a very few years–probably at that period when the fever of phrenology so raged among us, that no man's head was safe upon his own shoulders…. One might almost hear the last of the buried Miacomets, calling from his resting place–"Ye Vampires! take my cranium if ye will! but at least smooth the sod decently that hides the residue of my frame!" Little speaks of a graveyard in Quaise in "Abram Quary of Abram's Point."

Epilogue—Port of the *Pequod*

See Thomas Farel Heffernan's *Stove By a Whale* concerning Melville's interest in the *Essex* disaster. For Smalley's own account of how he killed a white whale, see his "I Killed 'Moby Dick.'" The Gay Head Wampanoag Aquinnah Research Library also contains a file of clippings concerning Amos Smalley. Nosapocket's stories of Maushop are in *SNET*. The Gay Head Indian Nanette Madison recorded a legend (circa 1955) describing Maushop's relationship with a white whale that echoes the Poot Pond legend's description of a whale swimming through an underground passage to an island pond: "Maushop's favorite pet was a large white whale, and knowing he most certainly would be pursued, Maushop dug a deep pool, connected to the sea by an underground passage. Today the pool is known as Witch Pond, because it is said to have strange properties…. Even now on foggy nights, some people claim to hear peculiar sounds from that direction, while others say they have felt a heavy moisture on their cheeks. Could it be Maushop's white whale, come up to spout?" (in *SNET*).

Russell Gardner, or Great Moose, provided the author with this previously unpublished Maushop legend entitled "Maushop's Return in the Twentieth Century, A Personal Account": "Over the centuries our old giant Maushop has been said to have left his den in the cliffs of Aquinnah and removed to other parts, returning periodically to his old haunts to aid his people. It has even been rumored that old Maushop had died. However, a recent event has, for the first time in history, provided physical evidence to the contrary....

"Early versions of Maushop's activities include his attempts to build a bridge from Gay Head to Cuttyhunk, whereby a crab bit his toe and he dropped the rocks from his apron, creating the so-called Devil's Bridge. It is also history that Captain Edward Harlow, an Englishman, took hostages at the Vineyard in 1611.

"These waters have been charted for close to four hundred years yet in the year 1992 the greatest ocean liner in the world struck an *uncharted* rock there. It was the Devil's Bridge and the ship was the *Queen Elizabeth II, an English ship*. You can't tell me that Maushop is dead. That old giant is still out there moving those rocks around, still looking after his people, the Wampanoag people."

For an account of Herman Melville's 1852 visit to Nantucket, see Susan Beegel's "Herman Melville: Nantucket's First Tourist." Ungar is not the only figure in *Clarel* that hearkens back to Melville's visit to Nantucket. There is also a character based on Captain Pollard (of the *Essex*)–see Walter E. Bezanson's "Historical and Critical Note" in the Northwestern-Newberry edition of the poem.

SELECT BIBLIOGRAPHY

Allen, Glover M. *The Whalebone Whales of New England*. Boston, 1916.

Anderson, Florence Bennett. *A Grandfather for Benjamin Franklin*. Boston, 1940.

Anderson, Virginia DeJohn. "King Philip's Herds: Indians, Colonists, and the Problem of Livestock in Early New England." *William and Mary Quarterly* 51 (1994).

Attaquin, Helen. *A Brief History of Gay Head, or "Aquinuih."* Published by the author, 1970.

Axtell, James. *The Invasion Within*. New York and Oxford, 1985.

——. "The White Indians in Colonial America." *The European and the Indian: Essays in the Ethnohistory of Colonial North America*. New York and Oxford, 1981.

Banks, Charles E. *History of Martha's Vineyard*. 1911. Reprint. Edgartown, Massachusetts, 1966.

Basset, Benjamin. "Fabulous Traditions and Customs of the Indians." *Massachusetts Historical Society Collections*. Vol. 1 (1792).

Baxter, James Phinney, ed. *Sir Ferdinand Gorges and His Province of Maine*. 3 vols. Boston, 1890.

Beck, Horace P. *Gluskap the Liar and Other Indian Tales*. Freeport, Maine, 1966.

Beegel, Susan F. "Herman Melville: Nantucket's First Tourist." *Historic Nantucket* (Fall 1991).

Berkhofer, Robert F., Jr. *The White Man's Indian: Images of the American Indian from Columbus to the Present*. New York, 1978.

Bliss, William Root. *September Days on Nantucket*. Boston and New York, 1902.

Bourne, Russell. *The Red King's Rebellion: Racial Politics in New England, 1675–1678*. New York and Oxford, 1990.

Bradford, William. *Of Plymouth Plantation, 1620–1647*. Edited by Samuel Eliot Morison. Reprint. New York, 1970.

Bragdon, Kathleen J. "'Another Tongue Brought In': An Ethnohistorical Study of Native Writings in Massachusetts." Ph.D. diss., Brown University, 1981.

——. "Native Economy on Eighteenth-Century Martha's Vineyard and Nantucket." *Papers of the 17th Algonquian Conference*. Edited by William Cowan. Ottawa, 1986.

——. *Native People of Southern New England, 1500–1650*. Norman, Oklahoma; and London, 1996.

Braun, Esther K., and David P. Braun. *The First Peoples of the Northeast*. Lincoln, Massachusetts, 1994.

Brenizer, Meredith Marshall. *The Nantucket Indians: Legends and Accounts before 1659*. Nantucket, 1976.

Brieger, Gert H., ed. *Theory and Practice in American Medicine: Historical Studies from the Journal of the History of Medicine and Allied Sciences.* New York, 1976.

Bullen, Ripley P., and Edward Brooks. "Three Burials at the Hughes Site, Nantucket, Massachusetts." *Bulletin of the Massachusetts Archaeological Society* 10 (1948).

Bushnell, David. "New England Names." *American Anthropologist* 13 (1911).

Butler, Eva M., and Wendell S. Hadlock. "Dogs of the Northeastern Woodland Indians." *Bulletin of the Massachusetts Archaeological Society* 10 (1949).

Byers, Edward. *The Nation of Nantucket: Society and Politics in an Early American Commercial Center, 1660–1820.* Boston, 1987.

Cadbury, Henry J. "An Off-Islander's Impressions, June, 1781." *Proceeedings of the Nantucket Historical Association* (1949).

Carlson, Catherine C. "Seasonality of Fish Remains from Locus Q-6 of the Quidnet Site, Nantucket Island, Massachusetts." *Bulletin of the Massachusetts Archaeological Society* 51 (1990).

Carpenter, Charles H., and Mary Grace Carpenter. *The Decorative Arts and Crafts of Nantucket.* New York, 1987.

Carpenter, Delores Bird, ed. "Early Encounters: Native Americans and Europeans in New England." From *The Papers of W. Sears Nickerson.* East Lansing, Michigan, 1994.

Chamberlain, Barbara Blau. *These Fragile Outposts: A Geological Look at Cape Cod, Martha's Vineyard, and Nantucket.* New York, 1964.

Chatwin, Bruce. *The Songlines.* New York, 1987.

———. *What Am I Doing Here* New York, 1989.

Cogley, Richard W. "Two Approaches to Indian Conversion in Puritan New England: The Missions of Thomas Mayhew, Jr., and John Eliot." *Historical Journal of Massachusetts* 28 (1995).

Cohen, Charles L. "Conversion Among Puritans and Amerindians: A Theological and Cultural Perspective." *Puritanism: Transatlantic Perspectives on a Seventeenth-Century Anglo-American Faith.* Edited by Frank Bremer. Boston, 1993.

Comstock, William. *The Life of Samuel Comstock.* Boston, 1840.

Cook, Sherburne F. *The Indian Population of New England in the Seventeenth Century.* Berkeley, 1976.

Crèvecoeur, Hector St. John de. *Letters from an American Farmer.* London, 1782. Reprint. Edited by Albert E. Stone. New York, 1981.

Cronon, William. *Changes in the Land: Indians, Colonists, and the Ecology of New England.* New York, 1983.

Cushman, Robert. "The Sin and Danger of Self Love" (1622). In *Chronicles of the Pilgrim Fathers.* Edited by John Masefield. New York, 1910.

Danforth, Samuel. "Letter, August 8, 1720." *Proceedings, of the Massachusetts Historical Society* , 4th ser., vol. 1.

Deloria, Vine, Jr. *Red Earth, White Lies: Native Americans and the Myth of Scientific Fact.* New York, 1995.

Dening, Greg. *Islands and Beaches: Discourse on a Silent Land. Marquesas, 1774–1880.* Chicago, 1980.

Desrocher, Tim. "The Red Men." *Nantucket Experience,* June 1982.

Diamond, Jared. *Guns, Germs, and Steel: The Fates of Human Societies.* New York and London, 1997.

Dilliplane, Timothy L. "European Trade Kettles," in *Burr's Hill, A Seventeenth-Century Wampanoag Burial Ground in Warren, Rhode Island.* Edited by Susan G. Gibson. Providence, 1980.

Dincauze, Dena F. "A Capsule Prehistory of Southern New England." In *The Pequots in Southern New England: the Fall and Rise of an American Indian Nation.* Edited by Laurence M. Hauptman and James D. Wherry. Norman, Oklahoma; and London, 1990.

Douglas-Lithgow, R. A. *Nantucket: A History.* New York, 1914.

Dudley, Paul. "An Essay upon the Natural History of Whales, with a Particular Account of the Ambergris Found in the *Sperma Ceti* Whale." Royal Society of London: *Philosophical Transactions* 33 (1725).

Dunn, Jerome P. "Squanto Before He Met the Pilgrims." *Bulletin of the Massachusetts Archaeological Society* (Spring 1993).

Dunwiddie, Peter W. "Postglacial Vegetation History of Coastal Islands in Southeastern New England." *National Geographic Research* 6 (1990).

Edwards, Everett J., and Jeanette Edwards Rattray. *"Whale Off!" The Story of American Shore Whaling.* New York, 1932.

Folger, Eva. *Nantucket: The Glacier's Gift.* New Haven, 1911.

Folger, Walter, Jr. "A Topographical Description of Nantucket, June, 1791." *Massachusetts Historical Society Collections,* 1st ser., vol. 3.

Ford, John W., ed. *Some Correspondence Between the Governors and Treasurers of the New England Company.* N.d. Reprint. New York, n.d.

Forman, Henry Chandlee. *Early Nantucket and Its Whale Houses.* 1966. Reprint. Nantucket, 1991.

Freeman, James. "Notes on Nantucket, 1807." *Massachusetts Historical Society Collections,* 2d ser., vol. 3.

Gardner, Arthur. *Wrecks Around Nantucket.* Nantucket, 1915.

Gardner, Russell H. "My Sanchekantakett." *The Dukes County Intelligencer.* (November 1970).

——. "A Rare Aboriginal Artifact from Martha's Vineyard Island, With a Living History." *Bulletin of the Massachusetts Archaeological Society* (Spring 1993).

——. "The Cape Cod–Nantucket–Martha's Vineyard Connection: A Traditional Lineage from Sachems of the Cape and Islands." *Nantucket Algonquian Studies* 15 (1994).

Goddard, Ives, and Kathleen Bragdon. *Native Writings in Massachusett.* Philadelphia, 1988.

Gookin, Daniel. *Historical Collections of the Indians in New England.* 1792. Reprint. New York, 1972.

Gookin, Warner Foote. *Capawack, alias Martha's Vineyard.* Edgartown, Massachusetts, 1947.

Guba, Emil. *Nantucket Odyssey.* Waltham, Massachusetts, 1965.

——. "The Trial and Execution of Nathan Quibby." *Historic Nantucket* (July 1967).

Hamell, George R. "Strawberries, Floating Islands, and Rabbit Captains: Mythical Realities and European Contact in the Northeast During the Sixteenth and Seventeenth Centuries." *Journal of Canadian Studies* (February 1987).

Hare, Lloyd C. *Thomas Mayhew: Patriarch to the Indians, 1593–1682.* New York, 1932.

Harkin, Michael. "History, Narrative, and Temporality: Examples from the Northwest Coast." *Ethnohistory* (Spring 1988).

Hart, Joseph C. *Miriam Coffin, or The Whale-Fishermen: A Tale.* 1834. Reprint, with foreword by Nathaniel Philbrick. Nantucket, 1995.

Hawley, Gideon. "Letter, 1794." *Massachusetts Historical Society Collections,* 4th ser., 1795

Heath, Dwight B., ed. *A Journal of the Pilgrims at Plymouth: Mourt's Relation.* New York, 1963.

Heffernan, Thomas Farel. *Stove by a Whale: Owen Chase and the Essex.* Hanover, New Hampshire; and London, 1981.

Hill, Jonathan D., and Robin M. Wright. "Time, Narrative, and Ritual: Historical Interpretations from an Amazonian Society." *Rethinking History and Myth: Indigenous South American Perspectives on the Past.* Edited by Jonathan D. Hill. Chicago, 1988.

Horner, George R. "Massasoit and his Sons: Wamsutta and Metacom." *Bulletin of the Massachusetts Archaeological Society* (Spring 1995).

Hosmer, S. D. "The Indian Churches on Nantucket." *Congregational Quarterly* 4 (1865).

Hough, Franklin B., ed. *Papers Relating to the Islands of Nantucket, Martha's Vineyard and Other Islands Adjacent, Known as Dukes County While under the Colony of New York.* Albany, 1856.

Hubbard, William. *A General History of New England.* Cambridge, Massachusetts, 1815.

Hussey, Christopher Coffin. *Talks About Old Nantucket.* Nantucket, 1901.

Hutchins, Francis G. *Mashpee: The Story of Cape Cod's Indian Town.* West Franklin, New Hampshire, 1979.

Jameson, J. Franklin, ed. *Narrative of New England, 1609–1664.* 1909. Reprint. New York, 1959.

Jenks, Samuel. "The Legend of Mudturtle." *Galaxy Magazine.* (July 2, 1827).

Kaplan, Sidney. *The Black Presence in the Era of the American Revolution, 1770–1800.* Washington, D.C., 1973.

Katz, William Loren. *Black Indians: A Hidden Heritage.* New York, 1986.

Kawashima, Yasuhide. *Puritan Justice and the Indian: White Man's Law in Massachusetts, 1630–1763.* Middletown, Connecticut, 1986.

Kellaway, William. *The New England Company, 1649–76: Missionary Society to the American Indians.* New York, 1961.

Kendall, Edward Augustus. *Travels through the Northern Parts of the United States in the Years 1807 and 1808.* Vol. 2. New York, 1809.

Leach, Douglas Edward. *Flintlock and Tomahawk: New England in King Philip's War.* 1958. Reprint. East Orleans, Massachusetts, 1992.

Leach, Robert J. "Quaker Intruders on Martha's Vineyard." *Vineyard Gazette,* August 4, 1942.

——. and Peter Gow. *Quaker Nantucket: The Religious Community Behind the Whaling Empire*. Nantucket, 1997.

Lemisch, Jesse. "Jack Tar in the Streets: Merchant Seamen in the Politics of Revolutionary America." *William and Mary Quarterly* 25 (1968).

Levermore, Charles Herbert, ed. *Forerunners and Competitors of the Pilgrims and Puritans*. 2 vols. Brooklyn, 1912.

Lewis, J. O. *Abraham Quary: A Sketch Contained in the Aboriginal Portfolio*. 1836. Reprint. Bridgewater, Connecticut, 1954.

Lindquist, Ole. "The Auskerry Whale, 1777: Processing and Economy." *Northern Scotland* 17(1997).

Linebaugh, Barbara. *The African School and the Integration of Nantucket Public Schools, 1825-1847*. Boston, 1978.

Linebaugh, Peter and Marcus Rediker. "The Many-Headed Hydra: Sailors, Slaves, and the Atlantic Working Class in the Eighteenth Century." *Journal of Historical Sociology*. (September 1990).

Little, Elizabeth A. "Sachem Nickanoose of Nantucket and the Grass Contest." *Historic Nantucket* 23 & 24 (1976).

—— and Marie Sussek. "Nantucket Indians who died of the Sickness, 1763-64." *Nantucket Algonquian Studies* 1 (1979).

——. "Probate Records of Nantucket Indians." *Nantucket Algonquian Studies* 2 (1980).

——. "The Writings of Nantucket Indians." *Nantucket Algonquian Studies* 3 (1981).

——. "Historic Indian Houses of Nantucket." *Nantucket Algonquian Studies* 4 (1981).

—— and Marie Sussek. "Index to Mary Starbuck's Account Book with the Indians." *Nantucket Algonquian Studies* 5 (1981).

——. "Essay on Nantucket Timber." *Nantucket Algonquian Studies* 6 (1981).

—— and Marie Sussek. "Zaccheus Macy's Account of the Indians of Nantucket: Three Versions." *Nantucket Algonquian Studies* 7 (1981).

——. "The Indian Contribution to Along-Shore Whaling at Nantucket." *Nantucket Algonquian Studies* 8 (1981).

——. "The Mattequecham Wigwam Murder." *Bulletin of the Massachusetts Archaeological Society* 42 (1981).

——. "Drift Whales at Nantucket: The Kindness of Moshup." *Man in the Northeast* 22 (1982).

——. "Indian Politics on Nantucket." *Papers of the Thirteenth Algonquian Conference*. Edited by William Cowan. Ottawa, 1982.

——. "Locus Q-6, Site M52/65, Quidnet, Nantucket, Massachusetts." *Bulletin of the Massachusetts Archaeological Society* 45 (1983).

——. "Indian Place Names at Nantucket." *Papers of the Fifteenth Algonquian Conference*. Edited by William Cowan. Ottawa, 1983.

——. "Observations on Methods of Collection, Use, and Seasonality of Shellfish on the Coasts of Massachusetts." *Bulletin of the Massachusetts Archaeological Society* 47 (1986).

——. "Nantucket Whaling in the Early 18th Century." *Papers of the Nineteenth Algonquian Conference*. Edited by William Cowan. Ottawa, 1988.

——. and John Pretola. "Nantucket: An Archaeological Record from the Far Island." *Bulletin of the Archaeological Society of Connecticut* 51 (1988).

——. "Indian Horse Commons at Nantucket Island, 1660–1760." *Nantucket Algonquian Studies* 9 (1990).

——. "Whaling off Nova Scotia, Newfoundland, and Greenland in the Early Eighteenth Century." *Nantucket Algonquian Studies* 10 (1987).

——. "Where are the Woodland Villages on Cape Cod and the Islands?" *Bulletin of the Massachusetts Archaeological Society* 49 (1988).

——. "History of the Town of Miacomet." *Nantucket Algonquian Studies* 12 (1988).

——. "Indian Whalemen of Nantucket: The Documentary Evidence." *Nantucket Algonquian Studies* 13 (1988).

——. "The Nantucket Indian Sickness." *Papers of the 21st Algonquian Conference.* Edited by William Cowen. Ottawa, 1990.

——. "Whales, Grass, and Shellfish: Land Use Issues at Nantucket in the Seventeenth Century." *Nantucket Algonquian Studies* 14 (1992).

——. "Abram Quary of Abram's Point, Nantucket Island." *Nantucket Algonquian Studies* 16 (1994).

——. "Daniel Spotso: A Sachem at Nantucket." *Northeastern Indian Lives, 1632–1816.* Edited by Robert S. Grumet. Amherst, Massachusetts, 1996.

Luedtke, Barbara E. "Regional Variation in Massachusetts Ceramics." *North American Archaeologist.* 7 (1986).

Macy, Obed. *The History of Nantucket.* 1835,1880. Reprint. Ellinwood, Kansas, 1985.

Macy, William F. *The Story of Old Nantucket.* Nantucket, 1915.

——. *The Nantucket Scrap Basket.* 1916. Reprint. Ellinwood, Kansas, 1984.

Mancall, Peter. *Deadly Medicine: Indians and Alcohol in Early America.* Ithaca and London, 1995.

Mandell, Daniel R. *Behind the Frontier: Indians in Eighteenth-Century Eastern Massachusetts.* Lincoln, Massachusetts; and London, 1996.

Martin, Calvin. ed. *The American Indian and the Problem of History.* Oxford and New York, 1987.

Matthiessen, Peter. *Men's Lives: The Surfmen and Baymen of the South Fork.* New York, 1986.

Mayhew, Experience. *Indian Converts: Or, Some Account of the Lives and Dying Speeches of a Considerable Number of the Christianized Indians of Martha's Vineyard, in New-England.* London, 1727.

Mayhew, Matthew. "A Brief Narrative of the Success Which the Gospel Had Among the Indians of Martha's Vineyard, 1694." *Massachusetts Historical Society Collections,* 2d ser., no. 119.

Mayhew, Thomas, Jr. In Henry Whitfield. "The Light appearing more and more towards the perfect Day, Or, A farther Discovery of the present state of the Indians in New-England." 1651. *Massachusetts Historical Society Collections,* 3d ser., vol. 4.

——. In Eliot and Mayhew. "Tears of Repentance: Or A further Narrative of the Progress of the Gospel Amongst the Indians in New-England." 1653. *Massachusetts Historical Society Collections,* 3d ser., vol. 4.

Melville, Herman. *Moby-Dick, or The Whale*. London, 1851. Evanston and Chicago, 1988.

——. *Clarel: A Poem and Pilgrimage in the Holy Land*. 1876. Evanston and Chicago, 1991.

Miller, Christopher I., and George R. Hamell. "A New Perspective on Indian–White Contact: Cultural Symbols and Colonial Trade." *Journal of American History* 73 (1986).

Mills, Earl, Sr., and Alicja Mann. *Son of Mashpee: Reflections of Chief Flying Eagle, A Wampanoag*. North Falmouth, Massachusetts, 1996.

Mitchell, Eliza. *Book of Reminiscences*. Nantucket Historical Association MS. Collection 23.

Morris, Preston. "Interesting Landmarks on Nantucket." *Inquirer and Mirror*, August 19, 1922.

Morison, Samuel Eliot. *Harvard College in the Seventeenth Century*. 2 vols. Cambridge, Mass, 1936.

Morton, Thomas. "New English Canaan (1637)." In *Tracts and Other Papers, Relating Principally to the Origin, Settlement, and Progress of the Colonies of North America, from the Discovery of the Country to the Year 1776*. Edited by Peter Force. New York, 1947.

Naeher, Robert. "Dialogue in the Wilderness: John Eliot and the Indian Exploration of Puritanism as a Source of Meaning, Comfort, and Ethnic Survival." *New England Quarterly*. September1989.

Neustadt, Kathy. *Clambake, A History and Celebration of an American Tradition*. Amherst, Massachusetts, 1992.

O'Brien, Jean. "Community Dynamics in the Indian-English Town of Natick, Massachusetts, 1650–1790." Ph.D. diss., University of Chicago (1990).

O'Callaghan, Edmund B., ed. *Documents Relating to the Colonial History of the State of New York*. Albany, New York, 1855.

O'Connell, Barry, ed. *On Our Own Ground: The Complete Writings of William Apess*. Amherst, Massachusetts, 1992.

Oldale, Robert N. *Cape Cod and the Islands: The Geological Story*. East Orleans, Massachusetts, 1992.

Paltsits, Victor Hugo, ed. *Minutes of the Executive Council of the Province of New York*. Albany, New York, 1910.

Pearce, Roy Harvey. *Savagism and Civilization, A Study of the Indian and the American Mind*. 1953. Rev. ed. Berkeley and Los Angeles, 1988.

Philbrick, Nathaniel. *Away Off Shore: Nantucket Island and Its People, 1602–1890*. Nantucket, 1994.

Preston, Douglas. *Talking to the Ground*. New York, 1995.

Quammen, David. *The Song of the Dodo, Island Biogeography in an Age of Extinctions*. New York, 1996.

Quinn, David B., and Alison M. Quinn, eds. *The English New England Voyages, 1602–1608*. London, 1983.

Ronda, James P. "Generations of Faith: The Christian Indians of Martha's Vineyard." *William and Mary Quarterly* 38 (1981).

Roy, Edward S. "A Steatite Vessel from Nantucket." *Bulletin of the Massachusetts Archaeological Society* 17 (1956).

Russell, Howard S. *Indian New England Before the Mayflower.* Hanover, New Hampshire, 1980.

Sansom, Joseph. "A Description of Nantucket." *PortFolio.* Vol. 5. Philadelphia, 1811.

Salisbury, Neal. *Manitou and Providence: Indians, Europeans, and the Making of New England, 1500–1643.* New York and Oxford, 1982.

Schroeder, Betty. "The True Lineage of King Philip (Sachem Metacom)." *New England Historical and Genealogical Register.* (July 1990).

Shurtleff, Nathaniel B., ed. *Records of the Colony of New Plymouth in New England.* Boston, 1855.

Simmons, William S. "Return of the Timid Giant: Algonquian Legends of Southern New England." *Papers of the Thirteenth Algonquian Conference.* Edited by William Cowan. Ottawa, 1982.

——. "Conversion from Indian to Puritan." *New England Quarterly* 52 (1979).

——. *Spirit of the New England Tribes: Indian History and Folklore, 1620–1984.* Hanover, New Hampshire; and London, 1986.

Slotkin, Richard. *Regeneration Through Violence: The Mythology of the American Frontier.* Middletown, Connecticut, 1973.

Smalley, Amos, as told to Max Eastman. "I Killed 'Moby Dick.'" *Reader's Digest,* May 1957.

Snow, Dean R., and Kim M. Lanphear. "European Contact and Indian Depopulation in the Northeast: The Timing of the First Epidemics." *Ethnohistory.* (Winter 1988).

Speck, Frank G. "Territorial Subdivisions and Boundaries of the Wampanoag, Massachusett, and Nauset Indians." *Indian Notes and Monographs* 44. Edited by F. W. Hodge. New York: Museum of the American Indian, Heye Foundation, 1928.

Spiess, Arthur E., and Bruce D. Spiess. "New England Pandemic of 1616–1622: Cause and Archaeological Implication." *Man in the Northeast* 34 (1987).

Stackpole, Edouard A. "The Fatal Indian Sickness of Nantucket That Decimated the Island Aborigines." *Historic Nantucket* (April 1975).

Starbuck, Alexander. *The History of Nantucket: County, Island, and Town.* 1924. Reprint. Rutland, Vermont, 1969.

Stockley, Bernard. "Preliminary Report: Ram Pasture I, A Stratified Site on Nantucket Island, Massachusetts." *Eastern States Archaeological Bulletin* 24 (1965).

Strong, John A. "Late Woodland Dog Ceremonialism on Long Island in Comparative and Temporal Perspective." *Bulletin of the New York State Archaeological Association* 19 (1985).

——. *The Algonquian Peoples of Long Island from Earliest Times to 1700.* Interlaken, New York, 1997.

Thomas, Lamont D. *Rise to Be a People: A Biography of Paul Cuffe.* Urbana, Illinois; and Chicago, 1986.

Thomas, Peter A. "Cultural Change on the Southern New England Frontier, 1630–1665." *Cultures in Contact: The Impact of European Contacts on Native American Cultural Institutions, A.D.1000–1800.* Edited by W. W. Fitzhugh. Washington D.C., 1985.

Thompson, Stith. *Tales of the North American Indians.* Bloomington, Indiana; and London, 1968.

Thoreau, Henry David. *The Maine Woods.* Vol. 3, *The Writings of Henry David Thoreau.* Boston and New York, 1906.

———. *Journal.* Edited by Francis H. Allen. New York, 1962.

Turner, Harry B. "Vanished Treasures." *Proceedings of the Nantucket Historical Association* (1916).

Vaughan, Alden T. *New England Frontier: Puritans and Indians, 1620–1675.* Boston, 1965.

Vecsey, George. *Imagine Ourselves Richly: Mythic Narratives of North American Indians.* New York, 1991.

Vickers, Daniel F. "The First Whalemen of Nantucket." *William and Mary Quarterly* (October 1983).

———. "Nantucket Whalemen in the Deep-Sea Fishery: The Changing Anatomy of an Early American Labor Force." *Journal of American History* (September 1985).

White, Richard. *The Middle Ground: Indians, Empires, and Republics in the Great Lakes Region, 1650–1815.* New York and Cambridge.

Wilbur, C. Keith. *The New England Indians.* Old Saybrook, Connecticut, 1978.

Williams, Roger. "Letter to John Winthrop, 1638." *Massachusetts Historical Society Collections,* ser. 1, vol. 4.

———. *A Key Into the Language of America.* 1643. Reprint. Edited by John J. Teunissen and Evelyn Hinz. Detroit, 1973.

Winslow, Edward. "Good News from New England, 1624." In *Chronicles of the Pilgrim Fathers.* Edited by A. Young. Boston, 1841.

Winthrop, John. *The History of New England from 1630 to 1649.* Edited by James Kendall Hosmer. 2 vols. New York, 1908.

Wood, William. *New England's Prospect.* Edited by Alden T. Vaughan. Amherst, Massachusetts, 1977.

Worth, Henry Barnard. *Nantucket Lands and Land Owners.* 1901. Reprint. Bowie, Maryland, 1992.

Wroth, L. Kinvin, and Hiller B. Zobel, eds. *Legal Papers of John Adams.* Cambridge, Massachusetts, 1965.

Wroth, Lawrence C., ed. *The Voyages of Giovanni da Verrazano, 1524–1528.* New Haven, 1970.

INDEX